RESTORATIVE JUSTICE FOR JUVENILES

A Comprehensive Guide to Principles, Practices, Healing, Accountability, and Restoring Our Youth

DR. MAXWELL SHIMBA

Published in Manhattan, New York by Shimba Publishing, LLC.

Shimba Publishing LLC

Table of Contents

Introduction

In the vast and often unforgiving landscape of the criminal justice system, a quiet revolution has been unfolding—one that dares to ask questions the punitive paradigm has long ignored. For centuries, societies have constructed elaborate systems of punishment designed to answer a single, simplistic question: "What must be taken from the offender in exchange for the harm they have caused?" This retributive lens, with its scales of justice and its ledger of debts paid through suffering, has dominated our collective imagination. But beneath the weight of this imposing framework, another current has been flowing, gathering strength from ancient wisdom, empirical research, and the persistent hope that justice might mean something more than the infliction of pain. This current is restorative justice, and when applied to our young people—those whose lives hang in the delicate balance between childhood's promise and adulthood's responsibilities—it becomes nothing less than a moral imperative.

The tapestry we are about to unravel together is intricate, woven from threads of theology, philosophy, psychology, and law. Each strand contributes something essential to the whole, and to understand restorative justice for juveniles in its fullness, we must trace each thread back to its source while watching how they intertwine to create something stronger than any single discipline could produce alone. This is not merely a program or a set of techniques; it is a worldview, a way of seeing crime, harm, and justice that fundamentally reorients our relationship to wrongdoing and to one another.

At its theological heart, restorative justice echoes the oldest and most profound truths of the Judeo-Christian tradition. The Hebrew scriptures are replete with a God who is *El Rachum v'Chanun*—compassionate and gracious, slow to anger, and abounding in steadfast love. When the prophet Hosea records God's lament, "For I desire mercy, not sacrifice, and acknowledgment of God rather than burnt offerings," we hear a divine preference for restoration over ritualistic punishment. The very concept of *tikkun olam*—the Jewish obligation to repair the world—speaks directly to the restorative impulse. When harm occurs, the fabric of creation is torn, and justice requires not merely that someone pay for the tear, but that we all participate in the mending.

The Christian tradition carries this imperative forward with even greater specificity. Consider the radical ethics of Jesus, who consistently disrupted the punitive logic of His day. When presented with a woman caught in adultery—a capital offense under the law—He did not ask what punishment she deserved. He invited those without sin to cast the first stone, and then, in one of the most restorative moments in all of scripture, He turned to the woman and asked, "Has no one condemned you? Neither do I condemn you. Go and sin no more." Here we see the essential restorative sequence: the harm is acknowledged, condemnation is withheld, and the offender is called toward transformation. The Greek word *metanoia*, often translated as repentance, literally means to change one's mind, to turn around, to reorient one's entire being. Restorative justice seeks precisely this metanoia in our young people—not mere compliance born of fear, but genuine transformation born of understanding and accountability.

The apostle Paul, in his second letter to the Corinthians, articulates what might be the most concise theology of restorative justice ever written. Speaking of the church's role in disciplining and then restoring a member, he writes, "The punishment inflicted on him by the majority is sufficient. Now instead, you ought to forgive and comfort him, so that he will not be overwhelmed by excessive sorrow. I urge you, therefore, to reaffirm your love for him." Paul understood something that punitive systems consistently miss: that there is a point at which punishment ceases to serve any constructive purpose and begins instead to destroy the very person we hope to restore. The goal, for Paul as for restorative justice, is not that the offender suffer enough, but that the offender be saved from being "overwhelmed by excessive sorrow"—that they be reaffirmed in love even as they are held accountable for their actions.

The theological foundations extend beyond the Abrahamic traditions. Indigenous peoples around the world have practiced restorative approaches for millennia, long before Western legal systems imposed their adversarial frameworks. The Navajo concept of *hózhó* speaks to the beauty, harmony, and balance that must be restored when wrongdoing has disrupted the community's equilibrium. Maori practices in New Zealand, which would eventually inspire that nation's transformative family group conferencing model, understood that when one person harms another, the entire web of relationships is damaged and requires collective healing. These indigenous wisdoms remind us that restorative justice is not an invention but a rediscovery—a returning to ways of being that human communities intuitively understood before the rise of centralized, punitive states.

Philosophically, restorative justice rests upon foundations as solid as any in Western thought, while challenging some of our most deeply held assumptions about the nature of justice itself. The retributive framework that dominates modern legal systems draws heavily from thinkers like Immanuel Kant, who argued that punishment is not merely permissible but morally required, regardless of any beneficial consequences it might produce. For Kant, the guilty must be punished because justice demands it—even if society would dissolve the next day, the last murderer in prison must first be executed. This view has a certain austere logic, but it fails to account for what we might call the relational nature of human existence. We are not isolated individuals whose actions affect only ourselves and our legal standing; we are beings-in-relationship, and harm ripples outward through networks of connection that cannot be captured by abstract legal categories.

The philosopher Martin Buber, in his seminal work *I and Thou*, distinguished between two fundamental ways of relating to others: the *I-It* relationship, in which we treat others as objects to be used or managed, and the *I-Thou* relationship, in which we encounter others in their full humanity, as subjects worthy of respect and response. Traditional punitive justice operates largely in the *I-It* mode. The offender becomes a case number, a set of charges, a body to be processed through the system. Their humanity, their story, their potential for transformation—these become irrelevant to the mechanical application of prescribed penalties. Restorative justice, by contrast, insists on the *I-Thou* encounter. It brings victims and offenders together not as legal abstractions but as human beings with stories, wounds, and the capacity for mutual recognition. In that encounter, something new becomes possible: not merely the application of law, but the emergence of understanding, the possibility of genuine remorse, and the groundwork for authentic repair.

The philosophical tradition of personalism, particularly as developed by thinkers like Emmanuel Mounier and Jacques Maritain, offers additional resources for understanding restorative justice. Personalism insists on the intrinsic dignity of every human person, a dignity that is not diminished by wrongdoing and cannot be restored through degradation. When we punish young people in ways that humiliate them, when we strip them of their names and replace them with numbers, when we treat them as problems to be managed rather than persons to be accompanied, we violate this dignity at the very moment when its affirmation is most needed. Restorative justice, with its emphasis on dialogue, accountability, and reintegration, seeks to honor the person even as it addresses the person's actions.

From the vantage point of psychology, the case for restorative justice with juveniles becomes even more compelling. Developmental psychology has taught us that the adolescent brain is fundamentally different from the adult brain—not defective, but under construction. The prefrontal cortex, responsible for impulse control, long-term planning, and the nuanced evaluation of consequences, is the last region of the brain to mature, often not reaching full development until the mid-twenties. Meanwhile, the limbic system, which governs emotional responses and reward-seeking behavior, is operating at peak intensity. This neurological reality means that adolescents are biologically predisposed to take risks, to prioritize immediate rewards over long-term consequences, and to be disproportionately influenced by peer presence. To punish them as if they were fully-formed adults is not justice; it is a fundamental misunderstanding of human development.

Attachment theory, pioneered by John Bowlby and Mary Ainsworth, adds another crucial dimension. We now understand that human beings are hardwired for connection, that our earliest relationships shape our capacity for trust, empathy, and self-regulation throughout our lives. Young people who end up in the juvenile justice system have often experienced profound disruptions in attachment—neglect, abuse, inconsistent caregiving, traumatic losses. Their offending behavior, while never excusable, is often understandable as a manifestation of unhealed wounds. Punitive responses that sever them further from positive relationships and community connections are precisely the opposite of what they need. Restorative justice, by contrast, seeks to strengthen bonds, to create opportunities for repair within relationships, and to provide the supportive connections that are essential for healthy development.

Trauma-informed psychology has revolutionized our understanding of what lies beneath much delinquent behavior. The Adverse Childhood Experiences (ACE) study, one of the largest investigations of childhood trauma ever conducted, found stunning correlations between early adversity and later physical, mental, and social problems. Children who experience abuse, neglect, household dysfunction, or community violence carry these experiences in their bodies and brains, often manifesting as hypervigilance, emotional dysregulation, and behavioral problems that bring them into contact with the justice system. When we encounter a young person who has committed harm, we must ask not only "What did they do?" but "What happened to them?" This is not to excuse their actions but to understand them—and understanding is the prerequisite for genuine change. Restorative justice creates space for this understanding to emerge, not through clinical diagnosis alone, but through the encounter with victims and community members who can see the young person's full humanity even as they name the harm done.

Positive psychology, particularly the work of Martin Seligman and his colleagues on character strengths and flourishing, offers a framework for thinking about what rehabilitation might mean. Rather than focusing exclusively on deficits and problems, positive psychology asks what enables human beings to thrive. It identifies character strengths like forgiveness, gratitude, perseverance, and social intelligence that can be cultivated even—perhaps especially—in the aftermath of failure. Restorative justice, by inviting young people to make amends, to understand the impact of their actions, and to reimagine their futures, provides a context in which these strengths can develop. The young person who completes a restitution agreement, who faces the person they have harmed and offers a genuine apology, who engages in community service that connects them to others in positive ways—this young person is not merely avoiding further punishment but actively building the capacities that will enable them to flourish as a contributing member of society.

The legal foundations of restorative justice, while more recent than its theological and philosophical roots, are no less significant. The American juvenile justice system was founded in 1899 with the establishment of the first juvenile court in Cook County, Illinois, based on the doctrine of *parens patriae*—the state as parent. The early juvenile court reformers believed that children were different from adults, that they deserved individualized attention and rehabilitation rather than punishment. This vision, however noble in its origins, was often betrayed in practice. Juvenile courts became increasingly punitive, children were transferred to adult facilities in growing numbers, and the very concept of rehabilitation was abandoned in favor of get-tough policies that treated young people as mini-adults deserving of adult consequences.

The tide began to turn with a series of Supreme Court decisions that granted juveniles some procedural protections—the right to notice of charges, the right to counsel, the privilege against self-incrimination—while still recognizing their distinctive status. But the most profound legal development for restorative justice has been the growing recognition that procedural justice matters as much as outcomes. Procedural justice theory, developed by Tom Tyler and others, demonstrates that people's willingness to accept legal decisions and comply with the law depends less on whether they got what they wanted than on whether they perceive the process as fair. When people feel heard, when they believe decision-makers are neutral and trustworthy, when they are treated with dignity and respect, they are more likely to view the legal system as legitimate and to internalize its norms.

Restorative justice embodies procedural justice in action. Victims who participate in restorative processes report feeling heard in ways that traditional court proceedings never allow. Offenders who face their victims and community members in a restorative conference experience accountability not as something done to them but as something they actively participate in. The process is transparent, inclusive, and focused on repairing harm rather than imposing suffering. Research consistently shows that both victims and offenders perceive restorative justice as more fair and legitimate than traditional court processing—and this perception of legitimacy translates into better outcomes for all involved.

Empirical research on restorative justice with juveniles has accumulated impressively over the past several decades, and the findings consistently support what the theological, philosophical, and psychological frameworks would predict. A meta-analysis by the RAND Corporation, examining dozens of rigorous studies, found that restorative justice programs reduce recidivism among juvenile offenders by an average of 10 to 35 percent compared to traditional court processing. The effects are particularly strong for violent offenses, suggesting that the intensive engagement required by restorative processes is especially valuable when harm has been most severe. A study by Lawrence Sherman and Heather Strang at the University of Cambridge, involving multiple randomized controlled trials across the United Kingdom and Australia, found that restorative justice not only reduced reoffending but also produced significant psychological benefits for victims—reduced fear, reduced anger, greater sense of closure.

The economic case for restorative justice is equally compelling. A study by the Washington State Institute for Public Policy, which has conducted some of the most sophisticated cost-benefit analyses of criminal justice programs in the nation, found that restorative justice for juveniles produces substantial net benefits to taxpayers and crime victims. Every dollar invested in restorative justice programs returns approximately eight dollars in benefits through reduced recidivism, lower criminal justice costs, and avoided victimization. These are not speculative projections but conservative estimates based on rigorous longitudinal data. In an era of tight budgets and competing demands for public resources, restorative justice offers the rare combination of better outcomes and lower costs—a genuine win-win for communities and taxpayers.

The theological imperative for restorative justice finds empirical support in studies of forgiveness and reconciliation. Psychologist Everett Worthington and his colleagues have developed a comprehensive model of forgiveness that distinguishes between decisional forgiveness—the choice to release resentment and treat the offender with goodwill—and emotional forgiveness—the replacement of negative emotions with positive ones. Their research demonstrates that forgiveness can be cultivated through structured interventions, that it produces measurable improvements in mental and physical health, and that it is particularly powerful when offenders have acknowledged harm and made genuine efforts at repair. These findings echo the ancient wisdom of Leviticus: "Do not hate a fellow Israelite in your heart. Rebuke your neighbor frankly so you will not share in their guilt. Do not seek revenge or bear a grudge against anyone among your people, but love your neighbor as yourself." The psychological research on forgiveness suggests that this ancient command is not merely moral exhortation but practical wisdom for human flourishing.

The philosophy of Martin Buber, with its insistence on the transformative potential of genuine encounter, finds empirical confirmation in studies of victim-offender dialogue. When victims and offenders meet face-to-face, something remarkable often happens that neither party anticipated. Victims who expected to confront a monster encounter a frightened and remorseful young person. Offenders who expected to face an angry accuser encounter a human being whose suffering they can no longer deny. These encounters do not always result in forgiveness, and restorative justice does not require forgiveness to be considered successful. But they do consistently produce something essential: recognition. The victim recognizes the offender's humanity; the offender recognizes the victim's reality. In that mutual recognition, the ground is prepared for whatever form of repair is possible.

From the standpoint of public health, restorative justice represents a prevention strategy as much as an intervention. The Centers for Disease Control and Prevention has identified youth violence as a significant public health problem, with annual costs exceeding $20 billion in medical expenses and lost productivity alone. But the CDC's approach to violence prevention emphasizes addressing root causes, building protective factors, and strengthening community connections—precisely the focus of restorative justice. When young people who have caused harm are reintegrated into their communities through restorative processes, they are not merely less likely to reoffend themselves; they become resources for preventing violence among their peers. They can speak from experience about the consequences of harmful choices, model accountability and growth, and serve as credible messengers to young people who might otherwise dismiss adult warnings as irrelevant.

The ecological perspective in psychology, developed by Urie Bronfenbrenner, understands human development as occurring within nested systems of influence: the microsystem of family and peers, the mesosystem of connections between these settings, the exosystem of community institutions, and the macrosystem of cultural values and norms. Delinquent behavior emerges not from individual pathology alone but from imbalances and disruptions across these systems. Interventions that focus only on the individual—therapy, skills training, punishment—are unlikely to succeed if they do not also address the relational and community contexts in which the young person lives. Restorative justice, by engaging victims, families, and community members, works across multiple ecological levels simultaneously. It intervenes not only in the young person's attitudes and behaviors but in the relationships and community structures that will either support or undermine their continued growth.

The theological concept of *shalom*—the Hebrew vision of comprehensive well-being, right relationship, and flourishing for all creation—provides a unifying framework for understanding what restorative justice seeks to accomplish. Shalom is not merely the absence of conflict but the presence of justice, not merely individual peace but communal wholeness. When the prophet Jeremiah laments, "They have healed the wound of my people lightly, saying 'Peace, peace,' when there is no peace," he warns against superficial resolutions that leave underlying injustices unaddressed. Restorative justice refuses to declare peace lightly. It insists on facing the wound directly, on understanding its depth, on engaging all those affected in the hard work of genuine healing. The goal is not a quick settlement but lasting shalom—a restoration of right relationship that makes future harm less likely and future flourishing more possible.

The psychological concept of post-traumatic growth, developed by Richard Tedeschi and Lawrence Calhoun, offers a framework for understanding how even the most painful experiences can become catalysts for positive transformation. Many survivors of trauma report not only recovery but growth—deeper relationships, renewed appreciation for life, increased personal strength, spiritual development, new possibilities. Restorative justice, when practiced with sensitivity and skill, can create conditions for post-traumatic growth among both victims and offenders. Victims who participate in restorative processes often describe a sense of empowerment, a release from the grip of fear and anger, a new ability to move forward with their lives. Offenders who face the harm they have caused and engage in genuine repair often experience profound personal transformation—a reorientation of values, a new sense of purpose, a commitment to becoming someone different. Neither outcome is guaranteed, and restorative justice does not promise transformation. But it creates the conditions in which transformation becomes possible.

The legal scholar Martha Minow, in her profound meditation *Between Vengeance and Forgiveness*, explores how societies respond to collective atrocities. She argues that the choice between vengeance and forgiveness is a false dichotomy, that there are other possibilities—truth commissions, reparations, institutional reforms, public acknowledgments of responsibility—that occupy a middle ground. The same insight applies to juvenile justice. The choice is not between harsh punishment and easy forgiveness. There is a third way, a way of accountability without degradation, of consequences without exclusion, of repair without retribution. This is the way of restorative justice, and it offers young people something that neither vengeance nor leniency can provide: the opportunity to confront what they have done, to understand its impact, to make things as right as possible, and to be restored to community not despite their wrongdoing but through the process of addressing it honestly and courageously.

The biblical witness, from Genesis to Revelation, is consistent in its insistence that God's justice is never merely punitive. When Cain murders Abel, God does not kill him but marks him for protection. When David commits adultery and murder, God confronts him through the prophet Nathan, leading to David's profound confession: "I have sinned against the Lord." The Psalms are filled with pleas for forgiveness and restoration, grounded in confidence in God's steadfast love. The prophets call Israel to repentance not as a condition of God's love but as a path back to the relationship God has always desired. Jesus announces a kingdom in which the last are first, the lost are found, the dead are raised to life. Paul proclaims that in Christ, God was reconciling the world to himself, not counting people's sins against them. The entire biblical narrative moves toward the ultimate restoration described in Revelation: "He will wipe every tear from their eyes. There will be no more death or mourning or crying or pain, for the old order of things has passed away."

Restorative justice for juveniles participates in this great arc of restoration. It does not pretend that harm is not real, that victims do not suffer, that communities are not wounded. It takes all of these with utmost seriousness, creating space for victims to speak their truth, for offenders to acknowledge their responsibility, for communities to express their pain and their hope. But it refuses to stop there. It insists that the story does not end with harm, that something new can emerge from the wreckage, that young people who have made terrible choices can become something other than their worst actions. It is, in the deepest sense, a practice of hope—hope that change is possible, that relationships can be healed, that communities can be strengthened, that the future need not be determined by the past.

As we prepare to journey through the chapters that follow, we carry with us this rich inheritance of wisdom from theology, philosophy, psychology, and law. We carry the stories of indigenous peoples who have kept restorative practices alive through centuries of colonization and oppression. We carry the insights of researchers who have documented what works and why. We carry the hope of victims who have found healing through encounter, of offenders who have found transformation through accountability, of communities that have found strength through collective engagement with harm. And we carry the conviction, grounded in faith and reason alike, that our young people deserve better than a justice system that simply processes them through punishment. They deserve a justice system that sees them, that holds them accountable while never giving up on them, that demands much of them while offering them even more. They deserve restorative justice.

The chapters ahead will explore the historical context that shaped our current juvenile justice system and the emergence of restorative alternatives. They will delve deeply into the principles that animate restorative practice: accountability that transforms rather than merely punishes, empathy that bridges the distance between victims and offenders, community involvement that strengthens the fabric of collective life. They will examine the victim-centered approach that distinguishes restorative justice from offender-focused rehabilitation models, ensuring that those who have been harmed are not forgotten in our concern for those who have caused harm. They will explore offender rehabilitation not as a vague aspiration but as a concrete process of change supported by psychological research and practical wisdom. They will consider the crucial role of community, not as an abstract concept but as a lived reality of mutual responsibility and support.

Subsequent chapters will survey the diverse practices that give restorative justice its vitality—victim-offender dialogues that create space for genuine encounter, restorative circles that engage multiple stakeholders in collective problem-solving, conferences that bring together all those affected by harm. They will examine the benefits that research has documented: reduced recidivism, improved victim satisfaction, stronger communities, cost savings for taxpayers. They will grapple honestly with the challenges and criticisms that restorative justice faces, from concerns about fairness and equity to questions about its applicability to serious offenses. They will explore the legal frameworks that support or impede restorative practice, offering guidance for advocates seeking to institutionalize these approaches. Case studies will bring restorative justice to life, showing how principles become practice in real cases with real young people. International perspectives will broaden our视野, revealing how different cultures have adapted restorative approaches to their unique contexts. Future directions will invite us to imagine what restorative justice might become as it continues to evolve. And practical guidance will equip readers to take the next steps in their own contexts, whether as practitioners, policymakers, or concerned community members.

Throughout this journey, we will return again and again to the fundamental insight that restorative justice is not merely a program or a technique but a way of seeing—a lens through which we understand crime, harm, accountability, and healing in fundamentally relational terms. It is a way of being that honors the dignity of every person while never minimizing the reality of harm. It is a way of hoping that refuses to write off any young person as beyond redemption while demanding that redemption, if it comes, come through honest confrontation with what they have done. It is, in short, a vision of justice worthy of our highest aspirations and our deepest faith.

Join us, then, as we unravel the intricate tapestry of restorative justice for juveniles—a tapestry woven from threads both ancient and new, from wisdom both secular and sacred, from hope both practical and transcendent. Join us as we explore what it means to repair harm, to rebuild lives, to restore our youth. Join us as we imagine a justice system that does not merely process cases but transforms lives, that does not merely punish wrongdoing but heals wounds, that does not merely exclude the dangerous but reintegrates the restored. Join us as we work toward the day when every young person who has caused harm will have the opportunity to make things right, to become someone new, to take their place in a community that has not given up on them. This is the promise of restorative justice. This is the journey we undertake together.

Dr. Maxwell Shimba
United States Institute for Restorative Justice

CHAPTER 01

THE CONCEPT OF RESTORATIVE JUSTICE FOR JUVENILES

In the world of juvenile justice, a transformative approach has emerged—one that fundamentally shifts our gaze from the narrow confines of punishment to the expansive horizon of healing and accountability. This is not merely a reform or an adjustment to existing systems; it is a paradigm shift of profound proportions, a reimagining of what justice itself might mean when applied to our youngest and most vulnerable offenders. As we stand at the crossroads of tradition and transformation, this book invites you on a journey to unravel the essence of restorative justice for juveniles, a concept that has steadily gained recognition for its profound impact on the criminal justice system and, more importantly, on the lives of young people caught in its web.

The concept of restorative justice for juveniles is rooted in a deceptively simple yet revolutionary proposition: that when a young individual commits an offense, the primary focus should not be solely on determining what punishment they deserve, but rather on understanding what harm has been caused and what must be done to repair it. This seemingly modest shift in focus—from "What law was broken and what penalty does it require?" to "Who was harmed and how can that harm be addressed?"—carries within it the seeds of a completely different way of understanding crime, accountability, and community. It is a distinction that echoes through the corridors of legal theory, resonates in the chambers of the human heart, and finds confirmation in the deepest wells of theological wisdom and psychological insight.

As we navigate these pages together, we will delve into the core principles that give restorative justice its distinctive character, explore the innovative practices that bring these principles to life in concrete situations, and bear witness to the numerous benefits that flow from this approach—benefits that extend not only to young offenders but to victims, families, and entire communities. This is a system that believes in second chances, not as cheap grace or easy forgiveness, but as the fruit of genuine accountability and meaningful repair. It is a system that understands rebuilding lives as a communal endeavor, one that requires the active participation of all those affected by harm. And it is a system that recognizes that stronger, more empathetic communities are not merely a fortunate byproduct of effective justice but its very purpose and goal.

To understand restorative justice fully, we must first understand what it is not. It is not a softening of justice, a letting off the hook, a failure to take crime seriously. On the contrary, restorative justice takes crime more seriously than punitive systems ever can, because it insists on engaging with its real consequences rather than its abstract legal categories. When a young person steals from a store, punitive justice asks: What law was broken? What penalty does the law prescribe? How can we ensure this young person suffers enough to deter future theft? These are not unimportant questions, but they are remarkably shallow. They tell us nothing about the store owner who now feels violated and fearful, nothing about the employees who must deal with inventory shrinkage and increased security, nothing about the neighborhood that loses a trusted business because insurance rates become prohibitive. Restorative justice asks the questions that matter: What was the real cost of this theft, in human terms? How can this young person come to understand those costs? What can be done to make things as right as possible? These questions are harder, more demanding, more uncomfortable—but they are the questions that lead to genuine justice.

The theological foundations of this approach run deep and cannot be ignored if we are to grasp its full significance. The sacred scriptures of the Judeo-Christian tradition, far from endorsing the punitive logic that dominates modern legal systems, consistently point toward a different understanding of justice—one centered on restoration rather than retribution. Consider the prophet Micah's famous articulation of what God requires: "He has shown you, O mortal, what is good. And what does the Lord require of you? To act justly and to love mercy and to walk humbly with your God." Notice the pairing: justice and mercy are not opposites to be balanced but companions to be embraced together. The Hebrew word for justice, *mishpat*, appears throughout the scriptures in contexts that make clear its restorative character. It is *mishpat* to care for the orphan and widow, to welcome the stranger, to ensure that the vulnerable are not crushed by the powerful. It is *mishpat* to restore what has been taken, to make right what has been wronged, to bring about *shalom*—that comprehensive well-being that is the ultimate goal of all God's dealings with humanity.

The life and teaching of Jesus bring this restorative vision into even sharper focus. When Jesus declares in the Sermon on the Mount, "Blessed are the merciful, for they will be shown mercy," he is not announcing a new idea but crystallizing a truth as old as humanity itself: that our treatment of others shapes our own destiny, that the mercy we extend becomes the mercy we receive. When he instructs his followers, "If you are offering your gift at the altar and there remember that your brother or sister has something against you, leave your gift there in front of the altar. First go and be reconciled to them; then come and offer your gift," he is establishing a hierarchy of values in which relationship takes precedence over ritual, reconciliation over religious observance. The priority is unmistakable: be reconciled before you worship. This is restorative justice as spiritual discipline.

The apostle Paul, drawing on his Hebrew heritage and his transformative encounter with the risen Christ, develops this theme with characteristic depth. In his letter to the Romans, he writes, "Do not take revenge, my dear friends, but leave room for God's wrath, for it is written: 'It is mine to avenge; I will repay,' says the Lord." This is not, as some have mistakenly read it, a command to leave vengeance to God so that we can get on with our own punitive business. It is rather a radical deconstruction of the very logic of vengeance, a recognition that the cycle of retaliation, once begun, has no natural end. Paul's alternative is stunning in its simplicity: "Do not be overcome by evil, but overcome evil with good." This is the essence of restorative justice—not responding to evil with more evil, not breaking the cycle of harm with further harm, but absorbing the impact of wrongdoing and responding in ways that transform rather than perpetuate the violence.

The philosophical underpinnings of restorative justice are equally profound, drawing on traditions of thought that challenge the individualism and abstraction of modern legal philosophy. The great Jewish philosopher Martin Buber, in his masterpiece *I and Thou*, distinguishes between two fundamental ways of relating to others: the *I-It* mode, in which we treat others as objects to be used, categorized, and managed; and the *I-Thou* mode, in which we encounter others in their full humanity, as subjects worthy of respect and response. Traditional punitive justice operates overwhelmingly in the *I-It* mode. The young offender becomes a case number, a set of charges, a body to be processed through the system. Their story, their wounds, their potential—all become irrelevant to the mechanical application of prescribed penalties. Restorative justice, by contrast, insists on the *I-Thou* encounter. It brings victims and offenders together not as legal abstractions but as human beings with names, faces, histories, and hopes. In that encounter, something new becomes possible: mutual recognition, genuine understanding, the groundwork for authentic repair.

The philosophical tradition of personalism, associated with thinkers like Emmanuel Mounier and Jacques Maritain, adds another crucial dimension. Personalism insists on the intrinsic dignity of every human person, a dignity that is not diminished by wrongdoing and cannot be restored through degradation. When we punish young people in ways that humiliate them, when we strip them of their names and replace them with numbers, when we treat them as problems to be managed rather than persons to be accompanied, we violate this dignity at the very moment when its affirmation is most needed. The young person who has caused harm is still a person, still bearing the image of God, still possessing inherent worth that no amount of wrongdoing can erase. Restorative justice, with its emphasis on dialogue, accountability, and reintegration, seeks to honor the person even as it addresses the person's actions.

From the vantage point of psychology, the case for restorative justice with juveniles becomes even more compelling, and the evidence is now overwhelming that this approach aligns with what we know about human development, trauma, and change. Developmental psychology has taught us that the adolescent brain is fundamentally different from the adult brain—not defective, but under construction, a work in progress that will not reach full maturity until the mid-twenties. The prefrontal cortex, responsible for impulse control, long-term planning, and the nuanced evaluation of consequences, is the last region of the brain to develop. Meanwhile, the limbic system, which governs emotional responses and reward-seeking behavior, is operating at peak intensity, creating a neurological mismatch that makes adolescents biologically predisposed to risk-taking, sensation-seeking, and poor decision-making under peer pressure. To punish young people as if they were fully-formed adults is not justice; it is a fundamental misunderstanding of human development, a category error with devastating consequences.

Attachment theory, pioneered by John Bowlby and Mary Ainsworth and confirmed by decades of research, reveals another crucial dimension. Human beings are hardwired for connection; our earliest relationships shape our capacity for trust, empathy, and self-regulation throughout our lives. Young people who end up in the juvenile justice system have often experienced profound disruptions in attachment—neglect, abuse, inconsistent caregiving, traumatic losses. Their offending behavior, while never excusable, is often understandable as a manifestation of unhealed wounds, a cry for connection expressed through actions that further alienate them from the very connections they need. Punitive responses that sever them further from positive relationships and community connections are precisely the opposite of what they need. They deepen the wound rather than healing it, confirm the young person's belief that they are worthless and unlovable, and drive them toward the only communities that will still accept them: gangs, criminal networks, other alienated and angry young people. Restorative justice, by contrast, seeks to strengthen bonds, to create opportunities for repair within relationships, and to provide the supportive connections that are essential for healthy development.

The research on adverse childhood experiences, or ACEs, has revolutionized our understanding of what lies beneath much delinquent behavior. The original ACE study, conducted by the Centers for Disease Control and Prevention and Kaiser Permanente, surveyed over seventeen thousand adults about their childhood experiences and current health status. The findings were staggering: childhood trauma was extraordinarily common, and its effects were cumulative and profound. Individuals who had experienced four or more types of adverse childhood experiences—physical abuse, sexual abuse, emotional neglect, household dysfunction, parental incarceration, and others—were dramatically more likely to experience a wide range of negative outcomes, including substance abuse, depression, chronic disease, and involvement in criminal behavior. Subsequent research has confirmed these findings across diverse populations and settings. When we encounter a young person who has committed harm, we must ask not only "What did they do?" but "What happened to them?" This is not to excuse their actions but to understand them—and understanding is the prerequisite for genuine change. Restorative justice creates space for this understanding to emerge, not through clinical diagnosis alone, but through the encounter with victims and community members who can see the young person's full humanity even as they name the harm done.

The psychology of shame and guilt, explored extensively by researchers like June Price Tangney and Ronda Dearing, adds another crucial layer to our understanding. Shame and guilt, though often used interchangeably in everyday speech, are fundamentally different emotions with profoundly different implications for behavior and change. Shame is the feeling that *I am bad*—a global, negative evaluation of the entire self. Guilt is the feeling that *I did something bad*—a negative evaluation of a specific behavior. Shame leads to hiding, denial, blame, and aggression; guilt leads to acknowledgment, remorse, and repair. Traditional punitive justice, with its emphasis on public condemnation, stigmatization, and exclusion, is a shame-generating machine. It tells young people, over and over, that they are worthless, that they are defined by their worst actions, that they have no future. Restorative justice, by contrast, distinguishes clearly between the person and the behavior. It says to the young offender: "You are a person of worth, a member of this community, someone capable of change. But what you did was wrong, and it caused real harm. Let's talk about that harm, and let's talk about what you can do to make it right." This is guilt, not shame—and guilt, as the research consistently shows, is the emotion that leads to genuine accountability and lasting change.

The legal foundations of restorative justice, while more recent than its theological and philosophical roots, are no less significant. The concept of procedural justice, developed by Yale psychologist Tom Tyler and his colleagues, has transformed our understanding of how people experience the legal system and why they comply with the law. Procedural justice theory posits that people's willingness to accept legal decisions and obey the law depends less on whether they got what they wanted—the outcome—than on whether they perceive the process that produced that outcome as fair. When people feel they have been heard, when they believe decision-makers are neutral and trustworthy, when they are treated with dignity and respect, they are more likely to view the legal system as legitimate and to internalize its norms. This perception of legitimacy, in turn, predicts compliance with the law and cooperation with legal authorities.

Tyler's research, conducted across multiple populations and settings, has consistently confirmed these propositions. In his seminal work *Why People Obey the Law*, he demonstrated that procedural justice judgments are more powerful predictors of compliance than either the favorability of outcomes or the fear of punishment. People obey the law not primarily because they fear getting caught but because they believe the law is legitimate and deserving of obedience. This insight has profound implications for juvenile justice. If we want young people to internalize legal norms and comply with the law over the long term, we must ensure that their encounters with the justice system are experienced as fair. Punitive approaches that treat young people harshly, that deny them voice, that communicate disrespect, that seem arbitrary or biased—these approaches undermine legitimacy and breed defiance rather than compliance.

Restorative justice embodies procedural justice in action. Victims who participate in restorative processes report feeling heard in ways that traditional court proceedings never allow. They have the opportunity to tell their stories, to ask questions, to express their feelings—and they experience this as profoundly validating. Offenders who face their victims and community members in a restorative conference experience accountability not as something done to them but as something they actively participate in. They are not passive recipients of punishment but active agents in determining how to make things right. The process is transparent, inclusive, and focused on repairing harm rather than imposing suffering. Research consistently shows that both victims and offenders perceive restorative justice as more fair and legitimate than traditional court processing—and this perception of legitimacy translates into better outcomes for all involved.

The concept of reintegrative shaming, developed by Australian criminologist John Braithwaite, adds another crucial theoretical dimension. Braithwaite distinguishes between two types of shaming: disintegrative shaming, which stigmatizes offenders and excludes them from the community; and reintegrative shaming, which condemns the offense while respecting the offender and creating a pathway back into the community. Disintegrative shaming, the dominant mode of traditional punishment, tells the offender: "You have done wrong, and therefore you are wrong. You are not one of us. You are excluded." This approach, Braithwaite argues, actually increases crime by cutting offenders off from the very relationships and communities that might support their return to law-abiding behavior. Reintegrative shaming, by contrast, tells the offender: "You have done wrong, and that wrong is serious. But you are still one of us. We expect better of you, and we will help you do better." This approach, embodied in restorative justice practices, strengthens rather than severs the bonds between offenders and their communities.

The empirical research on restorative justice with juveniles has accumulated impressively over the past several decades, and the findings consistently support what the theoretical frameworks would predict. A comprehensive meta-analysis by the RAND Corporation, examining dozens of rigorous studies, found that restorative justice programs reduce recidivism among juvenile offenders by an average of 10 to 35 percent compared to traditional court processing. The effects are particularly strong for violent offenses, suggesting that the intensive engagement required by restorative processes is especially valuable when harm has been most severe. A study by Lawrence Sherman and Heather Strang at the University of Cambridge, involving multiple randomized controlled trials across the United Kingdom and Australia, found that restorative justice not only reduced reoffending but also produced significant psychological benefits for victims—reduced fear, reduced anger, greater sense of closure. Victims who participated in restorative conferences were significantly less likely to want to harm the offender, less likely to experience post-traumatic stress symptoms, and more likely to feel that justice had been done.

The Washington State Institute for Public Policy, which has conducted some of the most sophisticated cost-benefit analyses of criminal justice programs in the nation, has consistently found that restorative justice for juveniles produces substantial net benefits to taxpayers and crime victims. Their most recent analysis, incorporating data from multiple rigorous studies, found that every dollar invested in restorative justice programs returns approximately eight dollars in benefits through reduced recidivism, lower criminal justice costs, and avoided victimization. These are not speculative projections but conservative estimates based on rigorous longitudinal data. In an era of tight budgets and competing demands for public resources, restorative justice offers the rare combination of better outcomes and lower costs—a genuine win-win for communities and taxpayers.

The principles of restorative justice for juveniles, which we will explore in depth throughout this book, flow directly from these theological, philosophical, psychological, and legal foundations. The first principle is accountability—but accountability understood not as passive suffering but as active responsibility. Restorative justice holds young offenders accountable for their actions by encouraging them to acknowledge the harm they have caused and take responsibility for their behavior. This is accountability with a purpose, accountability aimed at restoration rather than retribution. It asks the young person not "What will we do to you?" but "What will you do to make this right?" The difference is not semantic but substantive, shaping everything that follows.

The second principle is empathy—that capacity to understand and feel the impact of one's actions on others that is the foundation of moral development and prosocial behavior. Restorative justice fosters empathy in young offenders by creating opportunities for genuine encounter with those they have harmed. When a victim speaks directly to an offender about the fear, anger, sadness, and loss they have experienced, something shifts inside the young person. Statistics become stories, abstractions become realities, and the full human cost of their actions becomes impossible to deny. This empathy, once awakened, becomes a powerful motivator for change and a bulwark against future offending.

The third principle is community involvement—the recognition that crime harms not only individual victims but the entire fabric of community life, and that healing therefore requires the active participation of the community. Community members play crucial roles in restorative justice processes, participating in dialogues, circles, and conferences, helping to address the harm caused by the offense, and providing support for both victims and offenders. This involvement strengthens the community itself, building the trust, cooperation, and mutual responsibility that make communities safer and more resilient.

The practices of restorative justice for juveniles translate these principles into action. Victim-offender dialogues bring together those who have been harmed and those who have caused harm in structured conversations facilitated by trained mediators. These dialogues provide victims with the opportunity to express their feelings, ask questions, and participate in determining how the offender will make amends. They provide offenders with the opportunity to understand the impact of their actions, express remorse, and commit to repair. The agreements that emerge from these dialogues—restitution, community service, apologies, educational programs—are not imposed from above but crafted collaboratively, giving them a legitimacy and power that court-ordered penalties can never achieve.

Restorative circles extend this process to include the wider community. In a circle, victims, offenders, their supporters, and community members gather in a structured format that ensures everyone has the opportunity to speak and be heard. The circle process, with its talking piece, its focus on storytelling, and its commitment to consensus, creates a container for honest communication that can transform conflict into understanding. Circles have been used for generations by indigenous peoples around the world, and their adaptation to juvenile justice represents a return to ancient wisdom as much as an innovation in modern practice.

Restorative conferences are more formal gatherings that bring together all affected parties—victims, offenders, their supporters, and relevant community members—to discuss the offense, its consequences, and a plan for restitution or reconciliation. Conferences follow a structured script that ensures all voices are heard and all perspectives considered. They begin with the victim's account of the harm, move to the offender's response, engage supporters on both sides, and culminate in a collective agreement about what must be done. The power of the conference lies in its ability to surface the full humanity of all participants, to transform abstract legal categories into lived human experience, and to create a community of accountability and support around both victim and offender.

The benefits of restorative justice for juveniles flow directly from its principles and practices. The most rigorously documented benefit is reduced recidivism. By addressing the root causes of delinquency, fostering empathy and accountability, and reintegrating young people into communities of support, restorative justice breaks the cycle of criminal behavior that punitive approaches so often perpetuate. Young people who complete restorative processes are significantly less likely to reoffend than those processed through traditional courts—a finding that has been replicated across multiple studies, multiple jurisdictions, and multiple types of offenses.

Improved victim satisfaction is another consistently documented benefit. Victims who participate in restorative processes report higher levels of satisfaction, greater sense of closure, and more positive views of the justice system than those whose cases proceed through traditional courts. They appreciate having a voice, being heard, and participating in determining the outcome. They value the opportunity to ask questions and receive answers, to express their feelings and have them acknowledged, to see the offender as a human being rather than an abstract threat. For many victims, the restorative process provides something that no amount of punishment could ever provide: a sense that their experience matters, that their suffering is recognized, and that something has been done to make things right.

Stronger communities are the third great benefit of restorative justice. By involving community members in the resolution of crime, restorative justice builds social capital, strengthens networks of relationship, and creates the conditions for collective efficacy—that combination of mutual trust and shared expectations for action that research has shown to be the most powerful predictor of neighborhood safety. Communities that practice restorative justice become places where people know their neighbors, look out for one another, and work together to address problems before they escalate. They become places where young people are surrounded by adults who care about them, hold them accountable, and support their growth. They become, in short, the kinds of communities where crime is less likely to occur in the first place.

As we conclude this opening chapter, we stand at the threshold of a comprehensive exploration of restorative justice for juveniles—its history, its principles, its practices, its benefits, its challenges, and its future. We have seen how this approach draws on the deepest wells of theological wisdom, the richest traditions of philosophical reflection, the most rigorous findings of psychological research, and the most promising developments in legal theory. We have seen how it offers an alternative to the punitive logic that has dominated our justice system for too long, an alternative grounded not in soft sentimentality but in hard-headed recognition of what actually works to reduce crime, heal victims, and strengthen communities.

The chapters that follow will take us deeper into each of these dimensions. We will explore the historical context that shaped our current juvenile justice system and the emergence of restorative alternatives. We will examine in detail the principles that animate restorative practice: accountability, empathy, community involvement. We will consider the victim-centered approach that distinguishes restorative justice from offender-focused rehabilitation models, ensuring that those who have been harmed are not forgotten in our concern for those who have caused harm. We will explore offender rehabilitation not as a vague aspiration but as a concrete process of change supported by psychological research and practical wisdom. We will examine the crucial role of community, not as an abstract concept but as a lived reality of mutual responsibility and support.

We will survey the diverse practices that give restorative justice its vitality—victim-offender dialogues that create space for genuine encounter, restorative circles that engage multiple stakeholders in collective problem-solving, conferences that bring together all those affected by harm. We will examine the benefits that research has documented: reduced recidivism, improved victim satisfaction, stronger communities, cost savings for taxpayers. We will grapple honestly with the challenges and criticisms that restorative justice faces, from concerns about fairness and equity to questions about its applicability to serious offenses. We will explore the legal frameworks that support or impede restorative practice, offering guidance for advocates seeking to institutionalize these approaches. Case studies will bring restorative justice to life, showing how principles become practice in real cases with real young people. International perspectives will broaden our vision, revealing how different cultures have adapted restorative approaches to their unique contexts. Future directions will invite us to imagine what restorative justice might become as it continues to evolve. And practical guidance will equip readers to take the next steps in their own contexts, whether as practitioners, policymakers, or concerned community members.

Throughout this journey, we will return again and again to the fundamental insight that restorative justice is not merely a program or a technique but a way of seeing—a lens through which we understand crime, harm, accountability, and healing in fundamentally relational terms. It is a way of being that honors the dignity of every person while never minimizing the reality of harm. It is a way of hoping that refuses to write off any young person as beyond redemption while demanding that redemption, if it comes, come through honest confrontation with what they have done. It is, in short, a vision of justice worthy of our highest aspirations and our deepest faith.

The journey ahead is long, and the terrain is complex. But the destination—a justice system that truly serves our young people, our victims, and our communities—is worthy of every effort we can make. Let us begin.

CHAPTER 02

HISTORICAL CONTEXT OF JUVENILE JUSTICE

To understand where we are going, we must first understand where we have been. The historical context of restorative justice for juveniles is not merely a matter of academic curiosity; it is the living memory that shapes our present possibilities and constrains our future aspirations. The story of how human societies have responded to young people who break the law is a tale of profound significance, revealing not only our changing understandings of childhood, responsibility, and punishment but also our deepest convictions about justice itself. This history, with all its twists and turns, its moments of enlightenment and its periods of darkness, provides the essential backdrop against which the emergence of restorative justice must be understood.

The historical background of juvenile justice is a complex tapestry that has evolved over centuries, woven from threads of theology, philosophy, law, and social reform. In ancient societies, the concept of childhood as a distinct developmental stage with unique needs and vulnerabilities was largely unknown. Children were seen as miniature adults, expected to assume adult responsibilities and subject to adult consequences when they fell short. The Code of Hammurabi, dating to approximately 1754 BCE, made no distinction between adult and juvenile offenders; a child who struck his father would have his hands cut off, just as an adult would. The Twelve Tables of ancient Rome similarly imposed the same penalties regardless of age. In the Hebrew scriptures, while we find evidence of special consideration for children in some contexts—the book of Deuteronomy, for example, specifies that children shall not be put to death for the sins of their parents—the general approach was one of undifferentiated punishment. A stubborn and rebellious son could be brought before the elders and stoned to death by the men of his city, a provision that, whatever its actual enforcement, reveals a world in which youth offered no automatic protection from the harshest penalties.

The theological assumptions underlying these practices deserve our careful attention. In the ancient world, wrongdoing was understood primarily as an offense against the divine order, a violation of cosmic harmony that demanded restoration through punishment. The gods required satisfaction, and that satisfaction could only be achieved through the suffering of the offender. This sacrificial logic, deeply embedded in the religious consciousness of ancient peoples, left little room for considerations of age, development, or rehabilitative potential. If the gods demanded blood, the age of the one whose blood was shed mattered little. The biblical narrative, however, contained within itself seeds of a different understanding. The story of Cain and Abel, the first recorded instance of human violence, concludes not with Cain's execution but with his marking and protection. God's response to murder is not retributive death but restorative marking—a sign that preserves Cain's life even as it sets him apart. This subtle but profound deviation from the sacrificial logic of the ancient world hints at a divine justice that operates differently from human vengeance, a justice that seeks the preservation of life even in the face of death-dealing acts.

The Greco-Roman philosophical tradition, which would later merge with biblical theology to shape Western legal thought, offered similarly complex resources for thinking about young offenders. Aristotle, in his *Nicomachean Ethics*, distinguished between voluntary and involuntary actions, recognizing that ignorance, compulsion, and diminished capacity could affect moral responsibility. While he did not explicitly apply this framework to children, the implications were clear: those who lack full capacity cannot be held fully accountable for their actions. The Roman legal principle of *doli incapax*—the incapacity for criminal intent—would eventually codify this insight, holding that children below a certain age could not form the mental state necessary for criminal guilt. This principle, which would find its way into English common law and ultimately into American jurisprudence, represented an early recognition that childhood matters for justice, that young offenders are different from adult criminals in ways that the law must acknowledge.

The medieval period saw these insights develop unevenly across Europe. Christian theology, with its emphasis on mercy, redemption, and the possibility of transformation, provided resources for a more compassionate approach to young offenders. The concept of *purgatorium*, the purifying suffering that prepares souls for heaven, offered a framework for understanding punishment as remedial rather than merely retributive. Thomas Aquinas, synthesizing Aristotelian philosophy with Christian theology, articulated a theory of punishment that included both retributive and rehabilitative elements. Punishment, for Aquinas, served not only to satisfy the demands of justice but also to correct the offender and deter others from similar wrongdoing. This multifaceted understanding left room for considering the unique needs and capacities of young people, even if it did not yet produce a separate system for juvenile offenders.

The early modern period witnessed significant changes in European attitudes toward children and childhood. The Protestant Reformation, with its emphasis on individual conscience and direct access to scripture, heightened awareness of children's spiritual capacities and vulnerabilities. Puritan theologians in England and America wrote extensively about the proper upbringing of children, emphasizing the importance of moral education and the dangers of harsh punishment that might crush rather than correct. John Locke's *Some Thoughts Concerning Education* (1693) argued for treating children as rational beings capable of understanding and responding to reasoned guidance rather than mere force. Jean-Jacques Rousseau's *Émile* (1762) went further, presenting childhood as a distinct stage of development with its own logic and needs, a stage that should be protected from the corrupting influences of adult society. These philosophical developments prepared the ground for the emergence of a separate juvenile justice system, even if they did not yet produce one.

The Industrial Revolution of the eighteenth and nineteenth centuries created the social conditions that would finally necessitate such a system. As millions of families migrated from rural areas to rapidly growing cities, traditional structures of family and community support broke down. Children, left unsupervised while parents worked long hours in factories, flooded the streets of London, New York, and other industrial centers. Poverty, homelessness, and crime among young people reached unprecedented levels, creating what contemporaries called a "juvenile delinquency crisis." The response of the criminal justice system, which still made few distinctions between children and adults, was to arrest, prosecute, and imprison young offenders alongside hardened criminals. Children as young as seven were housed in adult jails, subjected to the same brutal conditions, and exposed to the corrupting influence of adult offenders.

The results were predictable and devastating. Rather than deterring crime, these practices seemed to produce it, turning troubled children into hardened criminals. The English reformer Mary Carpenter, drawing on her work with delinquent youth in the mid-nineteenth century, documented the ways in which imprisonment corrupted rather than corrected. In her influential book *Reformatory Schools for the Children of the Perishing and Dangerous Classes, and for Juvenile Offenders* (1851), she argued for separate institutions that would provide education, moral guidance, and vocational training rather than mere punishment. Carpenter's work, grounded in both Christian compassion and practical observation, influenced reformers on both sides of the Atlantic and helped create momentum for a new approach.

In the United States, the movement for separate juvenile justice institutions gained strength in the decades following the Civil War. The "child savers," as they came to be called—primarily middle-class women motivated by religious conviction and social concern—established houses of refuge and reform schools designed to rescue wayward youth from the corrupting influences of city life. These institutions, whatever their later failings, represented a genuine departure from the punitive logic that had previously governed responses to juvenile offending. They were based on the belief that young people could be changed, that proper guidance and education could redirect them toward productive citizenship, and that the state had a responsibility to provide such guidance when families failed to do so.

The crowning achievement of this reform movement came in 1899, with the establishment of the first juvenile court in Cook County, Illinois. This landmark institution embodied a revolutionary idea: that children who broke the law should be treated not as criminals but as wards of the state, entitled to guidance, protection, and rehabilitation rather than punishment. The legal doctrine underlying this innovation was *parens patriae*—a Latin term meaning "parent of the nation" that referred to the sovereign's responsibility to care for those unable to care for themselves. Under this doctrine, the juvenile court would act as a wise and loving parent, intervening not to punish but to save, not to condemn but to correct.

The early juvenile court judges saw themselves as benevolent figures, applying their wisdom and compassion to the task of rescuing wayward youth. Proceedings were informal, often held in the judge's chambers rather than a courtroom. Strict rules of evidence and procedure were relaxed in favor of flexible, individualized decision-making. The goal was not to determine guilt or innocence in an adversarial contest but to understand the young person's situation and craft a response that would serve their best interests. Probation officers, originally volunteers from charitable organizations, investigated the backgrounds of young offenders and recommended dispositions tailored to their needs. The entire apparatus was designed to be therapeutic rather than punitive, remedial rather than retributive.

This vision, for all its noble intentions, contained within itself the seeds of its own corruption. The informality and flexibility that seemed so progressive in theory often produced arbitrary and inconsistent results in practice. Young people could be incarcerated for years without the procedural protections that adult defendants enjoyed—no right to counsel, no right to confront witnesses, no right to trial by jury. The state, acting as parent, could deprive children of liberty on the basis of evidence that would never be admitted in an adult court, and could hold them until they were "reformed" according to standards that were never clearly defined. The rehabilitative ideal, untethered from procedural safeguards, became a license for unchecked state power over the lives of children.

The shortcomings of this approach became increasingly apparent as the twentieth century progressed. Sociological research revealed that juvenile courts were not protecting children so much as processing them through systems that often did more harm than good. Young offenders were frequently stigmatized and labeled as delinquents, a mark that followed them through life and shaped how others perceived and responded to them. This labeling, as sociologists like Howard Becker and Edwin Lemert would later demonstrate, could become a self-fulfilling prophecy, turning occasional offenders into committed delinquents who internalized the identities assigned to them by the system.

The practice of incarcerating juveniles in the same facilities as adults, though officially discouraged, continued in many jurisdictions, exposing young people to the influence of hardened criminals and subjecting them to violence and abuse. Even when separate juvenile institutions existed, they were often little better than the adult prisons they supposedly replaced—overcrowded, understaffed, focused on custody rather than treatment, and marked by the same brutality that characterized the adult system. The gap between the rehabilitative rhetoric and the punitive reality became impossible to ignore.

The lack of due process in juvenile proceedings, originally justified as necessary for flexible, individualized treatment, came under increasing criticism from legal scholars and civil liberties advocates. The Supreme Court, in a series of landmark decisions beginning in the 1960s, began to extend constitutional protections to juveniles. In *Kent v. United States* (1966), the Court held that juveniles facing waiver to adult court were entitled to a hearing, assistance of counsel, and a statement of reasons for the waiver decision. In *In re Gault* (1967), perhaps the most important juvenile justice decision in American history, the Court extended to juveniles the right to notice of charges, the right to counsel, the privilege against self-incrimination, and the right to confront and cross-examine witnesses. The Court made clear that neither the Fourteenth Amendment nor the Bill of Rights is for adults alone, and that the rehabilitative ideal could not justify the deprivation of fundamental constitutional rights.

These decisions, while essential for protecting juveniles from arbitrary state power, also revealed the tension at the heart of the juvenile court experiment. If juveniles were entitled to the same procedural protections as adults, in what sense was the juvenile court truly different? If the system was going to operate like a criminal court, why maintain the fiction of *parens patriae*? These questions fueled a growing movement to abolish the juvenile court altogether and treat young offenders as adults, subject to the same penalties and procedures. The get-tough movement of the 1980s and 1990s, fueled by fears of juvenile "superpredators" that never materialized, led to legislative changes that made it easier to transfer juveniles to adult court, imposed mandatory minimum sentences for certain offenses, and abandoned the rehabilitative ideal that had animated the original juvenile court.

The results of this punitive turn were disastrous. Young people transferred to adult courts and prisons were more likely to reoffend than those retained in the juvenile system, not less. They were more likely to be sexually assaulted, more likely to attempt suicide, less likely to complete their education, less likely to find employment upon release. The very outcomes the get-tough movement promised to prevent—more crime, more victims, more harm—were actually produced by the policies it enacted. States that doubled down on punishment saw their juvenile incarceration rates soar and their public safety outcomes worsen, a bitter irony that would eventually fuel a search for alternatives.

It was against this backdrop of failure—the failure of the original rehabilitative ideal to deliver on its promise, the failure of the punitive backlash to reduce crime, the failure of both approaches to address the real needs of victims, offenders, and communities—that restorative justice emerged as a compelling alternative. Restorative justice gained traction in the latter half of the twentieth century not as a theoretical abstraction but as a practical response to the limitations of both punitive and rehabilitative models. It offered a way forward that avoided the false choice between being soft on offenders and tough on crime, between abandoning accountability and embracing punishment.

The philosophical foundations of restorative justice, as they developed in this historical context, drew on resources that had been present but marginalized throughout the history of juvenile justice. The Hebrew prophetic tradition, with its emphasis on justice as right relationship and its critique of empty ritualism, provided a framework for understanding accountability as something more than suffering. The prophet Isaiah's condemnation of those who "deprive the poor of their rights and withhold justice from the oppressed" (Isaiah 10:2) was not a call for more punishment but for more genuine attention to the needs of those who had been wronged. The prophetic insistence that God desires mercy, not sacrifice, and acknowledgment of God rather than burnt offerings (Hosea 6:6) challenged the sacrificial logic that had dominated Western understandings of justice and opened space for a different approach.

The teachings of Jesus, particularly his parables of the lost sheep, the lost coin, and the prodigal son, offered a vision of restoration that went beyond either punishment or mere forgiveness. In these stories, the focus is not on what the lost one deserves but on what they need—to be found, to be welcomed, to be restored to community. The father of the prodigal son does not demand that his wayward child suffer before being accepted; he runs to meet him, embraces him, and throws a celebration. This is not cheap grace; the son has experienced the consequences of his choices and comes home in humility and need. But the father's response is not punitive; it is restorative, aimed at rebuilding relationship rather than exacting payment.

The psychological insights that informed restorative justice's emergence drew on developments that had been unfolding throughout the twentieth century. The work of Jean Piaget and Lawrence Kohlberg on moral development provided a framework for understanding how young people's capacity for moral reasoning evolves over time and how experiences of empathy and perspective-taking contribute to that development. Carol Gilligan's critique of Kohlberg's work, with its emphasis on an ethic of care that complements the ethic of justice, offered additional resources for understanding the relational dimensions of moral growth. Restorative justice, by creating opportunities for young offenders to encounter the human impact of their actions and to engage in dialogue with those they have harmed, provided precisely the kind of experience that research suggested could foster moral development.

The psychology of trauma, which emerged as a distinct field of study in the late twentieth century, added another crucial dimension. Researchers like Judith Herman and Bessel van der Kolk documented the ways in which traumatic experiences shape brain development, emotional regulation, and behavior, and the conditions under which healing can occur. Their work revealed that many young offenders are themselves victims of trauma, and that punitive responses that ignore this reality are not only ineffective but actively harmful. Restorative justice, with its emphasis on creating safe spaces for dialogue, acknowledging harm, and supporting all affected parties, aligned with what trauma research suggested about the conditions necessary for healing.

The philosophical tradition of dialogical ethics, associated with thinkers like Martin Buber and Emmanuel Levinas, provided theoretical resources for understanding what happens in restorative encounters. Buber's distinction between *I-It* and *I-Thou* relationships illuminated the difference between treating others as objects to be managed and encountering them as subjects worthy of response. Levinas's emphasis on the face of the Other as the source of ethical obligation—the way in which the vulnerable human other calls us to responsibility—captured something essential about the victim-offender encounter. When victims and offenders meet face-to-face, something shifts. The abstract categories of offender and victim become concrete human beings with names, stories, and needs. This encounter, in Levinas's terms, is the origin of ethics itself—the moment when we are called to respond to the other who faces us.

The legal scholar Howard Zehr, often called the grandfather of restorative justice, synthesized these theological, psychological, and philosophical insights into a coherent framework for practice. In his seminal work *Changing Lenses* (1990), Zehr articulated the fundamental questions that distinguish restorative from retributive justice. Where retributive justice asks, "What law was broken? Who broke it? What punishment do they deserve?" restorative justice asks, "Who has been harmed? What are their needs? Whose obligations are these?" This shift in questions, seemingly simple, carries profound implications for every aspect of justice practice. It reorients attention from abstract legal categories to concrete human experiences, from the past to the future, from suffering to repair.

Zehr's framework drew on his own experience working with victims and offenders in the context of the Mennonite Central Committee, a faith-based organization with deep roots in the Anabaptist tradition. The Anabaptist emphasis on peacemaking, community, and reconciliation provided a natural home for restorative justice, and many of the early experiments in restorative practice emerged from Mennonite and other peace church contexts. But the appeal of restorative justice soon extended far beyond its sectarian origins, resonating with people of diverse faiths and no faith who recognized in it something true about what justice should be.

The practice of victim-offender reconciliation, as it was initially called, began in small ways in the 1970s. The first recorded victim-offender meeting in North America took place in Kitchener, Ontario, in 1974, when a probation officer arranged for two young offenders to meet with the victims of their vandalism spree. The meeting was transformative: the victims received answers to their questions and restitution for their losses, the offenders understood for the first time the real impact of their actions, and all parties came away with a sense of closure that the court process had not provided. This modest experiment sparked a movement that would spread across Canada, the United States, and eventually the world.

In the United States, the first victim-offender reconciliation program was established in Elkhart, Indiana, in 1978, under the auspices of the Mennonite Central Committee. Similar programs soon appeared in other communities, each adapting the basic model to local circumstances. By the mid-1980s, victim-offender mediation had become an established practice in many jurisdictions, and the first systematic evaluations were beginning to appear. These evaluations, while limited in scope, suggested that participants in restorative processes were more satisfied than those processed through traditional courts, and that offenders who completed restorative programs were less likely to reoffend.

The 1990s saw explosive growth in restorative justice programming, along with increasing theoretical sophistication and empirical rigor. The development of family group conferencing in New Zealand, drawing on Maori traditions of collective decision-making, added a new model that emphasized the involvement of extended family and community members. The implementation of restorative justice in schools, workplaces, and other non-criminal contexts demonstrated its applicability beyond the justice system proper. The publication of major research studies, including the influential work of Lawrence Sherman and Heather Strang in the United Kingdom, provided rigorous evidence of restorative justice's effectiveness in reducing recidivism and improving victim outcomes.

The theological underpinnings of this movement continued to deepen as practitioners and scholars explored the resources of their respective traditions for understanding and supporting restorative practice. Catholic social teaching, with its emphasis on the dignity of the human person, the common good, and the principle of subsidiarity, offered a framework that aligned closely with restorative principles. The Jewish tradition, with its rich resources for understanding repentance (*teshuvah*), repair (*tikkun*), and the limits of punishment, provided another wellspring of insight. Islamic jurisprudence, with its emphasis on reconciliation (*sulh*) and restorative responses to harm, offered yet another perspective. Indigenous traditions around the world, many of which had maintained restorative practices despite centuries of colonization and suppression, contributed wisdom that enriched and challenged Western approaches.

The psychological research continued to accumulate, confirming and extending the insights that had animated the early restorative justice movement. Studies of shame and guilt, building on the work of June Price Tangney and others, demonstrated the importance of distinguishing between these emotions and designing interventions that foster guilt rather than shame. Research on forgiveness, conducted by Everett Worthington and his colleagues, identified the conditions under which forgiveness becomes possible and the benefits it produces for victims. Studies of empathy, building on the work of Martin Hoffman and others, showed how empathy develops and how it can be cultivated through appropriate experiences. Each of these research streams provided empirical support for what restorative practitioners had learned through experience: that face-to-face encounters between victims and offenders, when properly facilitated, can produce profound changes in both parties.

The legal framework for restorative justice continued to evolve as well. The United Nations, in its 2002 Basic Principles on the Use of Restorative Justice Programmes in Criminal Matters, provided international standards and guidance for the development of restorative practices. Many countries incorporated restorative justice into their juvenile justice legislation, creating formal mechanisms for referral and establishing quality standards for programs. In the United States, the federal Juvenile Justice and Delinquency Prevention Act was amended to encourage the use of restorative practices, and many states passed their own restorative justice legislation. These legal developments, while uneven and incomplete, represented significant progress toward the institutionalization of restorative justice.

Yet challenges remained, and remain today. The punitive impulse that has dominated Western justice systems for centuries does not yield easily to alternative approaches. Politicians continue to score points by promising to be tough on crime, and the public continues to harbor fears and misconceptions about restorative justice. Funding for restorative programs is often precarious, dependent on grants and soft money rather than stable institutional support. Training and quality assurance are uneven, leading to wide variation in program quality and outcomes. The overrepresentation of youth of color in the juvenile justice system, a persistent and shameful feature of American justice, raises questions about whether restorative programs will be implemented in ways that reduce or exacerbate racial disparities.

The historical context of juvenile justice, as we have traced it from ancient times to the present, reveals both the depth of the challenges we face and the resources available for addressing them. We have seen how societies have struggled to balance the demands of accountability with the possibilities of rehabilitation, the rights of victims with the needs of offenders, the requirements of public safety with the imperatives of human dignity. We have seen the failures of purely punitive approaches, which often increase the very behaviors they aim to suppress. We have seen the shortcomings of purely rehabilitative approaches, which can become vehicles for state control rather than genuine healing. And we have seen the emergence of restorative justice as a third way, one that honors the legitimate concerns of all parties while pointing toward a different kind of justice—a justice that repairs harm, rebuilds relationships, and restores communities.

The theological resources we have identified throughout this history—the prophetic call for mercy and justice, the teachings of Jesus about forgiveness and reconciliation, the wisdom of indigenous traditions about collective responsibility and healing—continue to nourish and guide the restorative justice movement. The psychological insights we have gained—about development, trauma, shame, empathy, and change—provide empirical grounding for restorative practices and guidance for their improvement. The philosophical frameworks we have inherited—from Buber and Levinas, from the personalist tradition, from dialogical ethics—illuminate what happens in restorative encounters and why it matters. The legal developments we have witnessed—from *parens patriae* to procedural justice, from the UN Basic Principles to state legislation—create structures within which restorative justice can flourish.

As we move forward into the subsequent chapters of this book, we will draw on this rich historical inheritance to explore in greater depth the principles, practices, and possibilities of restorative justice for juveniles. We will examine accountability, empathy, and community involvement as the foundational principles of restorative practice. We will explore victim-offender dialogues, restorative circles, and conferences as the primary vehicles through which these principles are realized. We will consider the benefits that research has documented and the challenges that practitioners continue to face. We will look at case studies that bring restorative justice to life, international perspectives that broaden our vision, and future directions that invite our imagination and commitment.

But before we turn to these explorations, let us pause to appreciate the full significance of the historical journey we have traced. The emergence of restorative justice for juveniles is not an accident or a fad. It is the fruit of centuries of struggle, reflection, and reform—a movement that has drawn on the deepest wells of human wisdom and the most rigorous findings of empirical research. It represents a return to insights that were present at the beginning of our legal tradition but were suppressed by the punitive logic that came to dominate. It embodies a hope that justice can be different, that responses to harm can heal rather than hurt, that communities can be strengthened rather than divided by the ways they address wrongdoing.

This hope, grounded in history and sustained by evidence, is what animates the pages that follow. It is a hope that we invite you to share as we continue this journey together into the heart of restorative justice for juveniles.

CHAPTER 03

PRINCIPLES OF RESTORATIVE JUSTICE

The principles of restorative justice for juveniles form the cornerstone of this transformative approach, the foundational truths upon which the entire edifice of restorative practice is constructed. These are not merely abstract concepts to be memorized and recited; they are living realities that must be embodied in every restorative encounter, breathed into every dialogue, and woven into every agreement. They represent a fundamental reorientation of our understanding of justice itself, a shift from asking what offenders deserve to asking what relationships require, from calculating penalties to repairing harm, from isolating wrongdoers to reintegrating them into the communities they have wounded. Three key principles stand out as the pillars upon which all else rests: accountability, empathy, and community involvement. Each of these principles, examined in depth, reveals layers of meaning that draw on the deepest resources of theology, philosophy, psychology, and law.

Accountability in restorative justice is a concept far richer and more demanding than the pale imitation that passes for accountability in traditional punitive systems. In the conventional approach, accountability is measured by what the offender suffers—how many days in detention, how many hours of community service, how many dollars in fines. The offender is a passive recipient of consequences determined by others, and their role is simply to endure what is imposed upon them. This is accountability reduced to its lowest common denominator, a transactional exchange of pain for pain that requires nothing of the offender's heart or mind. Restorative accountability, by contrast, is active rather than passive, internal rather than external, transformative rather than merely punitive. It requires that young offenders take genuine responsibility for their actions, not by accepting punishment but by acknowledging the harm they have caused and committing themselves to making things as right as possible.

This understanding of accountability finds deep resonance in the theological traditions that have shaped Western thought. The Hebrew scriptures speak repeatedly of confession, restitution, and turning from evil as the path to restoration. In the book of Leviticus, we find detailed provisions for what must happen when one person harms another: "When anyone sins and is unfaithful to the Lord by deceiving a neighbor about something entrusted to them or left in their care or about a stolen thing, or if they cheat their neighbor, or if they find lost property and lie about it, or if they swear falsely about any such sin that people may commit—when they sin in any of these ways and realize their guilt, they must return what they have stolen or taken by extortion, or what was entrusted to them, or the lost property they found, or whatever it was they swore falsely about. They must make restitution in full, add a fifth of the value to it and give it all to the owner on the day they present their guilt offering." Here we see the essential elements of restorative accountability: acknowledgment of wrongdoing, restitution for harm caused, and a ritual of reconciliation that restores the offender to right relationship with God and community.

The prophet Ezekiel articulates this vision with particular clarity, describing the kind of accountability that leads to life rather than death: "But if a wicked person turns away from all the sins they have committed and keeps all my decrees and does what is just and right, that person will surely live; they will not die. None of the offenses they have committed will be remembered against them. Because of the righteous things they have done, they will live." This is not a God who demands payment in suffering but a God who desires transformation in character. The wicked person who turns from sin and does what is just and right is restored not because they have suffered enough but because they have changed enough. This is accountability as metamorphosis, not as penalty.

The life and teachings of Jesus amplify this understanding. When Zacchaeus, the despised tax collector, encounters Jesus, his response is not to offer himself for punishment but to commit himself to restitution: "Look, Lord! Here and now I give half of my possessions to the poor, and if I have cheated anybody out of anything, I will pay back four times the amount." Jesus does not demand this; Zacchaeus offers it freely as the fruit of his transformation. And Jesus's response is telling: "Today salvation has come to this house." Salvation here is not a transaction completed but a relationship restored, a life reoriented, a future opened. This is accountability as the path to new life.

The philosophical foundations of restorative accountability draw on traditions of thought that emphasize responsibility, relationship, and the social nature of human existence. The philosopher Emmanuel Levinas, building on the work of Martin Buber, argued that the foundation of ethics lies in the face-to-face encounter with the Other. When we see the face of another person, we are called to responsibility, summoned to respond to their need. This responsibility is not chosen but given, not contractual but existential. It precedes our freedom and grounds our humanity. Restorative justice, by bringing victims and offenders into face-to-face encounter, creates the conditions for this primordial ethical response to emerge. The young offender who sits across from the person they have harmed cannot hide behind abstractions or legal categories. They are confronted with a human face, and that face calls them to accountability.

The personalist tradition in philosophy, represented by thinkers like Jacques Maritain and Emmanuel Mounier, insists on the intrinsic dignity of every human person and the social nature of human flourishing. Persons are not isolated individuals but beings-in-relationship, and their good is bound up with the good of others. Accountability, from this perspective, is not an external imposition but an internal requirement of our shared humanity. When we harm others, we harm ourselves, damaging the relational fabric that sustains us all. Restorative accountability is the process of repairing that damage, of restoring the relationships that constitute our common life.

From the vantage point of psychology, restorative accountability aligns with what research tells us about effective behavior change. The psychology of shame and guilt, explored extensively by researchers like June Price Tangney and Ronda Dearing, reveals that guilt—the feeling that one has done something bad—is associated with constructive responses like acknowledgment, apology, and repair. Shame—the feeling that one is bad—is associated with destructive responses like denial, blame, and aggression. Traditional punitive approaches, with their emphasis on public condemnation and stigmatization, tend to generate shame rather than guilt. They tell young people that they are worthless, that they are defined by their worst actions, that they have no future. The predictable result is defensiveness, resistance, and continued offending. Restorative accountability, by contrast, focuses on the behavior rather than the person, creating conditions for guilt rather than shame and opening pathways to genuine change.

The psychology of moral development, building on the work of Jean Piaget and Lawrence Kohlberg, reveals that moral reasoning develops through stages, moving from a focus on external consequences to internalized principles. Young offenders are often stuck in earlier stages of moral development, focused on what will happen to them rather than on the impact of their actions on others. Restorative accountability, by creating opportunities for perspective-taking and empathy, can catalyze movement to higher stages of moral reasoning. When a young person hears directly from a victim about the fear, anger, and loss they have experienced, abstract rules become concrete realities, and moral development becomes possible.

The legal framework for restorative accountability draws on concepts of restorative justice that have been incorporated into juvenile justice legislation around the world. The United Nations Basic Principles on the Use of Restorative Justice Programmes in Criminal Matters emphasize that restorative processes should be used only with the free and voluntary consent of the parties, that agreements should be reached voluntarily and contain only reasonable and proportionate obligations, and that failure to reach or implement an agreement should not be used as justification for more severe penalties in subsequent criminal proceedings. These principles ensure that restorative accountability is genuine and not coerced, that it serves the interests of all parties, and that it remains true to its restorative character.

The concept of reintegrative shaming, developed by Australian criminologist John Braithwaite, provides a theoretical framework for understanding how restorative accountability works. Braithwaite distinguishes between two types of shaming: disintegrative shaming, which stigmatizes offenders and excludes them from the community; and reintegrative shaming, which condemns the offense while respecting the offender and creating a pathway back into the community. Disintegrative shaming, the dominant mode of traditional punishment, tells the offender: "You have done wrong, and therefore you are wrong. You are not one of us. You are excluded." This approach, Braithwaite argues, actually increases crime by cutting offenders off from the very relationships and communities that might support their return to law-abiding behavior. Reintegrative shaming, by contrast, tells the offender: "You have done wrong, and that wrong is serious. But you are still one of us. We expect better of you, and we will help you do better." This approach, embodied in restorative justice practices, strengthens rather than severs the bonds between offenders and their communities.

The empirical research on restorative accountability is compelling. Studies consistently show that offenders who participate in restorative programs are more likely to complete restitution agreements, more likely to apologize to victims, and less likely to reoffend than those processed through traditional courts. A meta-analysis by the RAND Corporation found that restorative justice programs reduce recidivism among juvenile offenders by an average of 10 to 35 percent. The Washington State Institute for Public Policy, in its comprehensive cost-benefit analyses, has found that restorative justice produces substantial net benefits through reduced recidivism, lower criminal justice costs, and avoided victimization. These findings confirm what the theological, philosophical, and psychological frameworks would predict: that accountability, properly understood and practiced, transforms lives.

The second great principle of restorative justice is empathy—that capacity to understand and feel the inner experience of another person that is the foundation of moral development and prosocial behavior. In restorative justice, there is a deep emphasis on fostering empathy in both offenders and victims, creating opportunities for genuine encounter that can break through the walls of abstraction and indifference that so often surround wrongdoing. Juveniles are encouraged to see the human face of their actions, to understand in concrete and personal terms the impact they have had on others. This contrasts starkly with punitive methods that often dehumanize offenders, treating them as cases to be processed rather than persons to be transformed, and that offer victims no opportunity to be seen or heard.

The theological foundations of empathy are woven throughout the biblical narrative. The Hebrew scriptures command again and again that God's people care for the stranger, the orphan, the widow—those who are vulnerable and suffering. This command is grounded not in abstract principle but in lived experience: "You shall not wrong or oppress a stranger, for you were strangers in the land of Egypt." The memory of suffering becomes the basis for empathy with others who suffer. The prophets call Israel to "know the heart of the stranger" because they have known that heart themselves. This is empathy as divine command, rooted in the character of a God who hears the cry of the oppressed and acts on their behalf.

The life of Jesus exemplifies empathy in its fullest expression. The Gospels portray a man who is consistently moved with compassion by the suffering he encounters—the leper, the blind, the grieving, the hungry. This compassion is not mere sentiment but active response, leading to healing, feeding, and restoration. The letter to the Hebrews describes Jesus as a high priest who is "able to empathize with our weaknesses," having been "tempted in every way, just as we are." This is empathy as divine attribute, grounded in the incarnation itself—God's decision to enter human experience, to know human suffering from the inside, to be moved by human need.

The apostle Paul calls the early Christian community to this same empathetic posture: "Rejoice with those who rejoice; mourn with those who mourn." This is not merely a nice sentiment but a fundamental orientation of the Christian life, a recognition that we are members one of another, that the joys and sorrows of others are our own. Paul's image of the body—"If one part suffers, every part suffers with it; if one part is honored, every part rejoices with it"—captures the essence of empathy as participation in the experience of others. Restorative justice, by creating opportunities for victims and offenders to share their experiences with one another, embodies this Pauline vision of mutual participation in suffering and healing.

The philosophical foundations of empathy draw on traditions of thought that emphasize the interpersonal nature of human existence and the role of emotion in moral life. The Scottish Enlightenment philosopher Adam Smith, in his *Theory of Moral*

Sentiments, identified sympathy—what we would today call empathy—as the foundation of moral judgment. We judge the appropriateness of others' emotions by imagining ourselves in their situation and seeing whether we would feel the same. This capacity for sympathetic identification is, for Smith, what makes moral community possible. Without it, we would be isolated monads, unable to share the emotional experiences that bind us together.

The phenomenological tradition in philosophy, represented by thinkers like Edmund Husserl and Maurice Merleau-Ponty, explored the nature of empathy as a mode of access to other minds. Edith Stein, a student of Husserl who later became a Carmelite nun and was martyred at Auschwitz, wrote her doctoral dissertation on empathy, exploring how we come to know the experiences of others. She argued that empathy is not a matter of inference or analogy but a direct perception of the other's experience, a kind of intentional feeling that grasps the other's emotion as belonging to them while also resonating within us. This philosophical account of empathy illuminates what happens in restorative encounters: victims and offenders do not merely infer one another's feelings but directly perceive and participate in them, creating a shared emotional space that makes genuine understanding possible.

The psychology of empathy has been extensively researched, and the findings consistently support its central role in moral development and behavior change. Martin Hoffman, a leading researcher on empathy, has identified several modes of empathic arousal, from primitive motor mimicry to sophisticated perspective-taking. He has traced the development of empathy from infancy through adulthood and has shown how it becomes increasingly integrated with cognitive and moral capacities.

Hoffman's research demonstrates that empathy is not a fixed trait but a capacity that can be cultivated through appropriate experiences. Restorative justice, by creating opportunities for direct encounter between victims and offenders, provides precisely the kind of experience that fosters empathic development.

The neuroscience of empathy has revealed its biological foundations. Research using functional magnetic resonance imaging (fMRI) has shown that observing another person in pain activates many of the same brain regions as experiencing pain oneself. These "mirror neuron" systems provide a neural basis for empathy, allowing us to simulate the experiences of others within our own brains. This research suggests that empathy is not a cultural construction or a moral achievement but a biological given, a fundamental feature of human neural architecture. The task of restorative justice is not to create empathy where none exists but to activate and direct the empathic capacities that are already present, to create conditions in which young people can access and act on their natural ability to feel with others.

The psychology of perspective-taking, closely related to empathy, has been shown to reduce prejudice, increase prosocial behavior, and decrease aggression. When people are encouraged to imagine themselves in another's situation, they become more understanding, more helpful, and less hostile. Restorative justice practices, by explicitly inviting young offenders to imagine the experience of their victims, engage this powerful psychological mechanism. The question at the heart of restorative dialogue—"What do you think it was like for the person you harmed?"—is not merely rhetorical but transformative, calling forth the cognitive and emotional capacities that underlie moral behavior.

The third great principle of restorative justice is community involvement—the recognition that the broader community plays a vital role in the juvenile's rehabilitation and that addressing harm requires collective effort. Restorative justice actively engages the community in the process, seeking to mend the social fabric torn by the offense and to create a supportive environment for the young offender to reintegrate successfully. This principle stands in stark contrast to traditional punitive methods that isolate offenders from the community and focus solely on individual punishment without addressing the broader social context of their actions.

The theological foundations of community involvement are woven throughout the biblical narrative. The people of Israel understood themselves not as isolated individuals but as a covenant community, bound together by their relationship with God and with one another. When one member sinned, the whole community was affected; when one member suffered, the whole community mourned. The rituals of atonement described in Leviticus were not private affairs but communal ceremonies in which the entire people participated. The prophets called the whole nation to repentance, not merely individuals. This communal understanding of sin and redemption reflects a profound intuition that we are members one of another, that our fates are intertwined, that none of us can be fully well until all of us are well.

The New Testament develops this communal vision with even greater specificity. Paul's image of the church as the body of Christ—"Now you are the body of Christ, and each one of you is a part of it"—captures the essential interdependence of Christian community. Each member has a role to play, each is necessary for the health of the whole, and when one suffers, all suffer together. This is not merely a metaphor but a lived reality, a description of how the early Christian communities actually functioned. They shared their possessions, cared for the needy, and bore one another's burdens. They understood that following Jesus meant not individual salvation but communal transformation, not private piety but public witness.

The letter of James makes clear that this communal responsibility extends to accountability for wrongdoing: "My brothers and sisters, if one of you should wander from the truth and someone should bring that person back, remember this: Whoever turns a sinner from the error of their way will save them from death and cover over a multitude of sins." Here we see the community's role in restoration: not punishment but rescue, not exclusion but return. The one who wanders is brought back, the sinner is turned from error, and in this turning, life is saved and sins are covered. This is restorative justice as community practice.

The philosophical foundations of community involvement draw on traditions of thought that emphasize the social nature of human existence and the communal dimensions of justice. The communitarian tradition, represented by thinkers like Alasdair MacIntyre and Charles Taylor, argues that the Enlightenment's focus on the autonomous individual has obscured the ways in which our identities, values, and capacities are shaped by the communities in which we are embedded. We are not self-created monads but inheritors of traditions, participants in practices, members of communities. Our good is bound up with the good of these communities, and we cannot flourish apart from them. Restorative justice, by involving the community in the response to wrongdoing, honors this fundamental truth about human existence.

The pragmatist tradition, represented by thinkers like John Dewey and Richard Rorty, emphasizes the importance of democratic participation and collective problem-solving. Dewey argued that democracy is not merely a form of government but a mode of associated living, a way of addressing shared problems through collective intelligence. Restorative justice, with its circles and conferences that bring together all affected parties to determine how to repair harm, embodies this pragmatic vision. It treats wrongdoing not as a matter for experts alone but as a community problem requiring community solutions, and it trusts the collective wisdom of those most affected to craft responses that are both just and effective.

The sociology of crime and delinquency provides empirical support for the importance of community involvement. Research on collective efficacy, conducted by Robert Sampson and his colleagues, has shown that neighborhoods characterized by mutual trust and shared expectations for action have lower rates of crime, even when other factors like poverty and unemployment are taken into account. Collective efficacy—the combination of social cohesion and informal social control—is a powerful predictor of community safety. Restorative justice, by building social connections and encouraging collective responsibility, strengthens the very fabric of community life that prevents crime in the first place.

The research on social capital, developed by scholars like Robert Putnam, reveals the importance of networks of relationship for individual and community well-being. Social capital—the trust, norms, and networks that enable collective action—has been linked to better health, higher educational achievement, lower crime rates, and more effective governance. Communities rich in social capital are better able to address shared problems and support their members through difficulties. Restorative justice, by bringing community members together to address harm, builds social capital even as it repairs specific injuries. The connections forged in restorative processes become resources for future problem-solving and mutual support.

The psychology of belonging, explored by researchers like Roy Baumeister and Mark Leary, reveals that human beings have a fundamental need to belong, to form and maintain strong, stable relationships with others. When this need is thwarted, the consequences are severe: increased anxiety, depression, aggression, and antisocial behavior. Young offenders are often young people who have experienced profound failures of belonging—rejection by family, exclusion by peers, failure at school. Punitive responses that further exclude them from community only deepen this wound, confirming their worst fears about themselves and driving them toward the only communities that will still accept them: gangs, criminal networks, other alienated and angry young people. Restorative justice, by contrast, seeks to create pathways back into community, to offer the belonging that young people desperately need and cannot find elsewhere.

The differences between restorative justice and traditional punitive methods become clear when we examine how these principles are embodied in practice. Where punitive methods focus on healing over punishment, restorative justice seeks to address the underlying causes of delinquent behavior rather than simply imposing suffering in exchange for wrongdoing. This is not softness but wisdom, not leniency but effectiveness. Research consistently shows that punishment alone does not change behavior; it only suppresses it temporarily and often at the cost of increased resistance and resentment. Healing—addressing the wounds, building the capacities, restoring the relationships that enable prosocial behavior—is the only path to lasting change.

Where punitive methods encourage empathy over dehumanization, restorative justice creates opportunities for genuine encounter that can break through the walls of abstraction and indifference. The dehumanization that occurs in punitive systems is not merely a side effect but a feature; it is easier to punish people when we have first defined them as less than fully human. Restorative justice refuses this dehumanization, insisting that even those who have caused terrible harm remain persons worthy of respect and capable of change. This insistence is not sentimentality but realism; it recognizes that the only way to transform behavior is to engage the person, and that engagement requires seeing and being seen in one's full humanity.

Where punitive methods emphasize community engagement over isolation, restorative justice actively involves the community in the resolution process rather than separating offenders from the very relationships that might support their change. The isolation of offenders in prisons and detention centers is not merely a practical necessity but a symbolic statement: you are not one of us. This statement, repeated often enough, becomes self-fulfilling. Offenders internalize their exclusion and behave accordingly. Restorative justice, by keeping offenders connected to community even as they are held accountable for their actions, sends a different message: you are one of us, and we expect you to act like it. This message, too, can become self-fulfilling.

Where punitive methods aim for long-term solutions over short-term fixes, restorative justice seeks to create lasting change by addressing root causes rather than merely suppressing symptoms. The short-term fix of incarceration may temporarily remove a young person from the community, but it does nothing to address the factors that led to their offending—and often makes those factors worse. The long-term solution of restorative justice requires more time, more effort, more engagement—but it produces results that last. Young people who complete restorative programs are not merely less likely to reoffend; they are more likely to complete their education, find employment, form healthy relationships, and contribute to their communities.

The theoretical underpinnings of restorative justice—reintegrative shaming and procedural justice—provide a framework for understanding why these principles work. Reintegrative shaming, as developed by John Braithwaite, explains how communities can hold offenders accountable without excluding them, condemning the offense while affirming the offender. This approach activates the offender's conscience—the internalized norms that make wrongdoing uncomfortable—while also engaging the social disapproval that deters future offending. But unlike the stigmatizing shaming of traditional punishment, reintegrative shaming is followed by gestures of acceptance and inclusion, rituals that welcome the offender back into the community. This combination of accountability and acceptance, Braithwaite argues, is far more effective at reducing crime than either pure punishment or pure leniency.

Procedural justice, as developed by Tom Tyler, explains why people obey the law and accept legal decisions. Tyler's research demonstrates that people's willingness to comply with the law depends less on their fear of punishment than on their perception that legal authorities are legitimate and that legal processes are fair. When people feel they have been heard, when they believe decision-makers are neutral and trustworthy, when they are treated with dignity and respect, they are more likely to view the legal system as legitimate and to internalize its norms. Restorative justice embodies procedural justice in action. Victims and offenders alike have the opportunity to tell their stories, to participate in decision-making, to be treated as persons rather than cases. This experience of fairness and respect generates legitimacy, and legitimacy generates compliance.

The fusion of reintegrative shaming and procedural justice in restorative practice creates a powerful engine for transformation. The transparent, participatory process engages all parties in addressing harm and determining how to repair it. The community's expression of disapproval—the shaming—is balanced by gestures of acceptance and inclusion. The offender's experience of being heard and respected—the procedural justice—makes them more open to internalizing the community's norms. The victim's experience of having their voice honored and their needs addressed—also procedural justice—promotes healing and closure. All of this occurs in a context that is intentionally designed to foster healing and restoration for the justice-involved youth, the victim, and the wider community.

The biblical wisdom that undergirds these principles finds expression in the ancient practice of the Jubilee, described in Leviticus 25. Every fiftieth year, the Jubilee was to be proclaimed throughout the land: liberty to captives, return of property to original owners, rest for the land, restoration of relationships distorted by economic inequality and social dislocation. The Jubilee was not merely a humanitarian gesture but a theological declaration: the land belongs to God, the people belong to God, and the distortions introduced by human sin and failure cannot have the final word. Every fifty years, the slate was wiped clean, the relationships were restored, the community was renewed. This is restorative justice on a cosmic scale, a vision of shalom that encompasses all of creation.

Jesus announced his ministry in terms that echo the Jubilee: "The Spirit of the Lord is on me, because he has anointed me to proclaim good news to the poor. He has sent me to proclaim freedom for the prisoners and recovery of sight for the blind, to set the oppressed free, to proclaim the year of the Lord's favor." This is not merely a spiritual message but a social vision, a declaration that God's restorative justice is breaking into history, transforming lives, rebuilding communities. The early church understood itself as the community in which this vision was being realized, a place where "there were no needy persons among them" because those who had more shared with those who had less, where former enemies were reconciled, where the dividing walls of hostility were broken down.

The principles of restorative justice—accountability, empathy, community involvement—are not merely effective practices but faithful witnesses to this biblical vision. They embody the accountability that the prophets called for, the empathy that Jesus embodied, the community involvement that Paul cultivated. They are the practical outworking of the Jubilee vision, the concrete expression of God's restorative purposes for humanity. And they work. The research confirms it. The transformed lives testify to it. The healed victims and restored communities bear witness to it.

As we move forward into the subsequent chapters of this book, we will explore how these principles are embodied in specific practices—victim-offender dialogues, restorative circles, conferences, and other approaches. We will examine the benefits that flow from these practices and the challenges they face. We will consider case studies that bring restorative justice to life and international perspectives that broaden our vision. But always we will return to these foundational principles, these three pillars on which all else rests: accountability that transforms, empathy that connects, community that embraces. These are the gifts of restorative justice to young offenders, to victims, to communities—and to all of us who long for a justice system that truly serves the cause of healing and restoration.

CHAPTER 04

VICTIM-CENTERED APPROACH

Restorative justice's victim-centered approach is perhaps its most distinctive and revolutionary feature, the element that most fundamentally sets it apart from traditional punitive measures that have dominated Western legal systems for centuries. This approach places the needs and rights of victims at the very forefront of the justice process, recognizing their central role in addressing harm and seeking resolution. In doing so, it reverses a centuries-old pattern in which victims were systematically marginalized, their voices silenced, their suffering abstracted into legal categories, their needs subordinated to the interests of the state and the rights of the accused. To understand the victim-centered approach is to understand something essential about restorative justice itself: that justice is not done until those who have been harmed are made whole.

The historical marginalization of victims in Western legal systems is a story that must be understood if we are to appreciate the significance of the restorative alternative. In ancient societies, justice was largely a private matter between victims and offenders or their families. The injured party or their kin had the right to seek redress directly, through negotiation if possible, through vengeance if necessary. The emergence of state-centered legal systems, from ancient Rome through the development of English common law, gradually transformed this landscape. Crimes came to be understood as offenses against the king's peace, against the state, against abstract legal order rather than against actual human beings. The victim became a witness, a tool for the state's prosecution, rather than a party with standing and interests of their own. The state took over the role of pursuing justice, and the victim was left on the sidelines, watching a drama in which they had once been the central character but were now reduced to a bit part.

This transformation had profound consequences that persist to this day. Victims in traditional criminal proceedings have no formal role beyond that of witness. They do not participate in charging decisions, plea negotiations, or sentencing determinations. They are not consulted about whether a case should be diverted from prosecution or what conditions might be appropriate for an offender's release. They are often not even informed about the progress of "their" case, about court dates, about outcomes. When they are permitted to make a victim impact statement at sentencing, this statement comes at the end of the process, after all the important decisions have already been made, and it has no binding effect on the outcome. The message to victims is clear: what happened to you matters less than we say it does; your experience is less important than the legal categories into which it has been translated; your needs are subordinate to the procedural requirements of the system.

The psychological toll of this marginalization is severe and well-documented. Crime victims often experience what researchers call "secondary victimization" or "re-victimization" at the hands of the justice system. The very institutions established to address their suffering compound it through indifference, insensitivity, and exclusion. Victims report feeling used, ignored, and betrayed by a system that claims to serve them but in practice serves institutional interests. They describe the court process as alienating and disorienting, a labyrinth of procedures and jargon that leaves them feeling powerless and confused. They speak of the profound frustration of watching "their" case be resolved through plea bargains that they had no part in negotiating, resulting in sentences that bear no relation to their experience of the crime. For many victims, the justice system becomes a second injury, a wound added to the wound already suffered.

The victim-centered approach of restorative justice directly addresses this historical failure. In a victim-centered restorative justice process, victims are given the opportunity to express their feelings, concerns, and needs directly to the offender in a safe and structured setting. They have a voice in determining how the offender can make amends for the harm caused, which can include restitution, apologies, community service, or other forms of redress that address their specific needs. This empowerment of victims can be incredibly cathartic, allowing them to regain a sense of control and closure that is systematically denied in traditional criminal justice systems. The victim moves from the margins to the center, from passive observer to active participant, from object of the system's processing to subject of their own healing.

The theological foundations of this victim-centered approach run deep and cannot be ignored if we are to grasp its full significance. The Hebrew scriptures are filled with God's particular concern for those who have been wronged, for the vulnerable, the oppressed, the victimized. The psalmist repeatedly cries out to God for justice against those who have caused harm: "Arise, Lord, in your anger; rise up against the rage of my enemies. Awake, my God; decree justice. Let the assembled peoples gather around you, while you sit enthroned over them on high. Let the Lord judge the peoples. Vindicate me, Lord, according to my righteousness, according to my integrity, O Most High." This is not a detached, neutral God but a God who takes sides with the wronged, who hears the cry of the victim and responds.

The prophet Isaiah articulates God's concern for victims with particular power: "The Spirit of the Sovereign Lord is on me, because the Lord has anointed me to proclaim good news to the poor. He has sent me to bind up the brokenhearted, to proclaim freedom for the captives and release from darkness for the prisoners, to proclaim the year of the Lord's favor and the day of vengeance of our God, to comfort all who mourn, and provide for those who grieve in Zion—to bestow on them a crown of beauty instead of ashes, the oil of joy instead of mourning, and a garment of praise instead of a spirit of despair." Here we see God's restorative purpose focused on those who have suffered: the brokenhearted, the captives, the prisoners, those who mourn, those in despair. The good news is precisely that God sees their suffering and acts to restore them.

The life and teachings of Jesus amplify this victim-centered focus. Throughout the Gospels, Jesus consistently turns toward those who are suffering, marginalized, and oppressed. He heals the sick, feeds the hungry, touches the untouchable, speaks with the outcast. He declares that the greatest commandment is to love God and love neighbor, and he defines neighbor in terms that include the stranger, the enemy, the one in need. The parable of the Good Samaritan, perhaps his most famous teaching, centers on the question of who proves to be a neighbor to the man who fell among thieves. The priest and the Levite, religious professionals who might be expected to help, pass by on the other side. It is the Samaritan, a member of a despised and marginalized group, who stops, who sees the victim, who binds his wounds, who cares for him. The message is unmistakable: the victim matters, his suffering demands a response, and that response defines what it means to be a neighbor.

The early church understood itself as a community called to embody this victim-centered compassion. The book of Acts describes the believers sharing their possessions so that "there were no needy persons among them." The epistle of James defines "religion that God our Father accepts as pure and faultless" as this: "to look after orphans and widows in their distress and to keep oneself from being polluted by the world." Orphans and widows—the paradigmatic victims of ancient society, those without protectors or providers—are the special objects of God's concern and the church's care. The victim-centered approach of restorative justice stands in direct continuity with this biblical witness.

The philosophical foundations of the victim-centered approach draw on traditions of thought that emphasize the primacy of the other, the ethical demand of the vulnerable, and the irreducibility of human suffering. The philosopher Emmanuel Levinas, building on the work of Martin Buber, argued that ethics begins not with abstract principles or universal rules but with the face-to-face encounter with the Other. When we see the face of another person—particularly a person who is vulnerable, suffering, in need—we are called to responsibility. This responsibility is not chosen but given, not contractual but existential. It precedes our freedom and grounds our humanity. The face of the victim, in Levinas's framework, is the origin of ethics itself, the source of the command "You shall not kill" that is also a command "You shall respond."

Levinas's philosophy has profound implications for how we understand justice. If ethics begins with the face of the Other, then justice must be organized around responding to that face, meeting the needs it presents, honoring the claim it makes. Traditional punitive justice, with its focus on abstract rules and impersonal procedures, systematically screens out the face of the victim. The victim's suffering is translated into legal categories, their story is filtered through evidentiary rules, their presence is reduced to testimony. The face, with its immediate and irreducible demand, disappears. Restorative justice, by creating opportunities for victims and offenders to meet face-to-face, restores this ethical foundation. The victim's face is seen, their story is heard, their need is addressed. Justice becomes response rather than abstraction.

The personalist tradition in philosophy, represented by thinkers like Jacques Maritain and Emmanuel Mounier, insists on the intrinsic dignity of every human person and the social nature of human flourishing. This dignity is not earned or achieved but given, not conditional on virtue or status but inherent in personhood itself. Victims retain this dignity even when they have been violated; indeed, their dignity is precisely what has been assaulted by the crime. Justice requires not merely that offenders be punished but that victims' dignity be affirmed and restored. The victim-centered approach of restorative justice, with its emphasis on listening to victims, taking their needs seriously, and involving them in the resolution process, is a practical way of honoring this dignity.

The psychology of victimization provides empirical support for the victim-centered approach and reveals why traditional justice systems so often fail victims. Trauma research, pioneered by scholars like Judith Herman and Bessel van der Kolk, has documented the profound and lasting effects of victimization on psychological functioning. Victims of crime often experience symptoms of post-traumatic stress: intrusive memories, hypervigilance, emotional numbing, avoidance of reminders. They may struggle with feelings of shame, guilt, and self-blame, even when rationally they know they are not at fault. They may lose trust in others, in the world, in themselves. The experience of being victimized shatters fundamental assumptions about safety, predictability, and meaning that are essential for psychological well-being.

The process of recovery from trauma, Herman argues, requires three things: the establishment of safety, the reconstruction of the trauma story, and the restoration of connection with others. Each of these requirements is systematically undermined by traditional criminal justice processes. Victims are not made to feel safe in courtrooms where they must face the offender across a crowded room, where they may be subjected to aggressive cross-examination, where the outcome is uncertain and beyond their control. Their trauma story is not honored but filtered, truncated, and translated into legal language that strips it of its emotional meaning. Their connection with others is not restored but often further damaged by the isolation and alienation they experience in dealing with the system.

Restorative justice, by contrast, directly addresses each of these requirements. The restorative process is designed to be safe, with trained facilitators ensuring that all participants are treated with respect and that no one is subjected to intimidation or abuse. Victims have the opportunity to tell their full story, in their own words, to an audience that is required to listen. And the process aims to restore connection—between victim and offender to the extent possible, but also between victim and community, as community members witness the victim's suffering and commit to supporting their healing.

The psychology of voice and participation, explored by researchers like Tom Tyler and his colleagues, reveals why having a say in legal proceedings is so important for victims. Tyler's work on procedural justice demonstrates that people's satisfaction with legal outcomes depends less on whether they got what they wanted than on whether they perceive the process as fair. And the single most important factor in perceptions of fairness is the opportunity to participate—to tell one's story, to be heard, to have one's views considered. Victims in restorative processes consistently report higher levels of satisfaction than those whose cases go through traditional courts, precisely because they have this opportunity to participate. They are not passive recipients of a decision made by others but active participants in shaping the resolution.

The psychology of closure, while sometimes oversimplified in popular discourse, captures something real about what victims need. Closure is not about forgetting or moving on as if nothing happened; it is about integrating the experience into one's life story in a way that no longer dominates or defines. It is about reaching a point where the traumatic memory is no longer accompanied by overwhelming emotion, where the victim can think about what happened without being flooded by fear, anger, or grief. Research suggests that restorative processes can contribute to closure by providing victims with answers to their questions—Why me? Why did this happen? Does the offender understand what they did?—and by giving them the opportunity to express their feelings directly to the person who caused them harm. For many victims, this experience is profoundly cathartic, allowing them to release emotions that have been locked inside since the crime occurred.

The legal framework for victim-centered restorative justice has developed significantly in recent decades, reflecting growing recognition of victims' rights and needs. The United Nations Declaration of Basic Principles of Justice for Victims of Crime and Abuse of Power, adopted by the General Assembly in 1985, affirmed that victims are entitled to access to justice and fair treatment, restitution, compensation, and necessary material, medical, psychological, and social assistance. The declaration specifically recognized the value of informal mechanisms for resolving disputes, including mediation, and encouraged their use. Subsequent UN instruments, including the 2002 Basic Principles on the Use of Restorative Justice Programmes in Criminal Matters, have elaborated on these themes, emphasizing that restorative processes should be used only with the free and voluntary consent of victims and that victims should be able to withdraw such consent at any time.

Many countries have incorporated victim-centered restorative justice into their juvenile justice legislation, creating formal mechanisms for referral and establishing standards for practice. In New Zealand, the Family Group Conference process, which draws on Maori traditions, places victims at the center of decision-making about how to respond to youth offending. In Norway, the National Mediation Service provides victim-offender mediation as a voluntary option for victims and offenders at all stages of the justice process. In the United States, many states have passed legislation authorizing restorative justice practices and establishing victim rights that include the opportunity to participate in restorative processes. These legal developments, while uneven and incomplete, represent significant progress toward institutionalizing the victim-centered approach.

The empirical research on victim participation in restorative justice is remarkably consistent and compelling. Multiple studies across different countries and types of offenses have found that victims who participate in restorative processes report higher levels of satisfaction than those whose cases go through traditional courts. A meta-analysis by the RAND Corporation found that victims in restorative programs were significantly more likely to feel that justice had been done, that their needs had been addressed, and that they would recommend the process to others in similar situations. The landmark study by Lawrence Sherman and Heather Strang, involving multiple randomized controlled trials across the United Kingdom and Australia, found that victims who participated in restorative conferences experienced significant reductions in post-traumatic stress symptoms, anger, and desire for revenge compared to those whose cases proceeded through traditional courts.

The specific benefits that victims experience in restorative processes are multiple and mutually reinforcing. First and foremost is the benefit of voice and participation. Victims have the opportunity to express their feelings, concerns, and needs directly to the offender in a safe and structured setting. This is not the filtered, truncated testimony of the courtroom but full, authentic communication, unmediated by lawyers and evidentiary rules. Victims can say what they need to say, ask the questions that have been troubling them, and be heard by the person who most needs to hear them.

Second is the benefit of understanding and empowerment. Victim-centered restorative justice processes aim to help victims understand the motivations behind the offender's actions and, where appropriate, foster empathy. This understanding can be profoundly empowering for victims, as it allows them to see the human face of the offender and to make sense of an experience that may have seemed senseless and random. Understanding does not excuse the offense, but it can demystify it, reducing its power to terrify and confuse.

Third is the benefit of satisfaction and healing. Traditional punitive methods often leave victims feeling marginalized and dissatisfied with the justice system's handling of their cases. The process is slow, confusing, and alienating. The outcome often bears no relation to the victim's experience or needs. Restorative justice, by contrast, offers victims the opportunity for genuine satisfaction by addressing their emotional and practical needs directly. When victims see that their participation has made a difference, that the offender has heard them and is taking steps to make amends, they experience a sense of justice that no amount of punishment can provide.

Fourth is the benefit of redress and restitution. Victim-offender dialogues in restorative justice can lead to agreements for restitution or other forms of redress. This means that victims have a direct say in how the offender can make amends, which can be a powerful tool for restoring what was lost. Restitution agreements are tailored to the specific needs of each victim, rather than being imposed by a court according to rigid formulas. They may include financial compensation for losses, but they may also include services, actions, or symbolic gestures that address harms that money cannot measure.

Fifth is the benefit of closure and moving forward. Engaging in a restorative process can provide victims with a sense of closure and a path for moving forward after the offense. It allows them to actively participate in shaping the resolution rather than being passive observers of a drama that is supposedly about them but in which they have no role. This active participation is itself healing, restoring the sense of agency that crime so often destroys. Victims who have participated in restorative processes often describe the experience as transformative, allowing them to put the offense behind them and get on with their lives in ways they had not thought possible.

Sixth is the benefit of preventing re-victimization. Victim-centered restorative justice processes aim to prevent re-victimization by ensuring that victims are treated with dignity and respect throughout the process. This approach reduces the risk of secondary trauma that can result from traditional court proceedings, where victims may feel attacked, disbelieved, or ignored. By treating victims with the respect they deserve, restorative justice models the very behavior it seeks to promote—behavior that honors the dignity of every person and refuses to add injury to injury.

The theological vision that undergirds this victim-centered approach finds its most powerful expression in the cross of Christ. The cross is the ultimate symbol of victimization—an innocent man, tortured and executed by the powers of his day, suffering a death reserved for the worst criminals. And yet the cross is also the ultimate symbol of God's response to victimization. In the cross, God does not stand aloof from human suffering but enters into it, takes it into God's own life, experiences it from the inside. The God revealed in Jesus Christ is not a distant, unmoved mover but a suffering God, a God who weeps, a God who is crucified. And the resurrection that follows is God's victory over the powers that victimize, God's declaration that death and suffering do not have the final word, God's promise that those who suffer will be vindicated and restored.

This theological vision has profound implications for how we respond to victims. It tells us that victims matter, that their suffering is real, that God takes it seriously. It tells us that the goal of justice is not merely to punish offenders but to restore victims, to make them whole, to give them beauty for ashes and the oil of joy for mourning. It tells us that the church, as the body of Christ, is called to be a community of healing and restoration, a place where victims are welcomed, heard, and supported. And it tells us that restorative justice, with its victim-centered approach, is not merely a good idea or an effective program but a faithful response to the God who suffers with those who suffer and promises to make all things new.

The victim-centered approach of restorative justice also has profound implications for how we understand accountability. In traditional punitive systems, accountability is measured by what the offender suffers. The victim's role is to witness this suffering, to find satisfaction in seeing the offender get what they deserve. Restorative accountability is different. It is measured not by what the offender suffers but by what the offender does to make things right for the victim. The focus shifts from the offender's pain to the victim's need, from punishment to repair. This shift is not merely semantic but substantive, reflecting a fundamentally different understanding of what justice requires.

This understanding of accountability finds powerful expression in the biblical concept of restitution. Throughout the Hebrew scriptures, when one person harms another, the requirement is not that the offender suffer but that they make restitution—that they restore what was taken, repair what was broken, compensate for what was lost. The detailed provisions in Exodus and Leviticus for restitution in cases of theft, property damage, and personal injury reflect a justice system organized around making victims whole rather than making offenders suffer. Restorative justice reclaims this ancient wisdom, insisting that true accountability is accountability to the victim, not merely to the state or to abstract legal categories.

The victim-centered approach also transforms our understanding of forgiveness. In popular discourse, forgiveness is often understood as something victims do for offenders—a gift they bestow, a burden they take on. This understanding can create pressure on victims to forgive before they are ready, or to forgive in ways that deny the reality of their suffering. Restorative justice offers a different framework. It does not require or even expect forgiveness. What it requires is that victims be heard, that their needs be addressed, that they have the opportunity to participate in shaping the resolution. Forgiveness, if it comes, is a gift that victims may choose to give, not an obligation they must fulfill. And when forgiveness does come in the context of restorative justice, it is often deeper and more meaningful because it is grounded in genuine encounter and understanding rather than abstract principle or external pressure.

The psychological research on forgiveness, conducted by scholars like Everett Worthington and his colleagues, supports this understanding. Worthington distinguishes between decisional forgiveness—the choice to release the offender from the debt of the offense and to treat them with goodwill—and emotional forgiveness—the replacement of negative emotions like anger and fear with positive emotions like empathy and compassion. Both forms of forgiveness can be healing for victims, but they operate differently and require different conditions. Decisional forgiveness can be chosen relatively quickly, but it may not bring emotional relief. Emotional forgiveness takes longer and requires the kind of deep processing that restorative encounters can provide. When victims have the opportunity to tell their stories, to ask their questions, to see the offender's humanity, the conditions for emotional forgiveness are created.

The victim-centered approach also has implications for community. When a crime occurs, the harm ripples outward, affecting not only the direct victim but also family members, friends, neighbors, and the broader community. Restorative justice recognizes this reality by involving community members in the process, giving them the opportunity to express how the crime has affected them and to participate in determining how to address the harm. But the primary focus remains on the direct victim. Community involvement is not a substitute for victim participation but a supplement to it, a way of surrounding the victim with support and ensuring that their needs remain central.

The early church understood this dynamic intuitively. When a member of the community was wronged, the whole community gathered to address the wrong, to support the victim, and to restore the offender if possible. The letters of Paul are filled with instructions about how the community should respond to various kinds of wrongdoing, always with an eye to the needs of those who have been harmed and the restoration of those who have caused harm. This was not a formal legal process but a communal practice, grounded in the conviction that the body of Christ suffers when one member suffers and rejoices when one member is honored.

As we have explored in this chapter, the victim-centered approach of restorative justice is not merely a procedural innovation but a profound reorientation of our understanding of justice itself. It places the needs and rights of victims at the forefront, recognizing their central role in addressing harm and seeking resolution. It empowers victims by giving them voice and participation, offering them understanding and closure, providing them with redress and restitution. It protects victims from re-victimization by ensuring they are treated with dignity and respect throughout the process. And it does all this in ways that are grounded in the deepest theological, philosophical, and psychological insights about human suffering, healing, and restoration.

The journey of restorative justice is, at its heart, a journey toward the victim. It is a movement away from abstract legal categories and toward concrete human faces, away from institutional interests and toward personal needs, away from punishment and toward healing. It is a recognition that justice is not done until victims are made whole, that the measure of any justice system is not how efficiently it processes cases or how severely it punishes offenders but how well it serves those who have been harmed. And it is a hope that, by centering victims, we might create a justice system that truly deserves the name—a system that repairs harm, rebuilds lives, and restores our youth and our communities.

CHAPTER 05

OFFENDER REHABILITATION

Offender rehabilitation stands as a central and non-negotiable pillar of restorative justice for young offenders, representing perhaps the most hopeful and transformative dimension of this entire approach. Unlike traditional punitive approaches that often focus solely on punishment and confinement—warehousing young people in institutions where they are more likely to learn criminal skills than prosocial ones, more likely to be traumatized than healed, more likely to emerge as hardened offenders than responsible citizens—restorative justice places a strong and unwavering emphasis on the profound truth that individuals, even young people who have caused serious harm, can change and grow. This is not naive optimism but a conviction grounded in theological anthropology, philosophical understanding, psychological research, and decades of实践 evidence. Restorative justice seeks not merely to punish wrongdoing but to rehabilitate wrongdoers and facilitate their reintegration into society as responsible, law-abiding citizens who contribute to the common good rather than detract from it.

The very concept of rehabilitation rests on a set of assumptions about human nature that are fundamentally at odds with the assumptions underlying purely punitive approaches. Punitive systems assume that people are fixed, that their behavior reflects stable traits that punishment can suppress but not transform. The goal is deterrence—making offending so costly that rational actors will choose not to offend—and incapacitation—preventing offending by locking people away. Rehabilitation, by contrast, assumes that people can change, that their behavior is not fixed but fluid, that with appropriate support and intervention, even those who have caused serious harm can become different people. This assumption is not sentimentality but realism, grounded in the observation that most young people who offend eventually desist from crime, that criminal behavior is often a phase rather than a life sentence, and that the right interventions can accelerate the natural process of maturation and change.

The theological foundations of this rehabilitative vision run deep and cannot be ignored if we are to grasp its full significance. The entire biblical narrative is structured around the possibility and reality of transformation. The people of Israel are repeatedly called to turn from their ways and return to God, and the prophets announce that this turning is possible, that God stands ready to receive those who repent. The Hebrew word *shuv*, meaning to turn or return, appears hundreds of times in the scriptures, calling individuals and nations to transformation. The promise is not merely that God will forgive but that God will change hearts, will write the law on hearts, will give new spirits and new hearts. The prophet Ezekiel captures this vision with particular power: "I will give you a new heart and put a new spirit in you; I will remove from you your heart of stone and give you a heart of flesh." This is not rehabilitation as human achievement but as divine gift, not self-improvement but transformation from the inside out.

The life and ministry of Jesus exemplify this transformative possibility. He calls fishermen to become fishers of men, tax collectors to become disciples, zealots to become apostles. He eats with sinners and tax collectors, not condoning their sin but calling them to new life. The most dramatic transformations in the Gospels are those of people like Zacchaeus, the despised tax collector who, after encountering Jesus, commits himself to restitution and changed living. Jesus does not reject him because of his past but welcomes him into a different future. The woman caught in adultery, brought to Jesus by those eager to see her stoned, receives not condemnation but a call to transformation: "Go now and leave your life of sin." The past is not erased, but it need not determine the future. New life is possible.

The apostle Paul is himself the supreme example of this transformative possibility. The man who persecuted the church, who approved of Stephen's execution, who dragged Christians from their homes to prison—this same man becomes the greatest missionary and theologian in Christian history. Paul never forgot his past; he referred to himself as the "least of the apostles," unfit to be called an apostle because he persecuted the church. But his past did not define him. He was transformed by his encounter with the risen Christ, and his life became a testimony to the reality that God can change anyone. "If anyone is in Christ," Paul wrote, "the new creation has come: The old has gone, the new is here!" This is not mere metaphor but lived experience, the testimony of a man whose life had been radically reoriented and who spent the rest of his days inviting others into the same transformative possibility.

The philosophical foundations of rehabilitation draw on traditions of thought that emphasize human freedom, potential, and the capacity for change. The existentialist tradition, represented by thinkers like Jean-Paul Sartre and Simone de Beauvoir, insists that human beings are not fixed essences but projects, constantly creating themselves through their choices. "Existence precedes essence," Sartre declared, meaning that we are not born with predetermined natures but become who we are through our actions. This philosophy, whatever its excesses, captures something important about human freedom and the possibility of change. If we are not fixed, if we are always becoming, then even those who have made terrible choices can choose differently in the future. The past does not determine the future; we are always free to become something new.

The personalist tradition, represented by thinkers like Jacques Maritain and Emmanuel Mounier, emphasizes the inherent dignity of every human person and the social conditions necessary for human flourishing. This dignity is not earned or achieved but given, not conditional on virtue but inherent in personhood itself. It survives even the worst actions, even the most serious crimes. The young person who has caused harm retains this dignity and retains the capacity for growth and change that dignity implies. The task of a just society is not to strip away this dignity through degradation and punishment but to create the conditions in which it can be realized, in which the person can become who they are meant to be. Rehabilitation, from this perspective, is not a favor granted to offenders but an obligation owed to persons, a recognition of their inherent worth and potential.

The pragmatist tradition, represented by thinkers like John Dewey and William James, emphasizes the importance of experience and education in human development. Dewey argued that human beings learn through doing, through engaging with problems and reflecting on their experience. This insight has profound implications for rehabilitation. If we want young offenders to learn new ways of thinking and behaving, we must provide them with opportunities to practice those ways, to experience their benefits, to reflect on their effects. Purely punitive approaches that simply confine young people offer no such opportunities. They teach nothing except that power matters and that those with power will use it to hurt those without. Restorative justice, by contrast, creates opportunities for learning through experience—through facing victims, through making amends, through engaging with community, through reflecting on harm and how to repair it.

The psychology of rehabilitation provides empirical support for these philosophical and theological insights and reveals the mechanisms through which change occurs. Developmental psychology, building on the work of Jean Piaget and Lawrence Kohlberg, demonstrates that moral reasoning develops through stages and that this development can be facilitated by appropriate experiences. Young offenders are often stuck in earlier stages of moral development, focused on external consequences and personal consequences rather than on principles and the impact on others. Restorative justice, by creating opportunities for perspective-taking and empathy, can catalyze movement to higher stages. When a young person hears directly from a victim about the real impact of their actions, abstract rules become concrete realities, and moral development becomes possible.

The psychology of desistance—the process by which people stop offending—has become a major focus of criminological research in recent decades. Scholars like Shadd Maruna and John Laub have studied the lives of offenders over time, seeking to understand what leads some to desist from crime while others persist. Their findings consistently point to the importance of several factors: the development of a coherent prosocial identity, the establishment of meaningful relationships and social bonds, the acquisition of skills and employment, and the experience of being seen and treated as a person capable of change. These are precisely the factors that restorative justice seeks to foster. By treating young offenders as persons capable of change, by connecting them with supportive community members, by helping them develop skills and make amends, restorative justice creates the conditions for desistance to occur.

The psychology of trauma, pioneered by researchers like Judith Herman and Bessel van der Kolk, reveals another crucial dimension of rehabilitation. Many young offenders are themselves victims of trauma—physical abuse, sexual abuse, neglect, exposure to violence, loss of loved ones. The Adverse Childhood Experiences (ACE) study, conducted by the Centers for Disease Control and Prevention and Kaiser Permanente, found stunning correlations between childhood trauma and later involvement in criminal behavior. Children who experience four or more types of adverse experiences are dramatically more likely to be arrested as juveniles and adults, more likely to commit violent offenses, more likely to be incarcerated. This is not because trauma makes people bad but because trauma shapes the developing brain in ways that affect emotional regulation, impulse control, and social information processing. Traumatized children are hypervigilant, quick to perceive threat, quick to react with aggression. They have difficulty trusting others, difficulty forming healthy relationships, difficulty imagining a positive future.

Punitive responses that ignore this trauma are not only ineffective but actively harmful. They confirm the traumatized young person's belief that the world is hostile, that adults cannot be trusted, that they are worthless and beyond hope. They trigger the very hypervigilance and reactive aggression that trauma has produced. They reinforce the neural pathways that maintain problematic behavior rather than creating new pathways for healthier responses. Restorative justice, by contrast, recognizes the reality of trauma and seeks to address it. The supportive relationships, the opportunities for genuine connection, the experience of being heard and respected—all of these can be healing for traumatized young people. The process of facing the harm they have caused, while difficult, can also be empowering, helping them move from a victim identity to an agent identity, from passivity to responsibility.

The psychology of shame and guilt, explored extensively by researchers like June Price Tangney and Ronda Dearing, provides another crucial framework for understanding rehabilitation. Shame and guilt, though often used interchangeably in everyday speech, are fundamentally different emotions with profoundly different implications for behavior and change. Shame is the feeling that *I am bad*—a global, negative evaluation of the entire self. Guilt is the feeling that *I did something bad*—a negative evaluation of a specific behavior. Shame leads to hiding, denial, blame, and aggression; guilt leads to acknowledgment, remorse, and repair. Traditional punitive justice, with its emphasis on public condemnation, stigmatization, and exclusion, is a shame-generating machine. It tells young people, over and over, that they are worthless, that they are defined by their worst actions, that they have no future. Restorative justice, by contrast, distinguishes clearly between the person and the behavior. It says to the young offender: "You are a person of worth, a member of this community, someone capable of change. But what you did was wrong, and it caused real harm. Let's talk about that harm, and let's talk about what you can do to make it right." This is guilt, not shame—and guilt, as the research consistently shows, is the emotion that leads to genuine accountability and lasting change.

The legal framework for offender rehabilitation has evolved significantly over the past century, reflecting changing understandings of young offenders and the purposes of juvenile justice. The original juvenile court, established in 1899, was explicitly rehabilitative in its orientation, based on the doctrine of *parens patriae*—the state as parent—and the belief that young people could be saved from a life of crime through appropriate intervention. This vision, however noble in its origins, was often betrayed in practice, as juvenile institutions became warehouses for poor and minority youth, and as the rehabilitative ideal was used to justify indefinite confinement and unchecked state power. The due process revolution of the 1960s and 1970s, culminating in cases like *In re Gault* (1967), extended constitutional protections to juveniles but also raised questions about whether the juvenile court could survive as a genuinely rehabilitative institution.

The punitive turn of the 1980s and 1990s, driven by fears of juvenile "superpredators" and political demands to get tough on crime, largely abandoned the rehabilitative ideal in favor of punishment, deterrence, and incapacitation. States passed laws making it easier to transfer juveniles to adult court, imposed mandatory minimum sentences, and built more juvenile prisons. The results of this experiment were disastrous: increased recidivism, increased racial disparities, and no improvement in public safety. In recent years, there has been a pendulum swing back toward rehabilitation, driven in part by the evidence of what works and in part by fiscal concerns about the cost of incarceration. The Juvenile Justice and Delinquency Prevention Act, reauthorized in 2018, emphasizes evidence-based practices, alternatives to detention, and the importance of addressing the needs of youth. Restorative justice, with its focus on rehabilitation and reintegration, is increasingly recognized as a key component of this emerging approach.

The practice of rehabilitation in restorative justice involves multiple interconnected elements, each of which contributes to the overall goal of helping young offenders change and grow. The first element is acknowledging responsibility. Restorative justice encourages young offenders to acknowledge their responsibility for their actions, not as a formality or a legal requirement but as a genuine recognition of what they have done. This acknowledgment is the foundation on which everything else rests. Without it, there can be no genuine accountability, no meaningful repair, no lasting change. By taking ownership of their behavior and understanding its impact on victims and the community, young offenders begin the process of self-awareness and accountability that is essential for rehabilitation.

The second element is personal growth and change. Through restorative justice processes such as victim-offender dialogues and conferences, young offenders have the opportunity to reflect on their actions, their motivations, and the harm they have caused. This self-reflection can be a catalyst for personal growth and change, a moment of insight that reorients their understanding of themselves and their place in the world. The young person who sits across from the person they have harmed and hears directly about the fear, anger, and loss they have caused cannot remain unchanged. Something shifts inside them, some wall comes down, some new possibility opens up. This is not guaranteed—some young people will resist, will remain defensive, will refuse to engage—but for many, the encounter is transformative.

The third element is making amends. Restorative justice often involves developing plans for restitution or other forms of redress to repair the harm caused. This process allows young offenders to actively take steps to make amends for their actions, contributing to their rehabilitation in ways that passive punishment cannot. When a young person works to earn money to repay a victim, or performs community service that benefits those they have harmed, or writes a letter of apology that expresses genuine remorse, they are not merely completing a requirement but actively constructing a new identity. They are becoming someone who makes things right rather than someone who causes harm, someone who contributes rather than someone who takes. This active construction of a prosocial identity is at the heart of the rehabilitative process.

The fourth element is addressing underlying factors. Restorative justice recognizes that many young offenders have underlying issues contributing to their delinquent behavior, such as family problems, substance abuse, mental health challenges, learning disabilities, or trauma. The process aims to address these root causes through counseling, support, and access to necessary resources. This is not an afterthought but a central component of rehabilitation. You cannot help a young person change if you do not address the factors that drove their behavior in the first place. The restorative process, with its emphasis on understanding the full context of the offense and its connections to community partners, is well-positioned to identify these underlying factors and connect young people with appropriate services.

The fifth element is community involvement. Community members play a significant role in restorative justice processes, offering support, mentorship, and guidance to young offenders. This community involvement provides a positive influence and a sense of belonging that can be instrumental in rehabilitation. Young people who are disconnected from prosocial adults and positive peer groups are vulnerable to negative influences; young people who are embedded in supportive community networks have resources that can sustain them through difficult times. The community members who participate in restorative processes—as circle keepers, as support persons, as mentors—become part of the young person's network, offering relationship and accountability long after the formal process is complete.

The sixth element is reintegration into society. Restorative justice places a strong emphasis on helping young offenders reintegrate into society as responsible citizens. This reintegration is essential for reducing recidivism and ensuring that individuals do not become trapped in a cycle of criminal behavior. Reintegration is not a single event but an ongoing process, requiring support, monitoring, and opportunities for positive engagement. The community connections forged in restorative processes can provide this ongoing support, helping young people navigate the challenges of returning to school, finding employment, rebuilding family relationships, and establishing themselves as contributing members of society.

The diversity of restorative justice programs reflects recognition that different young people need different kinds of interventions. Research indicates that individuals convicted of different types of offenses may be directed to various restorative justice programs depending on their risk level to the community. For instance, nonviolent or younger justice-involved youths with no prior criminal history might find themselves in short-term, low-intensity programs like indirect mediation, where communication between victim and offender occurs through a mediator rather than face-to-face. These programs provide accountability and awareness without requiring the intensive engagement of direct encounter. In contrast, high-intensity programs emphasizing direct dialogues between victims and justice-involved youths, such as victim impact panels or conferences, may be reserved for youths with a history of repeated offenses or those posing a greater harm to the community. These programs require more from participants—more courage, more honesty, more vulnerability—but they also offer more in terms of potential transformation.

The timing of restorative interventions also varies. Restorative justice programming can intersect with justice-involved youth at different stages within the juvenile justice system, including arrest, referral, intake, and post-adjudication. Some restorative justice programs are designed as diversion options, diverting youths away from the formal justice system entirely. These programs offer the opportunity to avoid the stigma and consequences of formal processing while still providing accountability and support. Research suggests that diversion programs are particularly effective for first-time and low-risk offenders, preventing deeper involvement in the justice system while still addressing the offense.

Other restorative justice programs are structured as disposition outcomes, where youths are mandated to participate as part of their sentence. In these cases, restorative justice operates within the formal system rather than as an alternative to it. The challenge is to ensure that mandated participation does not become coerced participation, that young people are genuinely able to engage with the process rather than simply going through the motions. Skilled facilitators can create conditions in which even mandated participants experience the process as meaningful and transformative, but this requires careful attention to issues of power and voluntariness.

Additionally, some restorative justice programs are voluntary, requiring participants to admit responsibility for their actions, while others are court-mandated post-adjudication. Voluntary programs generally have higher rates of participant satisfaction and better outcomes, but mandated programs can also be effective when properly implemented. The key is the quality of facilitation and the extent to which participants experience the process as fair and respectful, even if they did not choose it voluntarily.

The application of restorative justice within school systems represents a particularly important frontier for offender rehabilitation. Statistics from the U.S. Department of Education for the 2017–18 school year reveal that out of 50.9 million students enrolled in public schools, 2.5 million students received at least one out-of-school suspension, and 101,600 students faced expulsion. These exclusionary disciplinary practices, disproportionately applied to students of color and students with disabilities, have been shown to increase rather than decrease problematic behavior. Students who are suspended or expelled are more likely to fall behind academically, more likely to drop out, more likely to become involved in the juvenile justice system—a phenomenon so well-documented that it has its own name: the school-to-prison pipeline.

Restorative justice approaches in schools offer an alternative to this destructive pattern. Rather than excluding students who cause harm, restorative practices bring together those affected to address the harm and determine how to repair it. Restorative circles, peer mediation, and restorative conferences can resolve conflicts, repair relationships, and hold students accountable while keeping them in school. The research on school-based restorative justice, while still emerging, is promising. Schools that implement restorative practices report reductions in suspensions and expulsions, improvements in school climate, decreases in racial disparities in discipline, and better academic outcomes. By addressing the underlying causes of behavioral problems and providing support rather than exclusion, school-based restorative justice embodies the rehabilitative ideal in the educational context.

The biblical vision that undergirds this rehabilitative approach finds its most powerful expression in the concept of *metanoia*—the Greek word typically translated as repentance but meaning literally a change of mind, a transformation of consciousness, a fundamental reorientation of one's entire being. John the Baptist appears in the wilderness proclaiming a baptism of *metanoia* for the forgiveness of sins. Jesus begins his ministry with the same call: "Repent, for the kingdom of heaven is at hand." This is not merely a call to feel sorry for past wrongs but a call to enter a new way of being, to see reality differently, to live in light of the coming kingdom. *Metanoia* is rehabilitation at the deepest level—not behavior modification but transformation of the self, not surface change but fundamental reorientation.

The parables of Jesus are filled with examples of this transformative possibility. The prodigal son, who has wasted his inheritance in reckless living, "comes to himself" in the far country and decides to return home. This is *metanoia*—a change of mind that leads to changed behavior. The father who runs to meet him, who embraces him before he can utter his confession, who throws a party to celebrate his return—this is the divine response to human transformation. The older brother, who cannot understand the celebration, represents those who cannot imagine that people can really change. But the father knows better. He knows that the one who was dead is alive again, the one who was lost is found.

The apostle Paul develops this theme with characteristic depth. In his letter to the Romans, he writes: "Do not conform to the pattern of this world, but be transformed by the renewing of your mind. Then you will be able to test and approve what God's will is—his good, pleasing and perfect will." Transformation comes through the renewing of the mind—not through external conformity but through internal change. This is rehabilitation as spiritual discipline, as the ongoing work of allowing one's thinking, one's values, one's whole orientation to be reshaped by the gospel. And this transformation has practical consequences: it enables discernment, the ability to recognize and choose what is good.

The psychological research on rehabilitation confirms what this theological vision suggests. Change is possible, but it requires the right conditions. It requires that people be treated as persons capable of change, not as fixed essences defined by their worst actions. It requires opportunities for genuine encounter with the consequences of one's actions and with those who have been affected by them. It requires supportive relationships that provide both accountability and encouragement. It requires access to resources and opportunities that enable new ways of living. It requires time—change does not happen overnight, and relapse is often part of the process. And it requires hope—the belief that a different future is possible, that one is not trapped forever in patterns of the past.

Restorative justice, at its best, provides all of these conditions. It treats young offenders as persons, not cases. It creates opportunities for genuine encounter with victims and community members. It builds supportive relationships that extend beyond the formal process. It connects young people with resources and opportunities. It takes the time necessary for genuine change. And it communicates, in every aspect of its practice, that a different future is possible, that young people can become something other than their worst actions, that rehabilitation is not only possible but expected.

The benefits of this rehabilitative approach extend far beyond the individual young person. Reintegrating young offenders as responsible citizens benefits society as a whole. It reduces the likelihood of future offenses, enhancing public safety and reducing the burden on the criminal justice system. It saves money that would otherwise be spent on incarceration and repeated processing through the courts. It helps create a more inclusive and compassionate community, one that does not give up on its young people but invests in their futures. It models for all of us what it means to believe in the possibility of change, to hope for transformation, to work for restoration.

The challenge of rehabilitation should not be underestimated. Not every young person who participates in restorative justice will be transformed. Some will remain resistant, defensive, unchanged. Some will reoffend despite the best efforts of all involved. Rehabilitation is not magic; it is hard work, requiring commitment from the young person, support from the community, and skill from practitioners. But the alternative—simply punishing and confining young people, writing them off as hopeless, abandoning them to the very conditions that produced their offending—is not only morally unacceptable but practically ineffective. It does not work, and it never has.

The restorative approach to rehabilitation is not naive optimism but hard-won hope. It is hope grounded in evidence that change is possible, in experience that many young people do desist from crime, in faith that every person bears the image of God and retains the capacity for transformation. It is hope that refuses to write off any young person as beyond redemption, that insists on seeing potential even in those who have caused great harm, that works tirelessly to create the conditions in which change can occur. And it is hope that, when realized, produces the most powerful testimony to the power of restorative justice: the young person who was once a source of harm becomes a source of healing, who was once a problem becomes part of the solution, who was once lost is found.

As we continue our journey through the principles and practices of restorative justice, we will see how this rehabilitative vision is embodied in specific programs and approaches. We will explore the research on what works and why. We will consider the challenges of implementing rehabilitation in a system still dominated by punitive thinking. And we will be invited to imagine what might be possible if we truly committed ourselves to the rehabilitation of every young person who comes into contact with the justice system. The vision is ambitious, the work is hard, but the goal—young people transformed, communities strengthened, futures opened—is worthy of all we can give.

CHAPTER 06

COMMUNITY INVOLVEMENT

Community involvement stands as the third great pillar of restorative justice for juveniles, and it may well be the most radical and challenging of the three. While accountability calls the individual offender to responsibility, and empathy opens the heart to the suffering of others, community involvement insists that justice is not merely a transaction between individuals but a communal endeavor, a matter of and for the whole. This principle recognizes what every traditional society has known and what modern individualism has obscured: that we are members one of another, that our lives are woven together in a fabric of relationship and mutual dependence, and that when one thread is torn, the whole fabric is weakened. The harm caused by juvenile delinquency extends beyond the immediate victim and offender; it ripples outward through families, neighborhoods, schools, and the entire community, leaving no one untouched. And if the harm is communal, the healing must be communal as well.

The importance of community involvement in juvenile restorative practices cannot be overstated, for it addresses dimensions of justice that individualistic approaches simply cannot reach. By actively involving the community in restorative justice processes, we foster a sense of shared responsibility that transforms justice from something done to people into something done with people. The community ceases to be a passive recipient of the justice system's outputs—more or less safe, more or less satisfied—and becomes an active participant in the justice process itself. Community members sit in circles with victims and offenders, listen to stories of harm and healing, offer their own perspectives and experiences, and join in crafting responses that address not only the immediate offense but the underlying conditions that made it possible. In this process, the community itself is restored, its social fabric rewoven, its capacity for collective action strengthened.

The theological foundations of community involvement are woven throughout the biblical narrative, from beginning to end. The Hebrew scriptures open not with the creation of an individual but with the creation of a people, a community bound to God and to one another by covenant. When God calls Abraham, it is with the promise that "all peoples on earth will be blessed through you." The people of Israel understand themselves not as a collection of isolated individuals but as a corporate body, a nation, a community whose identity is shaped by shared history, shared law, shared worship, shared destiny. When one member sins, the whole community is affected; when one member suffers, the whole community mourns. The rituals of atonement described in Leviticus are not private affairs but communal ceremonies in which the entire people participate. The Day of Atonement, Yom Kippur, is a day when "you shall deny yourselves and present a food offering to the Lord" and when the high priest makes atonement "for himself and his household and the whole community of Israel."

The prophets call the whole nation to repentance, not merely individuals. When Isaiah sees the Lord in the temple, his response is not "Woe is me, for I am a man of unclean lips" but "Woe is me, for I am a man of unclean lips, and I live among a people of unclean lips." His confession is personal and communal simultaneously, recognizing that his own uncleanness is bound up with the uncleanness of his people. When Jeremiah weeps over the destruction of Jerusalem, he weeps not for himself alone but for the whole community, for the city that was the sign of God's presence among his people. The communal dimension of sin and salvation is inescapable in the Hebrew scriptures.

The New Testament develops this communal vision with even greater specificity. Jesus calls twelve disciples, not one—a number that deliberately echoes the twelve tribes of Israel and signals the formation of a new community. He teaches his followers to pray not "My Father" but "Our Father," placing them from the start in a relationship of shared address to God. He instructs them in the practices of communal life: how to resolve conflicts, how to forgive one another, how to bear one another's burdens. The Sermon on the Mount, for all its focus on individual discipleship, is preached to a crowd, a community of hearers who are to embody its teachings together.

The early church understood itself as a community in the deepest sense. The book of Acts describes the believers as being "together and had everything in common," selling their possessions and goods and distributing the proceeds to all as any had need. They devoted themselves to the apostles' teaching and to fellowship, to the breaking of bread and to prayer. They were of one heart and soul, and no one claimed private ownership of any possessions. This was not communism as a political ideology but community as a theological reality, the embodiment of what it means to be the body of Christ. Paul's image of the church as a body is perhaps the most powerful biblical image of community: "For just as each of us has one body with many members, and these members do not all have the same function, so in Christ we, though many, form one body, and each member belongs to all the others." This is not mere metaphor but ontology: we actually belong to one another, our identities are bound up together, our fates are intertwined.

The philosophical foundations of community involvement draw on traditions of thought that challenge the individualism that has dominated Western philosophy since the Enlightenment. The communitarian tradition, represented by thinkers like Alasdair MacIntyre, Charles Taylor, and Michael Sandel, argues that the Enlightenment's focus on the autonomous individual has obscured the ways in which our identities, values, and capacities are shaped by the communities in which we are embedded. We are not self-created monads but inheritors of traditions, participants in practices, members of communities. Our good is bound up with the good of these communities, and we cannot flourish apart from them. MacIntyre famously argued that we come into the world "with a past" and that our lives are "embedded in the story of those communities from which we derive our identity." To be cut off from community is to be cut off from the sources of meaning and identity that make human flourishing possible.

The pragmatist tradition, represented by thinkers like John Dewey and Richard Rorty, emphasizes the importance of democratic participation and collective problem-solving. Dewey argued that democracy is not merely a form of government but a mode of associated living, a way of addressing shared problems through collective intelligence. Communities are not collections of pre-existing individuals but are constituted through shared activity, through the process of working together to solve common problems. Restorative justice, with its circles and conferences that bring together all affected parties to determine how to repair harm, embodies this pragmatic vision. It treats wrongdoing not as a matter for experts alone but as a community problem requiring community solutions, and it trusts the collective wisdom of those most affected to craft responses that are both just and effective.

The personalist tradition, represented by thinkers like Jacques Maritain and Emmanuel Mounier, insists on the social nature of the person. Persons are not isolated individuals but beings-in-relationship, and their fulfillment is found not in isolation but in communion with others. This is not to deny the reality or value of the individual but to insist that individuals are constituted by their relationships and find their fulfillment in community. The person and the community are not opposed but mutually implicating: persons need community to become who they are, and communities need persons to give them life and direction. Restorative justice, by involving the community in the response to wrongdoing, honors this mutual implication and creates opportunities for both persons and communities to be restored.

The psychological research on community and belonging provides empirical support for these philosophical and theological insights. The work of Roy Baumeister and Mark Leary on the need to belong demonstrates that human beings have a fundamental drive to form and maintain strong, stable relationships with others. This need is not optional but essential; when it is thwarted, the consequences are severe. People who lack strong social connections are more vulnerable to anxiety, depression, substance abuse, and a host of other problems. They are also more likely to engage in antisocial behavior, as the bonds that constrain such behavior are weakened or absent. Young offenders are often young people who have experienced profound failures of belonging—rejection by family, exclusion by peers, failure at school, disconnection from community. Their offending is, in part, a symptom of this belonging failure, a desperate attempt to find connection in the only communities that will still accept them: gangs, criminal networks, other alienated and angry young people.

The research on social capital, developed by scholars like Robert Putnam, reveals the importance of networks of relationship for individual and community well-being. Social capital—the trust, norms, and networks that enable collective action—has been linked to better health, higher educational achievement, lower crime rates, and more effective governance. Communities rich in social capital are better able to address shared problems and support their members through difficulties. They have higher levels of trust, stronger norms of reciprocity, and denser networks of relationship that facilitate cooperation and collective action. Restorative justice, by bringing community members together to address harm, builds social capital even as it repairs specific injuries. The connections forged in restorative processes become resources for future problem-solving and mutual support.

The research on collective efficacy, conducted by Robert Sampson and his colleagues, takes this insight a step further. Collective efficacy is the combination of social cohesion among neighbors and their willingness to intervene for the common good. Sampson's research, conducted in Chicago neighborhoods, found that collective efficacy is a powerful predictor of crime rates—more powerful than poverty, unemployment, or any other factor. Neighborhoods with high levels of collective efficacy have lower crime rates, even when they are disadvantaged in other ways. Restorative justice, by building social cohesion and encouraging collective responsibility, directly contributes to collective efficacy. The community that practices restorative justice becomes a community that can address its own problems, that has the relationships and norms necessary to prevent crime before it occurs.

The psychology of mentoring, explored by researchers like Jean Rhodes, reveals the power of positive relationships with caring adults to transform the lives of young people. Mentoring relationships have been shown to improve academic achievement, reduce substance abuse, decrease delinquency, and promote positive development. The key ingredients of effective mentoring are consistent presence, genuine caring, and the provision of both support and challenge. Young people who have mentors are more likely to stay in school, avoid trouble, and make positive life choices. Restorative justice, by involving community members as mentors and supporters of young offenders, harnesses this power of relationship. The community members who sit in circles with young offenders, who listen to their stories, who offer guidance and encouragement, become de facto mentors, providing the consistent caring presence that young people need.

The psychology of shame and reintegration, explored by John Braithwaite in his theory of reintegrative shaming, reveals the importance of community in the accountability process.

Braithwaite distinguishes between two types of shaming: disintegrative shaming, which stigmatizes offenders and excludes them from the community; and reintegrative shaming, which condemns the offense while respecting the offender and creating a pathway back into the community. Disintegrative shaming, the dominant mode of traditional punishment, tells the offender: "You have done wrong, and therefore you are wrong. You are not one of us. You are excluded." This approach, Braithwaite argues, actually increases crime by cutting offenders off from the very relationships and communities that might support their return to law-abiding behavior. Reintegrative shaming, by contrast, tells the offender: "You have done wrong, and that wrong is serious. But you are still one of us. We expect better of you, and we will help you do better." This approach, embodied in restorative justice practices, strengthens rather than severs the bonds between offenders and their communities.

The legal framework for community involvement in juvenile justice has evolved significantly in recent decades, reflecting growing recognition of the importance of community in responding to youth crime. The Juvenile Justice and Delinquency Prevention Act, originally passed in 1974 and most recently reauthorized in 2018, emphasizes the importance of community-based alternatives to incarceration and encourages the involvement of community members in the justice process. Many states have passed legislation authorizing restorative justice practices and establishing mechanisms for community participation. Some jurisdictions have created community justice boards or neighborhood accountability boards that involve trained community volunteers in responding to low-level offenses. These boards meet with offenders and their families, hear about the offense and its impact, and develop agreements for restitution, community service, and other forms of repair. The involvement of community members in these processes sends a powerful message: this matters to us, you matter to us, and we are willing to invest our time and energy in helping you get back on track.

The practice of community involvement in restorative justice takes many forms, each adapted to the specific context and needs of the community. In some communities, restorative circles bring together victims, offenders, their supporters, and community members in a structured dialogue that allows everyone to speak and be heard. The circle process, with its talking piece and its emphasis on storytelling, creates a container for honest communication that can transform conflict into understanding. Circles have been used for generations by indigenous peoples around the world, and their adaptation to juvenile justice represents a return to ancient wisdom as much as an innovation in modern practice.

In other communities, restorative conferences involve trained facilitators who bring together all affected parties to discuss the offense, its consequences, and a plan for restitution or reconciliation. These conferences follow a structured script that ensures all voices are heard and all perspectives considered. They begin with the victim's account of the harm, move to the offender's response, engage supporters on both sides, and culminate in a collective agreement about what must be done. The presence of community members in these conferences reinforces the message that the offense has affected more than just the immediate victim and that the community has a stake in the resolution.

In still other communities, community reparations boards bring together residents to review cases and recommend dispositions that address both the needs of the victim and the rehabilitation of the offender. These boards, composed of trained volunteers from the community, meet with offenders and their families, hear about the circumstances of the offense and the young person's background, and develop agreements that may include restitution, community service, counseling, educational programs, or other interventions. The involvement of community members in these decisions ensures that the response is tailored to local conditions and that the community takes ownership of the outcome.

The support that community involvement provides for victims cannot be overstated. Victims of crime often feel isolated, alone in their suffering, uncertain whether anyone cares about what has happened to them. The presence of community members in restorative processes can be profoundly validating, communicating that what happened matters, that the victim matters, that the community stands with them in their time of need. Community members can offer emotional support—a listening ear, a word of encouragement, a presence that says "you are not alone." They can offer practical support—help with transportation, childcare, or other needs that may arise as a result of the offense. And they can offer advocacy—ensuring that the victim's voice is heard and their needs are addressed in the resolution process. This support can be instrumental in the healing process for victims, helping them cope with the trauma of the offense and move forward with their lives.

The encouragement of accountability that community involvement provides for offenders is equally important. When young offenders see that their actions have affected not only an individual victim but also the broader community, they begin to understand the full scope of the harm they have caused. This understanding can be a powerful motivator for change, moving them from a narrow focus on their own consequences to a broader awareness of their impact on others. The presence of community members in restorative processes reinforces the message that the community has a stake in their behavior and that they are accountable not only to the victim and the state but to their neighbors, their peers, and everyone who shares their community. This collective accountability can be more powerful than any individual accountability, precisely because it taps into the fundamental human need for belonging and acceptance.

The guidance for offenders that community involvement provides is another crucial benefit. Community members can serve as positive role models and mentors for young offenders, offering examples of prosocial behavior and providing the kind of consistent, caring presence that young people need. Many young offenders lack positive adult role models in their lives; the adults they know may be absent, abusive, or themselves involved in criminal behavior. The community members who participate in restorative processes can fill this gap, offering guidance, encouragement, and support that can help young people imagine different futures for themselves. The relationships forged in restorative processes can continue long after the formal process is complete, providing ongoing support and accountability that reduce the likelihood of reoffending.

The resource accessibility that community involvement provides is yet another benefit. Communities often have access to a range of resources—counseling services, job training programs, educational opportunities, recreational activities, faith-based support—that can be invaluable in helping offenders address the underlying causes of their behavior and gain the skills needed to reintegrate successfully into society. These resources are often unknown to young offenders and their families, or inaccessible without the kind of connections that community members can provide. By connecting young people with these resources, community involvement addresses the practical needs that must be met if rehabilitation is to succeed.

The community restoration that occurs through restorative justice is perhaps the most profound benefit of community involvement. Restorative justice is not just about healing individuals but about restoring the social fabric of communities, repairing the tears that crime and conflict create. When community members come together to address harm, they engage in collective reflection on what happened, why it happened, and what must be done to prevent it from happening again. This reflection strengthens the bonds among community members, building the trust and mutual understanding that are essential for collective life. It creates a sense of shared ownership of community problems and shared responsibility for community solutions. And it models for young people what it means to be a community, to be people who care for one another and work together for the common good.

The prevention of recidivism that community involvement enables is the practical outcome of all these benefits. Community support and involvement are strong protective factors against reoffending. When young people have a sense of belonging, when they are connected to positive role models and mentors, when they have access to resources and opportunities, when they are held accountable by people who care about them, they are far less likely to return to criminal behavior. The community that embraces its young people, that invests in their futures, that refuses to give up on them even when they make mistakes, creates the conditions in which desistance becomes possible. This is not sentimentality but practicality: it is far cheaper, far safer, and far more humane to support young people in their communities than to incarcerate them and deal with the consequences of their reoffending.

The innovative community programs that have emerged across the nation in recent years demonstrate the power of community involvement to transform responses to crime and social problems. The Crisis Assistance Helping Out on the Streets (CAHOOTS) program in Eugene, Oregon, is a prime example of how communities can reimagine public safety. In this model, two-person teams composed of a mental health crisis worker and an emergency medical technician respond to a range of 911 and non-emergency calls involving mental health crises, intoxication, substance abuse, and homelessness. CAHOOTS provides voluntary services, including crisis intervention, counseling, and referrals to social services. This approach offers a more suitable and less intimidating response to behavioral health crises compared to traditional police involvement, ultimately mitigating the risk of escalations into police violence. Such alternatives also hold the potential to significantly reduce volatile police-citizen interactions in disadvantaged communities, all while being relatively cost-effective.

The success of CAHOOTS and similar programs has inspired communities across the country to explore civilian-based alternative responder programs for a wider range of situations. Beyond behavioral health crises, civilians may prove to be more effective responders in handling minor complaints, disturbances, disorderly conduct, and quality-of-life concerns. These types of calls constitute a substantial portion of police service requests, with conventional police responses often raising concerns about the use of harsh and racially discriminatory tactics, eroding trust within marginalized communities. Trained community members skilled in de-escalation and mediation might offer a peaceful resolution without police involvement. Given the negative impact of harsh order-maintenance policing on marginalized communities, these areas might contemplate programs redirecting quality-of-life and low-level calls to civilian community responders.

The potential for civilian responders to handle minor traffic violations is another promising development. Over-policing is particularly evident in traffic enforcement, with Black and Latino drivers experiencing a higher likelihood of being stopped, searched, cited, and arrested compared to their white counterparts. Minor traffic violations can serve as a pretext for invasive investigatory stops, contributing to a significant percentage of fatal police shootings. Proposals suggest that unarmed traffic monitors could issue citations for minor traffic violations while refraining from conducting background checks or criminal investigations. This approach could notably reduce the frequency of contentious police-civilian encounters, lessening the impact of over-policing in disadvantaged communities.

Community violence-interruption initiatives, such as the Cure Violence model, represent another innovative approach to community involvement in public safety. These programs train and employ community members as outreach workers and violence interrupters, offering credible messengers who can connect with at-risk youth. Violence interrupters work to mediate conflicts and de-escalate potentially violent situations, while outreach workers build long-term relationships with young individuals at risk of criminal involvement, guiding them towards better choices and access to services like education and job training. The success of these programs demonstrates that community members themselves, when properly trained and supported, can be the most effective responders to violence and conflict in their own neighborhoods.

School and community restorative justice programs are making significant strides in preventing crime and addressing conflicts without police involvement. In schools where punitive disciplinary measures have disproportionately affected students of color, restorative justice circles bring together students and teachers to collaboratively address conflicts and behavioral issues. Early reports from schools implementing restorative practices indicate reductions in suspensions, expulsions, and police referrals, improved graduation rates, and decreased racial disparities in discipline. These outcomes demonstrate that community-based approaches can be more effective than punitive measures in creating safe and supportive learning environments.

In the broader community, nonprofit organizations and community groups are organizing peacemaking circles and conflict resolution circles, where community members engage in guided conversations on various themes, addressing issues like violence, gang involvement, and goal setting. These programs offer a unique avenue to prevent crime and promote community safety while reducing negative police-civilian interactions. They create spaces where community members can come together to discuss shared concerns, build relationships, and develop collective strategies for addressing problems. The very process of coming together in circle strengthens the community's capacity to address its own challenges, building the social capital and collective efficacy that are the foundations of community safety.

While none of these initiatives eliminates the necessity for police intervention in violent crimes, collectively they hold the potential to reduce violence, enhance safety, and minimize adverse police-citizen interactions. They represent a reimagining of public safety that places community at the center, that trusts community members to be the primary agents of their own safety, and that invests in the relationships and resources that make communities strong. This reimagining is not a rejection of law enforcement but a recognition that law enforcement alone cannot create safe communities. Safety is built through relationships, through trust, through the everyday interactions of neighbors who know and care about one another. Restorative justice, with its emphasis on community involvement, is a practice of building this kind of safety.

The biblical vision that undergirds this community-centered approach is the vision of *shalom*—that comprehensive well-being, right relationship, and flourishing for all creation that is the goal of God's restorative work. *Shalom* is not merely the absence of conflict but the presence of justice, not merely individual peace but communal wholeness. It is the condition in which every person has what they need to flourish, in which relationships are characterized by trust and mutual respect, in which the community acts together for the common good. The prophets dreamed of *shalom*, painted pictures of it, called God's people to embody it. Isaiah imagined a day when "they will beat their swords into plowshares and their spears into pruning hooks. Nation will not take up sword against nation, nor will they train for war anymore." Micah imagined a day when "everyone will sit under their own vine and under their own fig tree, and no one will make them afraid." This is *shalom*—peace with justice, security with dignity, community with freedom.

The life and teachings of Jesus embody this *shalom* vision. He announced the coming of God's kingdom, a realm of right relationship where the last are first, the lost are found, the broken are healed. He taught his followers to pray for this kingdom to come, for God's will to be done on earth as it is in heaven. He gathered a community of disciples who were to embody this kingdom in their life together, who were to be salt and light, leaven and city on a hill. The early church understood itself as the community of the new age, the place where *shalom* was already breaking in, where the dividing walls of hostility were being torn down, where people from every nation and tribe and tongue were being reconciled to God and to one another.

The community involvement that restorative justice practices is a participation in this *shalom* vision. It is a recognition that justice is not something done to people by experts but something done with people by communities. It is an affirmation that every community has within itself the resources for healing, that the wisdom for addressing harm is present in the people who have been most affected by it. It is a commitment to building the kind of communities where crime is less likely to occur, where conflicts are resolved before they escalate, where young people are surrounded by caring adults who hold them accountable and support their growth. It is, in short, a practice of hope—hope that communities can be different, that people can change, that *shalom* is possible.

The challenges of community involvement should not be underestimated. Not every community is ready or willing to take on this role. Communities that have been fractured by poverty, racism, violence, and neglect may lack the social cohesion and trust necessary for effective restorative practice. Community members may be reluctant to get involved, may lack training and support, may burn out from the emotional demands of the work. The very communities that most need restorative justice may have the least capacity to practice it. These challenges are real, and they must be addressed through investment in community capacity, through training and support for community members, through the patient work of building relationships and trust.

But the alternative—continuing to rely on punitive systems that isolate offenders, marginalize victims, and exclude communities—is not acceptable. It has been tried for centuries, and it has failed. It has failed to reduce crime, failed to satisfy victims, failed to rehabilitate offenders, failed to build safe communities. The only way forward is the way of community involvement, the way of shared responsibility, the way of collective healing. It is a harder way, a more demanding way, a way that requires more of all of us. But it is also a more hopeful way, a more just way, a more faithful way.

As we continue our journey through the principles and practices of restorative justice, we will see how community involvement is embodied in specific programs and approaches. We will explore the research on what works and why. We will consider the challenges of building community capacity and the strategies for overcoming them. And we will be invited to imagine what might be possible if we truly committed ourselves to the vision of community-centered justice. The vision is ambitious, the work is hard, but the goal—communities restored, young people transformed, *shalom* realized—is worthy of all we can give.

CHAPTER 07

RESTORATIVE PRACTICES

Restorative practices encompass a diverse and richly textured range of methods and approaches aimed at addressing harm, fostering genuine accountability, and promoting deep healing in juvenile cases. These practices are not merely techniques or procedures to be mechanically applied; they are living expressions of the principles we have explored in previous chapters—accountability, empathy, community involvement—brought to life in concrete encounters between real human beings. They offer a fundamental alternative to punitive measures that have dominated Western justice systems for centuries, emphasizing dialogue over monologue, understanding over condemnation, and collaborative resolution over imposed punishment. In this chapter, we will explore the major restorative practices commonly applied in juvenile cases, examining not only how they work but why they work, drawing on the theological, philosophical, psychological, and legal foundations that give them their power and promise.

The practices we will explore—victim-offender dialogues, restorative circles, restorative conferences, restitution plans, peer mediation, and family group conferences—are not interchangeable options to be selected at random. Each has its own distinctive character, its own appropriate applications, its own strengths and limitations. But all share a common core: they bring together those who have been harmed and those who have caused harm, along with their supporters and the broader community, in processes designed to address the full human reality of crime. They recognize that crime is not merely a legal category but a wound in the fabric of human relationship, and that healing this wound requires the active participation of all those who have been affected. They embody the conviction that justice is not something done to people but something done with people, not a product of expert decision-making but a fruit of communal discernment.

The theological foundations of these practices are woven throughout the biblical narrative, from the communal rituals of ancient Israel to the reconciling ministry of Jesus to the restorative practices of the early church. The Hebrew scriptures are filled with examples of dialogue, confrontation, and reconciliation that prefigure modern restorative practices. When Nathan the prophet confronts David over his sin with Bathsheba and Uriah, he does not simply announce a divine verdict; he engages David in a dialogue that leads to self-awareness and confession. He tells a story, invites David's response, and then delivers the devastating application: "You are that man!" This is restorative encounter avant la lettre—the use of narrative to create understanding, the engagement of the wrongdoer in acknowledging his own wrongdoing, the opening of a path to repentance and restoration.

The life of Jesus is filled with restorative encounters that model the practices we will explore. He engages the woman at the well in dialogue that leads to her transformation and her witness to her entire village. He encounters Zacchaeus in a way that produces not condemnation but repentance and restitution. He restores Peter after his denial not with punishment but with questions that invite confession and recommissioning: "Simon son of John, do you love me?" Each of these encounters is unique, tailored to the particular persons and circumstances, but all share a common pattern: the creation of space for honest encounter, the invitation to acknowledgment and change, the offer of restoration and new beginning.

The early church developed practices of accountability and reconciliation that directly foreshadow modern restorative justice. In Matthew's gospel, Jesus instructs his followers in a process for addressing conflict: "If your brother or sister sins against you, go and point out their fault, just between the two of you. If they listen to you, you have won them over. But if they will not listen, take one or two others along, so that 'every matter may be established by the testimony of two or three witnesses.' If they still refuse to listen, tell it to the church." This is a graduated restorative process, moving from private dialogue to small-group mediation to communal discernment. It embodies the core restorative principles of direct encounter, involvement of supporters, and communal accountability. The goal throughout is not punishment but "winning them over"—restoration to right relationship.

The apostle Paul, in his letters, provides further evidence of restorative practices in the early church. In his first letter to the Corinthians, he addresses a case of serious sexual immorality, instructing the community to take action. But in his second letter, he writes of the need to forgive and comfort the repentant offender, "so that he will not be overwhelmed by excessive sorrow." This is restorative justice in action: accountability through communal confrontation, followed by restoration through communal welcome. The community's role is not exhausted by holding the offender accountable; it extends to receiving him back, reaffirming love for him, ensuring that he is not destroyed by his own remorse.

The philosophical foundations of restorative practices draw on traditions of thought that emphasize dialogue, encounter, and the social construction of meaning. The dialogical philosophy of Martin Buber, with its distinction between I-It and I-Thou relationships, provides a framework for understanding what happens in restorative encounters. In I-It relationships, we treat others as objects to be used, categorized, and managed. This is the mode of traditional punitive justice, where offenders become cases and victims become witnesses. In I-Thou relationships, we encounter others in their full humanity, as subjects worthy of respect and response. Restorative practices create the conditions for I-Thou encounter, bringing victims and offenders into direct relationship where each can see and be seen, hear and be heard, respond and be responded to.

The philosophy of Emmanuel Levinas, with its emphasis on the face of the Other as the source of ethical obligation, illuminates the transformative power of victim-offender encounter. When we see the face of another person—particularly a person who is vulnerable, suffering, in need—we are called to responsibility. This responsibility is not chosen but given, not contractual but existential. In restorative practices, victims and offenders see each other's faces, and in that seeing, something shifts. The abstract categories of victim and offender become concrete human beings with names, stories, and needs. The face of the victim calls the offender to accountability; the face of the offender calls the victim to see beyond the harm to the person who caused it. This mutual seeing is the beginning of healing for both.

The pragmatist philosophy of John Dewey, with its emphasis on learning through experience and democratic problem-solving, provides a framework for understanding the educational dimension of restorative practices. Dewey argued that we learn not by being told what to think but by engaging with problems, reflecting on our experience, and developing our own understandings. Restorative practices embody this pragmatist insight. Young offenders are not simply told that they have caused harm; they encounter that harm directly through the stories of those they have affected. They are not simply ordered to make amends; they participate in developing agreements that address the specific harm they have caused. This experiential learning is far more powerful than any abstract lesson, precisely because it engages the whole person—emotions, relationships, identity—in the process of change.

The psychology of restorative practices has been extensively researched, and the findings consistently support what practitioners have long known: that these practices work, and they work through identifiable psychological mechanisms. The psychology of voice and participation, explored by Tom Tyler and his colleagues, demonstrates that people's satisfaction with legal processes depends less on outcomes than on the opportunity to participate, to tell their story, to be heard. Restorative practices provide this opportunity to both victims and offenders, and the result is higher satisfaction, greater perception of fairness, and increased willingness to accept and comply with agreements.

The psychology of empathy, explored by researchers like Martin Hoffman, reveals that empathy can be cultivated through appropriate experiences and that increased empathy is associated with reduced aggression and increased prosocial behavior. Restorative practices, by creating opportunities for victims and offenders to share their experiences with one another, directly foster empathy. Offenders who hear directly from victims about the impact of their actions develop understanding that no lecture or punishment can provide. Victims who see offenders as human beings rather than monsters may find their anger and fear reduced, their capacity for forgiveness increased.

The psychology of shame and guilt, explored by June Price Tangney and Ronda Dearing, reveals the importance of distinguishing between these emotions and designing interventions that foster guilt rather than shame. Restorative practices, by focusing on the behavior rather than the person, by distinguishing clearly between the wrong done and the worth of the wrongdoer, create conditions for guilt rather than shame. Offenders can feel bad about what they did without feeling bad about who they are, and this guilt, unlike shame, leads to acknowledgment, remorse, and repair.

The legal framework for restorative practices has developed significantly in recent decades, providing structure and accountability for these approaches. The United Nations Basic Principles on the Use of Restorative Justice Programmes in Criminal Matters, adopted in 2002, establishes international standards for restorative practice. These principles emphasize that restorative processes should be used only with the free and voluntary consent of the parties, that agreements should be reached voluntarily and contain only reasonable and proportionate obligations, that failure to reach or implement an agreement should not be used as justification for more severe penalties, and that restorative processes should be available at all stages of the criminal justice process. These principles provide guidance for program development and ensure that restorative practices remain true to their restorative character.

Many countries have incorporated restorative practices into their juvenile justice legislation, creating formal mechanisms for referral and establishing standards for practice. In New Zealand, the Children, Young Persons, and Their Families Act 1989 made family group conferencing the primary response to youth offending, fundamentally transforming the juvenile justice system. In Norway, the National Mediation Service provides victim-offender mediation as a voluntary option for victims and offenders at all stages of the justice process. In the United States, many states have passed legislation authorizing restorative justice practices and establishing funding and oversight mechanisms. These legal developments, while uneven and incomplete, represent significant progress toward institutionalizing restorative practices.

Let us now turn to the specific restorative practices that are commonly applied in juvenile cases, examining each in depth and exploring its distinctive contributions to the work of repair and restoration.

Victim-Offender Dialogues (VODs)

Victim-offender dialogues, also known as victim-offender mediation, represent the foundational restorative practice from which many others have developed. These one-on-one meetings between the victim and the young offender, facilitated by a trained mediator, are the simplest and most direct form of restorative encounter. Yet within this simplicity lies profound power, the power of human beings meeting face-to-face to address the harm that one has caused the other.

The process of victim-offender dialogue typically begins long before the actual meeting. The mediator meets separately with both parties, explaining the process, assessing their readiness, and preparing them for the encounter. For victims, this preparation involves exploring what they hope to gain from the meeting, what questions they want to ask, what they want the offender to know about the impact of the offense. For offenders, it involves helping them understand the purpose of the meeting, encouraging them to take responsibility for their actions, and preparing them to listen openly to the victim's experience. This preparation is crucial; it ensures that both parties enter the dialogue with realistic expectations and with the support they need to engage constructively.

When the dialogue itself occurs, the mediator creates a safe and structured space for communication. The victim speaks first, describing the impact of the offense in their own words—the fear, the anger, the loss, the ongoing effects on their life. This is often the first time they have been able to tell their full story, to express the full range of their experience, to be heard by the person most responsible for their suffering. For many victims, this telling is itself healing, a release of emotions that have been locked inside since the crime occurred.

After the victim has spoken, the offender has the opportunity to respond. This may include acknowledging the harm, expressing remorse, answering the victim's questions, and explaining their own situation and motivations. For many offenders, this is the first time they have fully understood the human consequences of their actions. The abstract knowledge that stealing hurts people becomes concrete reality when they sit across from someone who has been stolen from. The intellectual understanding that violence causes suffering becomes visceral experience when they hear directly from someone who has been violated.

Following this exchange, the mediator guides the parties toward developing a plan for making amends. This plan, which becomes a written agreement, may include financial restitution for losses, community service, educational programs, or other actions that address the specific harm caused. The agreement is developed collaboratively, with input from both parties, ensuring that it addresses the victim's needs while being realistic about the offender's capacities. When the agreement is completed, the offender has the opportunity to demonstrate their commitment to change, and the victim has the satisfaction of seeing tangible repair.

The theological significance of victim-offender dialogue is profound. It embodies the biblical call to confession and reconciliation, the recognition that healing requires facing the truth about what we have done and who we have harmed. The prophet Isaiah's words capture something essential about this process: "Learn to do right; seek justice. Defend the oppressed. Take up the cause of the fatherless; plead the case of the widow." Victim-offender dialogue is a way of pleading the case of those who have been harmed, of ensuring that their voices are heard and their needs addressed. It is also a way of calling offenders to the righteousness that Isaiah envisions, the doing of right that flows from genuine encounter with the consequences of wrongdoing.

The psychological research on victim-offender dialogue is compelling. Studies consistently find that victims who participate in these dialogues experience significant reductions in fear, anger, and post-traumatic stress symptoms. They report feeling heard, validated, and empowered in ways that traditional court processes never provide. Offenders who participate are more likely to complete restitution agreements, more likely to express genuine remorse, and less likely to reoffend. A meta-analysis by the RAND Corporation found that victim-offender dialogue programs reduce recidivism by an average of 26 percent compared to traditional court processing. These findings confirm what practitioners have long known: that face-to-face encounter, properly facilitated, can transform both victims and offenders.

Restorative Circles

Restorative circles extend the restorative encounter beyond the dyad of victim and offender to include the wider circle of those affected by the offense. In a circle, victims, offenders, their supporters, and community members gather in a structured format that ensures everyone has the opportunity to speak and be heard. The circle process, with its talking piece and its emphasis on storytelling, creates a container for honest communication that can transform conflict into understanding and isolation into community.

The circle typically begins with a ceremonial opening—a reading, a moment of silence, a statement of purpose—that marks the space as different from ordinary conversation. The circle keeper, a trained facilitator, explains the process and the guidelines: speak from the heart, listen with respect, wait for the talking piece to come to you. The talking piece, an object passed from person to person, ensures that everyone who wants to speak can do so without interruption and that everyone has the obligation to listen while others hold the piece.

The conversation moves through stages, guided by the circle keeper. Participants may be invited to introduce themselves and share their connection to the offense. They may be asked to describe the impact of the offense on their lives. They may be invited to share what they need to move forward. Throughout, the circle maintains a rhythm of speaking and listening that allows each person's story to be heard and honored.

For victims, the circle offers the opportunity to be heard by a community that cares. The presence of supporters and community members validates their experience and communicates that they are not alone in their suffering. For offenders, the circle offers the opportunity to hear from multiple voices about the impact of their actions, deepening their understanding of the harm they have caused. For community members, the circle offers the opportunity to express their own experience of the offense and to participate in crafting a response that addresses not only the immediate harm but the underlying conditions that made it possible.

The agreement that emerges from a circle is a community document, reflecting the collective wisdom of all those who have participated. It may include restitution to the victim, community service that benefits the neighborhood, educational programs that address the offender's needs, and commitments from community members to provide support and mentorship. This collective ownership of the agreement strengthens accountability and ensures that the offender is surrounded by people who have a stake in their success.

The theological foundations of restorative circles are deeply rooted in indigenous traditions that have practiced circle processes for millennia. Many indigenous cultures understand justice as a matter of restoring balance and harmony within the community, a process that requires the participation of all those affected. The circle embodies this understanding, creating a space where every voice matters, where relationships are central, and where healing is a communal endeavor. The Christian tradition, with its emphasis on the body of Christ and the mutual belonging of all members, resonates deeply with this indigenous wisdom. When Paul writes that "if one part suffers, every part suffers with it," he is describing the reality that circles make visible: that we are connected, that harm to one is harm to all, and that healing requires the participation of all.

The psychological power of circles lies in their ability to create safety and equality. The circle format, with everyone seated in a circle facing one another, communicates that all participants are valued and that no one's perspective is more important than anyone else's. The talking piece ensures that everyone has the opportunity to speak without interruption, creating conditions for deep listening and genuine understanding. The presence of supporters provides emotional containment, allowing participants to express difficult feelings without being overwhelmed. The collective nature of the process builds social capital, strengthening the relationships and trust that are essential for community well-being.

Research on restorative circles, while less extensive than research on victim-offender dialogue, is promising. Studies of school-based circles have found reductions in disciplinary incidents, improvements in school climate, and decreases in racial disparities in discipline. Studies of community-based circles have found increased satisfaction among participants, greater perception of fairness, and reduced recidivism. The Washington State Institute for Public Policy, in its comprehensive cost-benefit analyses, has found that restorative circles produce positive returns on investment through reduced criminal justice costs and avoided victimization.

Restorative Conferences

Restorative conferences are more formal gatherings that bring together victims, offenders, their supporters, and relevant community members in a structured process facilitated by trained practitioners. Conferences follow a scripted format that ensures all voices are heard and all perspectives considered, while allowing flexibility to address the unique circumstances of each case.

The conference typically begins with the facilitator welcoming participants and explaining the process. The victim is then invited to speak about the offense and its impact, describing in detail what happened, how it has affected them, and what they have experienced since. Family members and supporters of the victim may also be invited to speak about how the offense has affected them. This opening phase ensures that the full human impact of the offense is acknowledged and witnessed.

After the victim and their supporters have spoken, the offender is invited to respond. This may include acknowledging responsibility, expressing remorse, and explaining their actions and motivations. The offender's supporters are then invited to speak about how the offense has affected them and what they have observed in the offender. This phase ensures that the offender is seen as a whole person, not defined solely by their worst action, and that the support available to them is made visible.

Following these narratives, the facilitator guides the group toward developing a plan for repair. Participants discuss what needs to happen to make things as right as possible, drawing on the victim's expressed needs, the offender's capacities, and the community's resources. The goal is to reach consensus on a written agreement that specifies the actions the offender will take to make amends—restitution, community service, educational programs, counseling, or other interventions. The agreement is signed by all parties and may be monitored by the facilitator or referred back to the court for oversight.

The legal status of conference agreements varies by jurisdiction. In some places, agreements are binding and enforceable through the court system; in others, they are voluntary and rely on the moral commitment of the parties for implementation. Either way, the process of developing the agreement collaboratively gives it a legitimacy and power that imposed penalties lack. Offenders who have participated in crafting their own restitution plans are far more likely to complete them than those who have been ordered to pay restitution by a court.

The theological significance of restorative conferences lies in their embodiment of the communal discernment that characterized the early church. When the apostles and elders gathered in Jerusalem to address the controversy over Gentile converts, they engaged in a process of listening, discussion, and consensus-building that resulted in a letter expressing "the decision of the Holy Spirit and us." This was not top-down decision-making but communal discernment, a process of seeking together what God was calling them to do. Restorative conferences, in their ideal form, are a secular analog of this process—a gathering of those affected by harm to seek together what justice requires.

The psychological dynamics of conferences are complex and powerful. The presence of supporters for both victim and offender creates a container of safety that allows difficult emotions to be expressed and processed. The structured format ensures that all voices are heard while preventing any single voice from dominating. The focus on developing a concrete agreement provides a forward-looking orientation that helps participants move from the pain of the past to the possibilities of the future. Research on conferences, including the rigorous randomized controlled trials conducted by Lawrence Sherman and Heather Strang in Australia and the United Kingdom, has found significant benefits for both victims and offenders. Victims who participated in conferences reported less fear, less anger, and greater sense of closure than those whose cases went to court. Offenders who participated in conferences had lower recidivism rates, particularly for violent offenses.

Restitution Plans

Restitution plans are agreements that specify how the offender will make amends for the harm caused. While restitution can be ordered by a court in traditional proceedings, the distinctive feature of restorative restitution is that it is developed collaboratively, with input from victims, offenders, and community members, and tailored to the specific circumstances of each case.

Restitution may take many forms. Financial restitution compensates victims for out-of-pocket losses—medical expenses, property damage, lost wages. This is the most straightforward form of restitution, but it is not always the most meaningful. For many victims, the symbolic value of restitution matters as much as the monetary value—the recognition that the offender is taking responsibility, the acknowledgment that the victim's loss matters. Community service allows offenders to give back to the community they have harmed, providing visible evidence of their commitment to change. Educational programs address the underlying factors that contributed to the offense—anger management, substance abuse treatment, literacy programs—helping offenders develop the skills and capacities they need to avoid future offending. Direct service to the victim, when appropriate and desired, can provide the most meaningful form of repair—mowing the lawn, painting the fence, repairing damage—actions that demonstrate concrete commitment to making things right.

The development of a restitution plan is a collaborative process that engages all parties in problem-solving. The victim identifies their needs and priorities. The offender identifies what they are capable of doing. Community members identify resources and opportunities that might support the plan. The facilitator helps the group craft an agreement that is specific, realistic, and meaningful. This collaborative process ensures that the plan addresses the real harm caused, that it is achievable for the offender, and that it has the support of all those affected.

The theological foundations of restitution are woven throughout the Hebrew scriptures. The law of Moses includes detailed provisions for restitution in cases of theft, property damage, and personal injury. When one person harms another, the requirement is not that the offender suffer but that they make restitution—restoring what was taken, repairing what was broken, compensating for what was lost. This focus on restitution reflects a profound understanding of justice as repair rather than punishment. The goal is not to make the offender suffer but to make the victim whole, to restore as much as possible what was taken away.

The story of Zacchaeus exemplifies this restorative understanding. When Zacchaeus encounters Jesus, he does not offer to suffer for his sins but to make restitution: "Look, Lord! Here and now I give half of my possessions to the poor, and if I have cheated anybody out of anything, I will pay back four times the amount." Jesus does not demand this; Zacchaeus offers it freely as the fruit of his transformation. And Jesus's response is telling: "Today salvation has come to this house." Salvation here is connected to restitution, to making things right with those who have been wronged.

The psychology of restitution is powerful. For offenders, completing a restitution agreement provides concrete evidence of their capacity for positive action, building self-efficacy and supporting the development of a prosocial identity. For victims, receiving restitution provides tangible evidence that their suffering has been recognized and that something has been done to make it right. The psychological benefits of restitution extend beyond the material; they include the symbolic value of being taken seriously, of having one's losses acknowledged, of seeing the offender take responsibility.

Peer Mediation

Peer mediation is a restorative practice in which trained young people facilitate conversations between their peers who are involved in conflicts or disputes. This approach is particularly common in schools, where peer mediation programs train students to help their classmates resolve conflicts peacefully, constructively, and restoratively.

The peer mediation process typically begins when a conflict is identified by teachers, administrators, or the students themselves. Trained peer mediators, working in pairs, meet with each party separately to explain the process, assess willingness to participate, and prepare them for the joint session. The joint session then brings the parties together in a structured conversation guided by the mediators. The mediators help each party express their perspective, identify the underlying issues, and develop a mutually acceptable resolution. The agreement is written down and may include commitments to changed behavior, restitution, or other actions.

The power of peer mediation lies in its use of credible messengers. Young people often listen more openly to their peers than to adults, who may be perceived as authority figures rather than allies. Peer mediators speak the language of their peers, understand their concerns, and can connect with them in ways that adults cannot. The experience of being helped by a peer also models positive behavior and demonstrates that young people can be part of the solution to problems rather than merely the source of them.

The theological significance of peer mediation lies in its embodiment of the priesthood of all believers—the conviction that every member of the community has gifts to offer and a role to play in the work of reconciliation. The early church understood that the ministry of reconciliation was not reserved for a few professionals but entrusted to the whole community. Paul writes that God "gave us the ministry of reconciliation" and "entrusted to us the message of reconciliation." This ministry is given to all who are in Christ, not to a clerical elite. Peer mediation enacts this conviction, empowering young people to exercise the ministry of reconciliation among their peers.

The psychology of peer mediation is supported by research on peer influence and social learning. Young people are strongly influenced by their peers, for better or worse. Peer mediation harnesses this influence for positive purposes, using peer relationships to promote constructive conflict resolution. The training that peer mediators receive also benefits them directly, building communication skills, empathy, and confidence that serve them well in all areas of life. Studies of peer mediation programs have found reductions in disciplinary incidents, improvements in school climate, and positive effects on the mediators themselves.

Family Group Conferences

Family group conferences, also known as family group decision-making, are restorative practices that involve the extended family and significant others of the young offender in collective decision-making about how to respond to the offense. This approach, which originated in New Zealand and draws on Maori traditions, recognizes the central role of family in the lives of young people and the importance of harnessing family resources for rehabilitation and support.

The family group conference process typically begins with a referral from the court or other authority. A coordinator meets with the young person and their family to explain the process and prepare them for the conference. The conference itself brings together the young person, their immediate and extended family, the victim if they choose to participate, relevant professionals, and a facilitator. The conference proceeds through several stages: information sharing, in which professionals present the facts of the case and the concerns that have been raised; private family time, in which the family meets alone to develop a plan; and agreement, in which the plan is presented to the full group for discussion and approval.

The private family time is the distinctive feature of the family group conference. During this time, the family has the opportunity to discuss the situation openly, without professionals present, and to develop a plan that draws on their own resources and understanding. This plan may include provisions for the young person's care and supervision, consequences for the offense, restitution to the victim, and supports for the family. When the family presents their plan to the full group, professionals have the opportunity to raise concerns and offer resources, but the plan remains fundamentally the family's creation.

The theological foundations of family group conferences lie in the biblical understanding of family as the primary context for nurturing and shaping young people. The Hebrew scriptures are filled with injunctions to parents to teach their children, to pass on the faith, to guide and discipline with love. The commandment to honor father and mother reflects the recognition that family relationships are foundational to human flourishing. Family group conferences honor this biblical vision by treating the family as the primary resource for addressing juvenile offending, rather than as an obstacle to be overcome or a problem to be managed.

The psychological wisdom of family group conferences lies in their recognition of the power of family relationships. Families know their children in ways that professionals never can; they have insights into what will work and what will not; they have resources—emotional, relational, practical—that can support change. Involving the family in decision-making also increases the likelihood that plans will be implemented, because family members have ownership of them and are committed to their success. Research on family group conferences has found high levels of satisfaction among participants, increased engagement of families in the justice process, and reduced recidivism compared to traditional court processing.

The Integration of Practices

These restorative practices are not mutually exclusive; they can be combined and adapted to meet the needs of specific cases and communities. A case might begin with a victim-offender dialogue, move to a family group conference to develop a comprehensive plan, and then use circles for ongoing support and accountability. Schools might use peer mediation for everyday conflicts and restorative conferences for more serious incidents, while also building a restorative culture through classroom circles. Communities might organize peacemaking circles to address neighborhood conflicts and violence interrupters to mediate potentially violent situations. The key is not fidelity to a particular model but fidelity to the principles that underlie all restorative practices: accountability, empathy, community involvement, and the commitment to repair harm and rebuild relationships.

The empirical evidence for the effectiveness of restorative practices is strong and growing. Multiple meta-analyses have found that restorative justice programs reduce recidivism, with effects ranging from 10 to 35 percent depending on the program and population. The effects are particularly strong for violent offenses, suggesting that the intensive engagement required by restorative processes is especially valuable when harm has been most severe. Victims who participate in restorative practices report higher levels of satisfaction, greater sense of closure, and reduced fear and anger compared to those whose cases go through traditional courts. Restorative practices also produce significant cost savings through reduced recidivism, lower criminal justice costs, and avoided victimization.

The theological vision that animates these practices is the vision of *shalom*—that comprehensive well-being, right relationship, and flourishing for all creation that is the goal of God's restorative work. *Shalom* is not merely the absence of conflict but the presence of justice, not merely individual peace but communal wholeness. The practices we have explored in this chapter are means of pursuing *shalom* in the specific context of juvenile offending. They are ways of repairing the harm that has been done, restoring the relationships that have been damaged, and rebuilding the communities that have been wounded. They are practices of hope—hope that change is possible, that healing can occur, that *shalom* can be realized even in the aftermath of harm.

As we continue our journey through the principles and practices of restorative justice, we will explore the benefits that flow from these practices, the challenges they face, and the future directions they might take. But for now, let us pause to appreciate the richness and power of the practices themselves—the simple yet profound act of victims and offenders meeting face-to-face, the communal wisdom of circles, the structured engagement of conferences, the tangible repair of restitution, the peer empowerment of mediation, the family ownership of family group conferences. These practices are gifts to our communities, tools for the work of restoration, signs of the *shalom* that is possible when we commit ourselves to justice that heals.

CHAPTER 08

BENEFITS OF RESTORATIVE JUSTICE

The benefits of restorative justice in the context of juvenile cases are profound, far-reaching, and increasingly well-documented by decades of research and practice across diverse settings and cultures. These benefits extend far beyond the immediate outcomes of individual cases to encompass transformations in the lives of young offenders, the healing of victims, the strengthening of communities, and the very fabric of society itself. To understand restorative justice fully is to appreciate not only its principles and practices but also its fruits—the tangible, measurable, and deeply human outcomes that demonstrate its power to repair harm, rebuild lives, and restore our youth. In this chapter, we will explore these benefits in depth, drawing on the theological, philosophical, psychological, and legal foundations that explain why restorative justice works and the empirical evidence that confirms it does.

The benefits of restorative justice are not accidental or incidental; they flow directly from its core principles and practices. Because restorative justice focuses on addressing the root causes of delinquent behavior rather than merely punishing its symptoms, it produces lasting change rather than temporary suppression. Because it gives victims voice and participation, it produces satisfaction and healing rather than frustration and secondary trauma. Because it involves the community in the resolution process, it produces stronger social bonds and collective efficacy rather than isolation and fear. Because it holds offenders accountable in meaningful ways, it produces genuine responsibility and personal growth rather than resentment and defiance. These outcomes are not mutually exclusive but mutually reinforcing, creating a virtuous cycle of healing and restoration that benefits everyone touched by crime.

The theological vision that undergirds these benefits is the vision of *shalom*—that comprehensive well-being, right relationship, and flourishing for all creation that is the goal of God's restorative work. The prophets dreamed of *shalom*, painted pictures of it, called God's people to embody it. Isaiah imagined a day when "they will beat their swords into plowshares and their spears into pruning hooks. Nation will not take up sword against nation, nor will they train for war anymore." Micah imagined a day when "everyone will sit under their own vine and under their own fig tree, and no one will make them afraid." This is *shalom*—peace with justice, security with dignity, community with freedom. The benefits of restorative justice are signs of *shalom* breaking into the present, glimpses of what is possible when we align our justice practices with God's restorative purposes.

The philosophical foundations of these benefits lie in traditions of thought that emphasize human flourishing, social connection, and the common good. The Aristotelian tradition, with its emphasis on *eudaimonia*—human flourishing achieved through virtuous activity in community—provides a framework for understanding how restorative justice contributes to the good life. Young offenders who complete restorative processes are not merely less likely to reoffend; they are more likely to develop the virtues—responsibility, empathy, self-control—that enable flourishing. Victims who participate in restorative processes are not merely more satisfied; they are more likely to experience the healing that allows them to flourish despite the harm they have suffered. Communities that practice restorative justice are not merely safer; they are more likely to be places where all members can flourish together.

The psychological research on the benefits of restorative justice has accumulated impressively over the past several decades, and the findings are remarkably consistent across different settings, populations, and methodologies. Let us now examine each of the key benefits in depth, exploring both the evidence for them and the mechanisms through which they are produced.

1. Reduced Recidivism Rates

Perhaps the most rigorously documented benefit of restorative justice for juveniles is the substantial reduction in recidivism rates among young offenders who participate in restorative processes. Recidivism—the tendency of offenders to reoffend after being processed by the justice system—is the single most important measure of a justice program's effectiveness in promoting public safety. If a program does not reduce reoffending, it fails in its most basic purpose, regardless of how satisfying it may be to participants or how efficiently it may operate. The evidence that restorative justice reduces recidivism is now overwhelming.

A comprehensive meta-analysis by the RAND Corporation, examining dozens of rigorous studies with tens of thousands of participants, found that restorative justice programs reduce recidivism among juvenile offenders by an average of 10 to 35 percent compared to traditional court processing. This range reflects variation in program quality, participant characteristics, and outcome measures, but the direction of the effect is consistent across studies: restorative justice works better than punishment at preventing future offending. The effects are particularly strong for violent offenses, where the reduction in recidivism is often even larger. This finding is especially significant, as violent offenses cause the greatest harm to victims and communities and are often the most difficult to address through traditional approaches.

The Washington State Institute for Public Policy, which has conducted some of the most sophisticated cost-benefit analyses of criminal justice programs in the nation, has consistently found that restorative justice for juveniles produces substantial reductions in recidivism. Their most recent analysis, incorporating data from multiple rigorous studies, found that restorative justice programs reduce recidivism by approximately 15 percent compared to traditional court processing. This reduction translates into significant benefits for taxpayers and crime victims: fewer future offenses, lower criminal justice costs, and less victimization. The Institute's analysis also found that restorative justice produces positive returns on investment, with every dollar spent on restorative programs returning multiple dollars in benefits.

Why does restorative justice reduce recidivism? The mechanisms are multiple and mutually reinforcing. First, restorative justice addresses the root causes of delinquent behavior rather than merely punishing its symptoms. Through dialogue with victims, reflection on harm, and engagement with community, young offenders come to understand why they acted as they did and what they need to change. The restitution plans and support services that emerge from restorative processes address these underlying factors directly, providing counseling, education, job training, and other interventions that equip young people for prosocial lives.

Second, restorative justice fosters genuine accountability rather than passive compliance. Young offenders in traditional systems often experience punishment as something done to them, an external imposition that requires nothing from them internally. They serve their time, pay their fines, and return to their communities unchanged, often more angry and alienated than before. Restorative justice, by contrast, requires active engagement. Offenders must acknowledge their responsibility, listen to victims, participate in developing agreements, and take concrete steps to make amends. This active engagement produces internal change—changed attitudes, changed values, changed sense of self—that external punishment cannot achieve.

Third, restorative justice builds social bonds that support desistance. The research on desistance—the process by which people stop offending—consistently finds that social bonds are crucial. Offenders who develop strong connections to prosocial others—family, mentors, community members—are far more likely to desist from crime than those who remain isolated. Restorative justice, by involving community members as supporters and mentors, helps build these bonds. The relationships forged in restorative processes become resources for ongoing support and accountability, reducing the likelihood of reoffending long after the formal process is complete.

Fourth, restorative justice reduces the stigma and labeling that drive continued offending. Labeling theory, developed by sociologists like Howard Becker and Edwin Lemert, argues that when society labels people as criminals, they internalize that label and behave accordingly. Traditional punishment is a labeling machine, stamping young people with the mark of "offender" and excluding them from the community. Restorative justice, by distinguishing clearly between the person and the behavior, by condemning the offense while affirming the offender, by creating pathways back into community, reduces this stigmatizing effect. Young people who complete restorative processes are not marked for life; they are welcomed back, given the opportunity to be seen as something other than their worst action.

The theological significance of reduced recidivism is profound. The God of the Bible is a God of new beginnings, of second chances, of transformation. The prophet Isaiah declares, "Forget the former things; do not dwell on the past. See, I am doing a new thing!" The apostle Paul writes, "If anyone is in Christ, the new creation has come: The old has gone, the new is here!" Reduced recidivism is evidence that new creation is possible, that young people can leave their past behind and become something new. It is a sign that the restorative purposes of God are being realized in the lives of young offenders, that the promise of transformation is not empty words but living reality.

2. Improved Victim Satisfaction

The second great benefit of restorative justice for juveniles is improved victim satisfaction. Victims of crime have long been the forgotten party in traditional criminal justice systems, marginalized to the role of witness and denied any meaningful participation in the resolution of "their" cases. Restorative justice reverses this historical injustice, placing victims at the center of the process and giving them voice, participation, and genuine influence over outcomes. The result is levels of satisfaction that traditional systems rarely achieve.

Research consistently finds that victims who participate in restorative processes report significantly higher levels of satisfaction than those whose cases go through traditional courts. A meta-analysis by the RAND Corporation found that victim satisfaction rates in restorative programs averaged 80 to 90 percent, compared to 50 to 60 percent in traditional proceedings. The landmark study by Lawrence Sherman and Heather Strang, involving multiple randomized controlled trials across the United Kingdom and Australia, found that victims who participated in restorative conferences were more satisfied, more likely to feel that justice had been done, and more likely to recommend the process to others in similar situations.

Why are victims more satisfied with restorative justice? The reasons are multiple. First, restorative justice gives victims voice. In traditional court proceedings, victims have limited opportunities to speak, and when they do, their statements come at the end of the process, after all important decisions have been made. In restorative processes, victims speak first, and their stories shape everything that follows. They can express the full impact of the offense—the fear, the anger, the loss, the ongoing effects—in their own words, to an audience that is required to listen. This experience of being heard is profoundly validating, communicating that what happened matters and that the victim matters.

Second, restorative justice gives victims answers. Crime often leaves victims with unanswered questions: Why me? Why did this happen? Does the offender understand what they did? In traditional proceedings, these questions go unanswered; the focus is on legal guilt or innocence, not on the victim's need to understand. In restorative processes, victims can ask these questions directly, and offenders are expected to answer. The answers may not always be satisfying, but they provide information that victims can use to make sense of their experience and begin the process of healing.

Third, restorative justice gives victims participation. In traditional proceedings, victims are passive observers of a drama that is supposedly about them but in which they have no role. Decisions are made by prosecutors, defense attorneys, and judges, with no input from the person most affected. In restorative processes, victims participate actively in shaping the resolution. They have a say in what the offender will do to make amends, what form restitution should take, what conditions will address their needs. This participation restores the sense of agency that crime so often destroys, empowering victims to move from passivity to activity, from helplessness to efficacy.

Fourth, restorative justice gives victims closure. The experience of being heard, of receiving answers, of participating in resolution—all of these contribute to a sense of closure that traditional proceedings rarely provide. Victims who complete restorative processes often describe a release, a letting go of anger and fear that had been locked inside since the crime occurred. They are able to move forward with their lives in ways that were not possible before.

The theological significance of victim satisfaction lies in the biblical emphasis on God's care for those who have been wronged. The psalmist cries out, "Hear my cry for help, my King and my God, for to you I pray." The prophets announce God's special concern for the vulnerable, the oppressed, the victimized. Jesus pronounces blessing on those who mourn and promises they will be comforted. Restorative justice, by attending to the needs of victims, by giving them voice and participation and closure, embodies this divine concern. It is a way of saying to victims: You matter. Your suffering matters. God sees you, and we see you too.

3. Healing and Emotional Recovery

Closely related to improved satisfaction is the benefit of healing and emotional recovery. Crime inflicts wounds that go far beyond physical injury or property loss—wounds to the psyche, to the spirit, to the sense of safety and trust that makes human life possible. Victims of crime often experience symptoms of post-traumatic stress: intrusive memories, hypervigilance, emotional numbing, avoidance of reminders. They may struggle with feelings of shame, guilt, and self-blame. They may lose trust in others, in the world, in themselves. The process of healing from these wounds is long and difficult, and it requires conditions that traditional justice systems rarely provide.

Restorative justice creates these conditions. By giving victims voice and participation, it helps them move from passivity to agency, from helplessness to empowerment. By providing answers to their questions, it helps them make sense of their experience and integrate it into their life story. By allowing them to express their feelings directly to the person who caused them harm, it provides catharsis and release. By demonstrating that the community cares about what happened, it restores the sense of belonging that crime so often destroys.

The research on healing and emotional recovery in restorative justice is compelling. The Sherman and Strang study found that victims who participated in restorative conferences experienced significant reductions in post-traumatic stress symptoms compared to those whose cases went to court. They were less fearful of being revictimized, less angry at the offender, and more able to put the experience behind them. These effects were particularly strong for victims of violent crime, who often suffer the most severe psychological wounds.

Why does restorative justice promote healing? The psychology of trauma provides answers. Judith Herman, in her classic work *Trauma and Recovery*, identifies three stages of recovery from trauma: the establishment of safety, the reconstruction of the trauma story, and the restoration of connection with others. Restorative justice addresses each of these stages. The safe and structured environment of restorative processes helps victims feel safe enough to engage with their trauma. The opportunity to tell their full story, in their own words, helps them reconstruct the trauma narrative in a way that restores meaning and control. The presence of supportive community members and the encounter with the offender, when properly facilitated, helps restore connection with others.

The theology of healing is woven throughout the biblical narrative. The psalmist cries out, "Heal me, Lord, and I will be healed; save me and I will be saved, for you are the one I praise." The prophet Isaiah announces God's promise: "I will turn their mourning into gladness; I will give them comfort and joy instead of sorrow." Jesus spends much of his ministry healing the sick, the blind, the lame, the broken. The early church understood healing as a sign of the kingdom, a foretaste of the time when all tears would be wiped away. Restorative justice, by promoting healing and emotional recovery for victims, participates in this divine work of restoration.

4. Accountability and Responsibility

The fourth great benefit of restorative justice is the cultivation of genuine accountability and personal responsibility in young offenders. Traditional punitive approaches often produce the opposite: offenders focus on their own suffering, feel that they are victims of an unfair system, and emerge more angry and alienated than before. Restorative justice, by contrast, creates conditions in which offenders can acknowledge what they have done, understand its impact, and take active steps to make things right.

Accountability in restorative justice is not something done to offenders but something they do. Through victim-offender dialogues, they hear directly about the harm they have caused. Through restitution plans, they take concrete steps to repair that harm. Through engagement with community, they experience both the disapproval of their actions and the support for their change. This active accountability produces internal change that passive punishment cannot achieve.

The research on accountability in restorative justice is consistent: offenders who participate in restorative processes are more likely to acknowledge responsibility, express remorse, and complete restitution agreements than those processed through traditional courts. They are also less likely to reoffend, suggesting that the accountability they experience is genuine and lasting. A study by the University of Pennsylvania found that juvenile offenders who participated in restorative conferences were significantly more likely to express genuine remorse and to understand the impact of their actions than those who went through traditional court proceedings.

Why does restorative justice produce genuine accountability? The mechanisms are multiple. First, restorative justice creates conditions for guilt rather than shame. As we have seen, guilt—the feeling that one has done something bad—leads to acknowledgment and repair, while shame—the feeling that one is bad—leads to denial and blame. Restorative justice, by distinguishing clearly between the person and the behavior, by condemning the offense while affirming the offender, fosters guilt rather than shame. Offenders can feel bad about what they did without feeling bad about who they are, and this guilt motivates them to make things right.

Second, restorative justice provides direct feedback on the consequences of actions. In traditional systems, offenders may never learn the full impact of what they have done. They hear about harm through the abstract language of legal proceedings, filtered through lawyers and rules of evidence. In restorative processes, they hear directly from victims—from the people who have been most affected. This direct feedback is far more powerful than any abstract lesson, creating understanding that cannot be achieved through punishment alone.

Third, restorative justice offers a pathway to repair. Offenders who acknowledge their responsibility are not left in a state of guilt with no way to address it. They are given the opportunity to make amends, to take concrete steps that demonstrate their commitment to change. This opportunity is itself motivating, providing a way to move from remorse to restoration, from guilt to growth.

The theological significance of accountability lies in the biblical understanding of repentance. The Hebrew word *shuv* and the Greek word *metanoia* both mean turning—turning from wrongdoing, turning toward God, turning toward right relationship. This turning is not merely feeling sorry but changing direction, reorienting one's whole life. Restorative justice, by creating conditions for genuine accountability and responsibility, facilitates this turning. It helps young offenders not merely regret what they have done but become different people, people who make different choices and live different lives.

5. Community Building

The fifth great benefit of restorative justice is community building. By involving the community in the resolution process, restorative justice strengthens the social fabric, builds trust and cooperation, and creates the conditions for collective efficacy—that combination of social cohesion and shared expectations for action that research has shown to be the most powerful predictor of neighborhood safety.

The research on collective efficacy, conducted by Robert Sampson and his colleagues in Chicago neighborhoods, found that communities with high levels of collective efficacy have lower crime rates, even when they are disadvantaged in other ways. Collective efficacy is built through relationships, through trust, through the everyday interactions of neighbors who know and care about one another. Restorative justice, by bringing community members together to address harm, builds these relationships. The connections forged in circles and conferences become resources for future problem-solving and mutual support.

The research on social capital, developed by Robert Putnam and others, reveals the importance of networks of relationship for community well-being. Social capital—the trust, norms, and networks that enable collective action—has been linked to better health, higher educational achievement, lower crime rates, and more effective governance. Restorative justice builds social capital by creating opportunities for community members to work together on shared problems. The trust developed in restorative processes carries over into other areas of community life, strengthening the fabric of relationships that makes communities work.

Why does restorative justice build community? First, it creates opportunities for positive interaction. In many communities, residents have few opportunities to come together around shared concerns. Restorative processes provide structured opportunities for community members to meet, talk, and work together. These interactions build relationships that would not otherwise exist.

Second, it demonstrates that the community cares. When community members show up for circles and conferences, they communicate that what happens matters, that people matter, that the community is not indifferent to the suffering of its members. This demonstration of care strengthens the bonds of mutual responsibility that hold communities together.

Third, it empowers community members to address their own problems. Restorative justice trusts that those most affected by crime have wisdom about how to address it. By giving community members a role in resolving conflicts and repairing harm, it builds their capacity to solve problems collectively. This empowerment is itself community-building, as residents come to see themselves as agents of their own safety rather than passive recipients of services provided by others.

The theological significance of community building lies in the biblical vision of God's people as a community of mutual care and responsibility. The early church understood itself as a body, each member belonging to all the others. They shared their possessions, cared for the needy, bore one another's burdens. They were not merely individuals who happened to believe the same things but a community bound together by love. Restorative justice, by building community in the context of addressing harm, participates in this vision. It creates communities that are not merely collections of individuals but bodies, each member connected to all the others, each member responsible for all the others.

6. Enhanced Communication and Empathy

The sixth benefit of restorative justice is enhanced communication and empathy between victims and offenders, and among all participants in restorative processes. Communication and empathy are not merely nice additions to justice but essential components of healing and accountability. Without communication, victims cannot express their needs and offenders cannot understand the impact of their actions. Without empathy, victims remain isolated in their suffering and offenders remain insulated from the consequences of their behavior.

Restorative processes facilitate open and honest communication in ways that traditional proceedings cannot. In court, communication is mediated by lawyers, filtered through rules of evidence, constrained by formal procedures. Victims and offenders rarely speak directly to one another, and when they do, it is in highly structured ways that limit genuine exchange. In restorative processes, communication is direct, personal, and unmediated. Victims and offenders speak to one another, ask questions, express feelings, and work together toward resolution. This direct communication builds understanding that cannot be achieved through any other means.

This communication, in turn, fosters empathy. Empathy—the capacity to understand and feel the inner experience of another—is both a natural human capacity and a skill that can be cultivated. Restorative processes cultivate empathy by creating conditions in which victims and offenders can see each other's humanity. Victims see offenders not as monsters but as human beings, often young people with their own struggles and wounds. Offenders see victims not as abstract categories but as real people who have suffered real harm. This mutual seeing is the beginning of empathy, and empathy is the beginning of healing.

The research on empathy in restorative justice is compelling. Studies have found that offenders who participate in restorative processes show significant increases in empathy for their victims, and that this increased empathy is associated with reduced recidivism. Victims who participate in restorative processes often report increased empathy for offenders, not in the sense of excusing their behavior but in the sense of understanding them as human beings. This empathy does not replace accountability but complements it, creating conditions for genuine resolution rather than mere settlement.

Why does restorative justice enhance communication and empathy? First, it creates a safe space for honest expression. The structured format, the presence of facilitators, the support of community members—all of these create conditions in which participants feel safe enough to speak openly and listen deeply. Without this safety, genuine communication cannot occur.

Second, it provides opportunities for perspective-taking. When victims describe their experience, offenders are invited to imagine what it would be like to be in that situation. When offenders explain their actions, victims are invited to understand what led to those actions. This mutual perspective-taking builds empathy and understanding.

Third, it models respectful communication. The facilitators and community members who participate in restorative processes model ways of speaking and listening that participants can learn from and internalize. Over time, these models shape how participants communicate in other contexts, improving their relationships with family, peers, and community members.

The theological significance of enhanced communication and empathy lies in the biblical understanding of love. The greatest commandment, Jesus teaches, is to love God and love neighbor. Love requires knowing the neighbor, understanding the neighbor, seeing the neighbor as a human being worthy of care. Empathy is the capacity that makes this knowing possible. Restorative justice, by enhancing communication and empathy, cultivates the capacity for love. It helps victims and offenders see one another as neighbors, as human beings deserving of respect and care, as members of the same community and children of the same God.

7. Prevention of Secondary Victimization

The seventh benefit of restorative justice is the prevention of secondary victimization—the additional trauma that victims often experience in their dealings with the criminal justice system. Secondary victimization occurs when the very institutions established to address crime compound its effects through indifference, insensitivity, and exclusion. Victims who navigate traditional court proceedings often report feeling used, ignored, and betrayed by a system that claims to serve them but in practice serves institutional interests.

Restorative justice aims to prevent secondary victimization by ensuring that victims are treated with dignity and respect throughout the process. From the initial contact through the final agreement, restorative processes are designed to honor victims' experience, attend to their needs, and protect them from further harm. Victims are never pressured to participate; their consent is required at every stage. They are never subjected to aggressive cross-examination or made to feel that they are on trial. They are never ignored or marginalized; their voices are central to everything that happens.

The research on secondary victimization in restorative justice is consistent: victims who participate in restorative processes report lower levels of secondary trauma than those whose cases go through traditional courts. They feel heard, validated, and respected. They do not experience the system as a second injury but as a source of support and healing. A study by the University of Minnesota found that victims who participated in restorative conferences reported significantly lower levels of distress related to the justice process than those whose cases went to court.

Why does restorative justice prevent secondary victimization? First, it gives victims control. In traditional systems, victims have no control over the process; decisions are made by others, often without their input or even their knowledge. In restorative processes, victims have control over their participation, their voice, their role in shaping outcomes. This control restores the sense of agency that crime destroys.

Second, it treats victims with respect. From the way they are greeted to the way their stories are received to the way their needs are addressed, restorative processes communicate that victims matter. This respectful treatment is itself healing, counteracting the disrespect inherent in victimization.

Third, it avoids the adversarial dynamic that produces secondary trauma. Traditional court proceedings are adversarial by design; victims are witnesses for one side, subjected to cross-examination by the other. This adversarial dynamic can be profoundly traumatizing, especially for victims of violent crime. Restorative processes are collaborative rather than adversarial, focused on problem-solving rather than winning and losing. This collaborative dynamic protects victims from the additional trauma of adversarial combat.

The theological significance of preventing secondary victimization lies in the biblical command to "not mistreat or oppress a foreigner, for you were foreigners in Egypt." This command is grounded in empathy—because you know what it feels like to be mistreated, you should not mistreat others. The justice system that mistreats victims violates this command, adding injury to injury. Restorative justice, by treating victims with dignity and respect, obeys it.

8. Personal Growth and Rehabilitation

The eighth benefit of restorative justice is the opportunity it provides for personal growth and genuine rehabilitation in young offenders. Rehabilitation is not merely the absence of reoffending but the presence of positive development—the acquisition of skills, the formation of character, the development of a prosocial identity. Restorative justice creates conditions for this kind of deep change.

Young offenders who participate in restorative processes have opportunities for growth that traditional punishment cannot provide. They learn to take responsibility for their actions, to understand the impact of their behavior on others, to make amends for harm caused. They develop empathy, communication skills, and problem-solving abilities. They experience the support of community members who believe in their potential and invest in their futures. They come to see themselves not as criminals defined by their worst actions but as persons capable of change, worthy of respect, able to contribute to their communities.

The research on personal growth and rehabilitation in restorative justice is compelling. Studies have found that young offenders who participate in restorative processes show improvements in empathy, moral reasoning, and prosocial attitudes. They are more likely to complete educational programs, find employment, and form healthy relationships. They are less likely to reoffend, not merely because they fear punishment but because they have become different people.

Why does restorative justice promote personal growth? First, it provides opportunities for reflection. The restorative process invites young offenders to reflect on their actions, their motivations, the harm they have caused. This reflection is the beginning of self-awareness, and self-awareness is the beginning of change.

Second, it provides opportunities for learning. The encounter with victims teaches lessons that no lecture can convey. The development of restitution plans teaches problem-solving skills. The engagement with community teaches social skills. Every aspect of the restorative process is a learning opportunity.

Third, it provides opportunities for identity reconstruction. Young offenders in restorative processes are treated not as criminals but as persons capable of change. This treatment invites them to see themselves differently, to imagine different futures, to become different people. The identity of "offender" is replaced by the identity of "person who made a mistake and is making it right." This new identity is the foundation for lasting change.

The theological significance of personal growth and rehabilitation lies in the biblical understanding of transformation. The apostle Paul writes, "Do not conform to the pattern of this world, but be transformed by the renewing of your mind." This transformation is not merely behavior modification but fundamental change—a new way of thinking, a new way of being, a new creation. Restorative justice, by creating conditions for personal growth and rehabilitation, participates in this transformative work. It helps young people become, in Paul's words, "new creations"—people who have left their old selves behind and are living new lives.

Cost Savings and System Benefits

Beyond these direct benefits to victims, offenders, and communities, restorative justice also produces significant cost savings for the justice system. By reducing recidivism rates, it decreases the burden on law enforcement, courts, and correctional facilities. Fewer reoffenses mean fewer arrests, fewer court appearances, fewer incarcerations. These savings can be substantial, especially when multiplied across many cases over many years.

The Washington State Institute for Public Policy's cost-benefit analyses have consistently found that restorative justice produces positive returns on investment. Their most recent analysis found that every dollar spent on restorative justice programs returns approximately eight dollars in benefits through reduced criminal justice costs and avoided victimization. These are not speculative projections but conservative estimates based on rigorous data. In an era of tight budgets and competing demands for public resources, restorative justice offers the rare combination of better outcomes and lower costs.

Restorative justice also produces system benefits beyond direct cost savings. By diverting cases from overloaded courts, it reduces pressure on the judicial system and allows judges and prosecutors to focus their attention on more serious cases. By providing alternatives to incarceration, it reduces pressure on overcrowded juvenile detention facilities. By engaging community members in the justice process, it builds public trust and legitimacy, which are essential for effective law enforcement and crime prevention.

Communication and Community Engagement

The benefits of restorative justice cannot be realized without effective communication and community engagement. Communities may initially hold reservations about restorative justice programs, concerned that they are soft on crime or that they will not adequately protect public safety. Addressing these concerns through transparent communication is essential for building the broad foundation of support that programs need to succeed.

Successful programs implement comprehensive communication plans founded on honesty and transparency. They collaborate with local media to explain the program's purpose and keep the community informed of its progress. They engage community opinion leaders—clergy, business owners, elected officials—to publicly express their support. They share accurate facts and genuine human stories that demonstrate the program's effectiveness and its benefits for real people.

Programs must also be prepared for the inevitable challenges that arise. Every restorative justice program will eventually face a case that goes wrong—an offender who reoffends, a victim who is dissatisfied, a community member who criticizes the process. Having a contingency communication plan ready for such situations is essential. Programs that respond quickly, honestly, and transparently to challenges can maintain public trust and continue their work. Programs that are caught off guard, that try to hide problems or deflect blame, can lose the credibility they have worked so hard to build.

The theological significance of effective communication lies in the biblical understanding of truth-telling. The prophets spoke truth to power, calling God's people to accountability. Jesus described himself as "the way, the truth, and the life." The early church was committed to speaking the truth in love. Restorative justice programs that communicate honestly and transparently embody this commitment. They tell the truth about their work—its successes and its failures, its strengths and its limitations—and in doing so, they build the trust that makes their work possible.

The Cumulative Impact

The benefits of restorative justice are not isolated from one another but mutually reinforcing. Reduced recidivism benefits victims by preventing future harm and benefits communities by enhancing safety. Improved victim satisfaction contributes to healing and emotional recovery, which in turn strengthens communities. Accountability and responsibility in offenders contribute to personal growth and rehabilitation, which reduces recidivism. Enhanced communication and empathy benefit all parties, creating conditions for healing and growth. Prevention of secondary victimization protects victims from additional trauma, supporting their recovery. Community building strengthens the social fabric, creating conditions in which all these benefits can flourish.

This cumulative impact is what makes restorative justice more than the sum of its parts. It is not merely a set of techniques for achieving discrete outcomes but a holistic approach to justice that transforms everyone it touches. Young offenders are not merely less likely to reoffend; they are more likely to become contributing members of their communities. Victims are not merely more satisfied; they are more likely to experience genuine healing and closure. Communities are not merely safer; they are more cohesive, more resilient, more capable of addressing their own problems.

The theological vision that encompasses all these benefits is the vision of the kingdom of God—that new order of reality that Jesus announced and embodied, in which the last are first, the lost are found, the broken are healed, and all things are made new. Restorative justice is not the kingdom, but it is a sign of the kingdom, a foretaste of what is possible when God's restorative purposes are realized. Its benefits are glimpses of the *shalom* that is to come, when all tears will be wiped away, when death and mourning and crying and pain will be no more, when everything will be made new.

As we continue our journey through the principles and practices of restorative justice, we will explore the challenges it faces, the legal frameworks that support it, the case studies that illustrate it, and the future directions it might take. But for now, let us celebrate the benefits we have explored—the reduced recidivism, the improved victim satisfaction, the healing and emotional recovery, the accountability and responsibility, the community building, the enhanced communication and empathy, the prevention of secondary victimization, the personal growth and rehabilitation, the cost savings and system benefits. These are not abstract outcomes but real changes in real lives, evidence that restorative justice works, that it is worthy of our support, and that it offers hope for a better way of responding to juvenile offending.

CHAPTER 09

CHALLENGES AND CRITICISM

The path of restorative justice, for all its promise and proven benefits, is not without its obstacles and detractors. To present restorative justice as an unalloyed good, a perfect solution to the complex problems of juvenile offending, would be dishonest and ultimately harmful to the movement itself. Every human institution, every practice, every approach to the profound challenges of justice is necessarily imperfect, limited by human fallibility, constrained by resources, and shaped by contexts that vary widely across communities and cultures. The honest advocate of restorative justice must confront these limitations directly, acknowledging the challenges that arise in practice and the criticisms that have been leveled by thoughtful observers. Only by doing so can we work to address these concerns, refine our approaches, and build restorative justice programs that are as fair, effective, and safe as humanly possible.

The challenges facing restorative justice are not arguments against its value but invitations to greater rigor, deeper reflection, and more careful implementation. They remind us that restorative justice is not a magic wand but a human practice, subject to all the limitations and possibilities that attend any human endeavor. They call us to humility, to ongoing learning, to the recognition that we do not have all the answers and must remain open to critique and correction. And they point us toward the theological truth that all human systems are fallen, that even our best efforts are imperfect, and that we must rely on grace as much as technique in the work of restoration.

The theological tradition is rich with resources for understanding and responding to these challenges. The prophets of Israel were relentless critics of injustice, even—perhaps especially—when it appeared in the guise of religious practice. Amos thundered against those who trampled the poor and pushed the needy aside, even as they offered their sacrifices and sang their hymns. Jesus confronted the religious leaders of his day, calling them whitewashed tombs and blind guides, not because they were evil but because their righteousness had become self-righteousness, their concern for the law had become indifference to mercy. The honest acknowledgment of challenges and criticisms is itself a faithful practice, a recognition that we stand always in need of examination and reform.

The philosophical tradition, too, offers resources for engaging with criticism. The Socratic method, with its relentless questioning of assumptions and its insistence on following the argument wherever it leads, models the kind of critical reflection that restorative justice requires. The pragmatist tradition, with its emphasis on learning from experience and adapting practice based on results, provides a framework for responding to challenges with humility and flexibility. The critical theory of the Frankfurt School, with its attention to power, ideology, and the ways that seemingly benign practices can reproduce injustice, offers tools for examining restorative justice with the depth it deserves.

The psychological research on bias, power, and interpersonal dynamics provides empirical grounding for understanding the challenges that arise in restorative practice. We know that human beings are subject to unconscious biases that can distort judgment and produce unfair outcomes. We know that power differentials can undermine the voluntariness of participation and the genuineness of agreements. We know that trauma can be triggered by well-intentioned interventions and that safety must be vigilantly maintained. These psychological realities are not arguments against restorative justice but factors that must be taken into account in its design and implementation.

The legal framework for restorative justice, still developing in many jurisdictions, both reflects and shapes the challenges the movement faces. Questions about the relationship between restorative processes and formal legal proceedings, about the enforceability of restorative agreements, about the rights of participants and the obligations of facilitators—these are legal questions that require careful attention and ongoing refinement. The law can be both a support for restorative justice and an obstacle to it, depending on how it is structured and applied.

With this context in mind, let us examine the major challenges and criticisms that restorative justice for juveniles faces, exploring each in depth and considering how they might be addressed.

1. Fairness and Equity Concerns

Perhaps the most fundamental set of challenges facing restorative justice relates to issues of fairness and equity. Critics raise legitimate questions about whether restorative processes can be consistently fair across diverse cases and populations, and whether they might inadvertently reproduce or even exacerbate existing inequalities in the justice system.

The concern about selectivity is particularly acute. Restorative justice programs typically have discretion over which cases they accept, and this discretion can lead to patterns of selection that favor certain types of offenders or offenses over others. Research has documented that restorative programs often serve younger, first-time, and nonviolent offenders, while excluding older, repeat, and violent offenders. While this selectivity may be justified on grounds of safety and appropriateness, it can also produce disparities in treatment that raise fairness concerns. Offenders who are deemed suitable for restorative justice receive the benefits of that approach—lower recidivism, greater satisfaction, more support—while those who are excluded are left with traditional punishment, which research shows is less effective. This two-track system can be fair if the selection criteria are clear, consistently applied, and based on legitimate factors, but it can be deeply unfair if selection is arbitrary, biased, or influenced by factors like race, class, or the quality of legal representation.

The concern about power imbalances is equally important. Restorative processes bring together victims and offenders who may have very different levels of power, resources, and support. A victim who is articulate, educated, and confident may be able to participate effectively, while a victim who is traumatized, intimidated, or unsupported may struggle to have their voice heard. An offender who has strong family support, access to legal advice, and the resources to complete restitution agreements may fare well, while an offender who is isolated, impoverished, and unsupported may be unable to meet the expectations placed upon them. These power imbalances can undermine the voluntariness of participation and the fairness of outcomes, particularly if facilitators are not trained to recognize and address them.

The psychological research on power and voice is relevant here. Studies have shown that people in positions of power are more likely to speak, more likely to be heard, and more likely to have their preferences reflected in group decisions. People with less power may defer to those with more power, may be reluctant to express disagreement, may internalize the belief that their perspective matters less. In restorative processes, these dynamics can play out in ways that undermine the very goals of the approach. A victim who defers to an offender, or an offender who defers to a victim, may not be able to participate authentically, and the agreement that emerges may reflect power rather than genuine consensus.

The theological response to these concerns is grounded in the biblical emphasis on justice for the poor and vulnerable. The prophets repeatedly condemn those who use their power to exploit the powerless, who "sell the righteous for silver and the needy for a pair of sandals," who "trample the heads of the poor into the dust of the earth." Restorative justice must be vigilant against the same dynamics, ensuring that its processes do not become vehicles for the powerful to further advantage themselves at the expense of the vulnerable. This requires intentional design, careful facilitation, and ongoing attention to the ways that power operates in every human interaction.

Addressing fairness and equity concerns requires multiple strategies. First, programs must develop clear, transparent, and consistently applied criteria for case selection, based on legitimate factors like offense severity, offender risk, and victim preferences. These criteria should be reviewed regularly and adjusted as needed to ensure they are not producing unintended disparities. Second, programs must train facilitators to recognize and address power imbalances, using techniques that ensure all participants have the opportunity to speak and be heard. This may include meeting separately with parties before the joint session, providing support persons for those who need them, and intervening when one party dominates the conversation. Third, programs must collect data on participant demographics and outcomes, monitoring for patterns of disparity and adjusting practices accordingly. Fourth, programs must engage with communities to understand their concerns about fairness and equity, and to involve community members in shaping practices that are responsive to local conditions.

2. Victim Participation Concerns

The second major set of challenges relates to victim participation. While restorative justice aims to empower victims and give them voice, the reality of victim participation is complex and sometimes problematic. Critics raise legitimate concerns about whether victims may be pressured into participating, whether the process may retraumatize rather than heal, and whether victims receive adequate support throughout the process.

The concern about pressure to participate is significant. Victims may feel pressure from multiple sources—from the justice system, which may present restorative justice as the only way to get their needs addressed; from family members, who may encourage them to participate for the sake of closure; from their own sense of obligation, feeling that they should participate because it might help the offender or because it's the "right" thing to do. This pressure can undermine the voluntariness that is essential to restorative justice, turning what should be a freely chosen process into one that feels coerced. Victims who participate under pressure may not be able to engage authentically, and the experience may compound rather than heal their trauma.

The concern about retraumatization is equally serious. Victim-offender dialogue involves confronting the person who caused harm, hearing their account of what happened, and revisiting painful memories and emotions. For some victims, this confrontation can be healing, providing catharsis and closure. For others, it can be retraumatizing, reopening wounds that had begun to heal and exposing them to additional emotional pain. The risk of retraumatization is particularly acute when victims are not adequately prepared, when facilitators are not sufficiently skilled, or when offenders are not genuinely accountable. A victim who encounters a defensive, minimizing, or blaming offender may experience the dialogue as a second injury rather than a healing encounter.

The concern about inadequate support is also important. Victims need support throughout the restorative process—before, during, and after the encounter. They need preparation that helps them understand what to expect and how to participate effectively. They need accompaniment during the encounter, whether from support persons, victim advocates, or skilled facilitators. They need follow-up after the encounter, to process their experience and address any ongoing needs. When this support is lacking, victims may be left to navigate the process alone, increasing the risk of negative outcomes.

The psychological research on trauma and recovery is directly relevant to these concerns. Trauma researchers emphasize the importance of safety, control, and choice in the healing process. Victims must feel safe enough to engage with their traumatic memories; they must have control over whether and how they participate; they must have genuine choices about what happens to them. Restorative processes that are imposed, that remove control, that limit choice, are likely to be retraumatizing rather than healing. The challenge for restorative justice is to create conditions that maximize safety, control, and choice for victims, while still allowing for genuine encounter with offenders.

The theological response to these concerns is grounded in the biblical emphasis on care for the vulnerable. The psalmist cries out, "O Lord, hear my prayer, listen to my cry for mercy; in your faithfulness and righteousness come to my relief." Victims of crime are vulnerable, and the justice system—including restorative justice—must be organized around their care. This means ensuring that their participation is truly voluntary, that they are protected from harm, and that they receive the support they need. It means treating victims not as means to the end of offender rehabilitation but as ends in themselves, persons of dignity whose healing matters for its own sake.

Addressing victim participation concerns requires multiple strategies. First, programs must ensure that victim participation is genuinely voluntary, with clear information about what participation entails, what alternatives exist, and the right to withdraw at any time. This informed consent process should be documented and revisited throughout the process. Second, programs must conduct thorough victim preparation, including assessment of readiness, exploration of hopes and fears, and development of coping strategies. This preparation should be tailored to each victim's unique circumstances and needs. Third, programs must provide ongoing support, including accompaniment during the encounter and follow-up afterward. This support may be provided by victim advocates, counselors, or trained volunteers. Fourth, programs must screen cases carefully for appropriateness, considering factors like the nature of the offense, the relationship between victim and offender, and the victim's readiness. Cases that pose high risk of retraumatization should not proceed, or should proceed only with extraordinary safeguards.

3. Offender Accountability Concerns

The third set of challenges relates to offender accountability. Critics question whether offenders who participate in restorative justice genuinely take responsibility for their actions, or whether they simply go through the motions to avoid harsher consequences. They also question whether restorative justice effectively deters reoffending, particularly for more serious or chronic offenders.

The concern about genuine accountability is fundamental. Restorative justice depends on offenders acknowledging their responsibility and committing to repair. But offenders may have multiple motivations for participating—some genuine, some strategic. An offender who participates only to avoid detention, who says what they think the victim wants to hear, who makes promises they have no intention of keeping, is not experiencing genuine accountability. The process becomes a performance rather than a transformation, and the benefits that restorative justice promises are unlikely to materialize.

The challenge for facilitators is to discern genuine accountability from its counterfeits. This requires skill in reading nonverbal cues, in probing beneath surface responses, in creating conditions that invite authenticity rather than performance. It also requires attention to the structural factors that may incentivize inauthenticity. Offenders who are offered restorative justice as an alternative to detention, who are told that participation will lead to lesser charges or lighter sentences, face powerful incentives to say whatever is necessary to achieve those outcomes. The voluntariness that is essential to restorative justice is compromised when participation is coerced by the threat of worse alternatives.

The concern about reoffending risk is also significant. While research shows that restorative justice reduces recidivism on average, it does not eliminate it entirely. Some offenders who participate in restorative processes will reoffend, sometimes seriously. When this happens, critics may point to the failure as evidence that restorative justice does not work, and supporters may scramble to explain why this particular case did not produce the expected outcome. The reality is that no intervention works for everyone, and restorative justice is no exception. The question is not whether it occasionally fails but whether it fails less often than the alternatives.

The psychological research on motivation and behavior change is relevant here. Genuine change requires internal motivation, not merely external compliance. Offenders who change because they have internalized new values, because they genuinely understand the harm they have caused, because they have developed empathy for victims—these offenders are likely to sustain their change over time. Offenders who change only to avoid punishment, who comply with external requirements without internal transformation, are likely to revert to old patterns when the external pressure is removed. Restorative justice aims to produce internal motivation, but it does not always succeed.

The theological response to these concerns is grounded in the biblical understanding of the human heart. The prophets understood that outward compliance is not enough; God looks at the heart. Jesus condemned the Pharisees for their outward righteousness, which masked inner corruption. Genuine accountability, in the biblical view, is not merely saying the right words but being transformed from the inside out. Restorative justice must aim for this deep transformation, while recognizing that it cannot guarantee it. The work of change is ultimately mysterious, involving factors beyond any program's control.

Addressing offender accountability concerns requires multiple strategies. First, programs must attend carefully to the voluntariness of offender participation. Offenders should understand their options, including the alternatives to restorative justice, and should choose participation freely rather than under coercion. This does not mean that restorative justice cannot be offered as an alternative to traditional processing, but it does mean that the choice should be genuine and informed. Second, programs must train facilitators to assess genuineness and to probe beneath surface responses. Facilitators should be skilled in asking questions that invite reflection, in creating conditions that encourage honesty, and in recognizing signs of inauthenticity. Third, programs must build in follow-up and accountability after the agreement is reached. Offenders should know that their progress will be monitored, that they will be held to their commitments, and that failure to follow through will have consequences. This ongoing accountability supports the internalization of change.

4. Resource Limitations

The fourth set of challenges relates to resource limitations. Implementing restorative justice programs effectively requires significant resources—trained facilitators, adequate facilities, support services for victims and offenders, data collection and evaluation systems. Many communities, particularly those with the highest crime rates and the greatest need for effective interventions, lack these resources.

The concern about training and implementation is particularly acute. Restorative justice is not a simple technique that can be learned in a brief workshop; it is a complex practice that requires deep understanding, sophisticated skills, and ongoing development. Facilitators must understand the dynamics of trauma, power, and communication. They must be skilled in managing intense emotions, in creating safety, in guiding groups toward consensus. They must be able to work with diverse populations and adapt their approach to individual circumstances. Developing this expertise takes time, money, and commitment—resources that are often in short supply.

The concern about monitoring and evaluation is equally important. Restorative justice programs need to know whether they are achieving their goals, whether they are serving participants well, whether they are producing unintended consequences. This requires data collection, analysis, and ongoing adjustment. But data collection is expensive, analysis requires expertise, and adjustment requires flexibility. Programs that lack resources for evaluation may continue practices that are ineffective or even harmful, simply because they do not have the information needed to improve.

The psychological research on program implementation emphasizes the importance of fidelity and quality. Programs that are implemented with high fidelity to their design, with well-trained staff, and with adequate resources produce better outcomes than those that are implemented poorly. The challenge for restorative justice is to maintain quality as programs scale up and spread to new communities. Without attention to implementation quality, the benefits demonstrated in well-designed programs may not be realized in everyday practice.

The theological response to resource limitations is grounded in the biblical call to share resources and care for the vulnerable. The early church shared their possessions so that "there were no needy persons among them." Communities that have resources are called to share with those that do not, ensuring that all have access to effective interventions. This is not charity but justice, a recognition that the well-being of all is bound up with the well-being of each.

Addressing resource limitations requires multiple strategies. First, advocates must make the case for investment in restorative justice, demonstrating its cost-effectiveness and its benefits for communities. The Washington State Institute for Public Policy's cost-benefit analyses provide powerful evidence that restorative justice produces positive returns on investment, saving money in the long run even as it requires investment upfront. Second, programs must seek diverse funding sources, including government grants, private foundations, and community contributions. Diversifying funding reduces vulnerability to cuts in any single source. Third, programs must invest in training and capacity building, developing the expertise needed to implement restorative justice effectively. This may include partnerships with universities, professional associations, and experienced programs. Fourth, programs must build evaluation into their design from the beginning, allocating resources for data collection and analysis. This investment pays off in improved outcomes and stronger evidence for the program's effectiveness.

5. Cultural Sensitivity Concerns

The fifth set of challenges relates to cultural sensitivity. Restorative justice programs must be culturally sensitive and adaptable to the diverse communities they serve, but achieving this sensitivity is challenging and requires ongoing attention.

The concern about cultural awareness is fundamental. Restorative justice, like all justice practices, is shaped by cultural assumptions about conflict, relationship, accountability, and healing. The family group conference model, for example, draws on Maori traditions and may be particularly appropriate for Maori communities. But when that model is exported to other cultural contexts without adaptation, it may not fit local understandings and practices. Similarly, the victim-offender dialogue model, developed primarily in Western contexts, may not align with the communication styles and conflict resolution practices of other cultures.

The challenge is to develop restorative practices that are culturally appropriate for the communities they serve. This requires deep engagement with community members, respect for local traditions, and willingness to adapt practices rather than imposing a one-size-fits-all model. It also requires attention to power dynamics between cultural groups, ensuring that the practices of dominant groups are not imposed on marginalized communities under the guise of universal best practices.

The psychological research on cultural competence emphasizes the importance of understanding cultural differences in communication, emotion, and relationship. Different cultures have different norms about directness, about the expression of emotion, about the role of family and community in conflict resolution. Facilitators who are not aware of these differences may misinterpret participants' responses, may create discomfort, may fail to create the conditions for genuine encounter. Cultural competence is not a static achievement but an ongoing process of learning and adaptation.

The theological response to cultural sensitivity concerns is grounded in the biblical vision of a diverse community united in Christ. The book of Revelation depicts a multitude from every nation, tribe, people, and language, gathered around the throne of God. This diversity is not erased but celebrated; each brings their unique gifts and perspectives to the worship of God. Restorative justice, in its ideal form, honors this diversity, creating practices that are adapted to local cultures while remaining faithful to restorative principles.

Addressing cultural sensitivity concerns requires multiple strategies. First, programs must engage with diverse communities in the design and implementation of restorative practices. Community members should have meaningful roles in shaping how restorative justice is practiced in their communities. Second, programs must recruit and train facilitators from diverse backgrounds, ensuring that participants can work with facilitators who understand their cultural context. Third, programs must provide ongoing training in cultural competence, helping facilitators recognize and respond to cultural differences. Fourth, programs must be willing to adapt their practices based on community feedback, recognizing that what works in one context may not work in another.

6. Safety Concerns

The sixth set of challenges relates to safety. Bringing victims and offenders together, particularly in cases involving violence or serious harm, raises legitimate safety concerns that must be addressed.

The concern about physical safety is obvious. Victims and offenders may have reason to fear one another, and bringing them together could create opportunities for further harm. Even when physical violence is unlikely, the emotional intensity of restorative encounters can be overwhelming, and participants may feel psychologically unsafe. Ensuring the safety and well-being of all participants is the first responsibility of any restorative justice program.

The challenge is to create conditions in which participants can engage safely with one another. This requires careful screening to identify cases where safety risks are too high to proceed. It requires thorough preparation to ensure that participants are ready for the encounter and have strategies for managing difficult emotions. It requires skilled facilitation to maintain a safe environment during the encounter. And it requires follow-up to ensure that participants are safe after the encounter and have access to support if needed.

The psychological research on safety in therapeutic settings emphasizes the importance of creating conditions in which participants can explore difficult material without being overwhelmed. This requires attention to the physical environment, to the pacing of the encounter, to the availability of support. It requires facilitators who are attuned to signs of distress and prepared to intervene when necessary. It requires participants who have been adequately prepared and who have coping strategies they can use.

The theological response to safety concerns is grounded in the biblical understanding of sanctuary. In ancient Israel, cities of refuge were established where those accused of crime could find safety from avengers. The church has historically offered sanctuary to those in need. Restorative justice must be a place of sanctuary, a safe space where victims and offenders can meet without fear. This requires vigilant attention to safety and a commitment to protecting the vulnerable.

Addressing safety concerns requires multiple strategies. First, programs must conduct thorough screening to identify cases that are appropriate for restorative processes and those that are not. Cases involving ongoing violence, significant power imbalances, or participants who are not ready should not proceed. Second, programs must provide thorough preparation for all participants, including assessment of readiness, development of safety plans, and identification of support resources. Third, programs must ensure that facilitators are skilled in managing safety during encounters, including the ability to pause or terminate the process if safety is threatened. Fourth, programs must provide follow-up support, including access to counseling and other services, to address any ongoing safety concerns.

7. Limited Applicability Concerns

The seventh set of challenges relates to limited applicability. Restorative justice may not be suitable for all cases, and identifying which cases are appropriate is a significant challenge.

The concern about suitability is particularly acute for cases involving serious violence, repeat offending, or offenders who deny responsibility. Some critics argue that restorative justice is only appropriate for minor, first-time offenses and that its applicability to more serious cases is limited. Others argue that restorative justice can be appropriate even for serious cases, but only with extraordinary safeguards and skilled facilitation. The question of where to draw the line is contested and context-dependent.

The challenge is to develop criteria for case selection that are principled, practical, and consistently applied. These criteria must balance multiple factors: the nature and severity of the offense, the wishes of the victim, the readiness of the offender, the availability of resources, and the safety of all participants. There is no simple formula for determining appropriateness; it requires judgment, experience, and ongoing learning.

The psychological research on readiness for change provides some guidance. Offenders who are in the contemplation or preparation stages of change may be good candidates for restorative justice, while those in precontemplation may not be ready. Victims who have some distance from the trauma and some capacity to engage may be good candidates, while those in acute distress may need more time and support before they are ready. Assessing readiness requires skill and attention.

The theological response to limited applicability concerns is grounded in the biblical understanding that not all situations are the same. Jesus responded differently to different people—

challenging the Pharisees, comforting the afflicted, calling the disciples, healing the sick. There is no one-size-fits-all approach to ministry, and there is no one-size-fits-all approach to justice. The challenge is to discern what is appropriate in each situation, guided by principles of love, justice, and mercy.

Addressing limited applicability concerns requires multiple strategies. First, programs must develop clear criteria for case selection, based on research and experience, and must apply these criteria consistently. These criteria should be reviewed regularly and adjusted as needed. Second, programs must be willing to say no to cases that are not appropriate, even when there is pressure to accept them. Protecting the integrity of restorative practice sometimes means declining to use it. Third, programs must invest in research on what works for whom, building the evidence base for case selection decisions. Fourth, programs must remain humble about their limitations, recognizing that restorative justice is not a panacea and that some cases will require other approaches.

Challenges in Evaluating Restorative Justice

Beyond the challenges in practice, restorative justice faces significant challenges in evaluation. Assessing the effectiveness of restorative justice programs is methodologically complex, and the limitations of existing research make it difficult to draw definitive conclusions.

The challenge of securing adequate control groups is fundamental. To know whether restorative justice works, we need to compare outcomes for participants with outcomes for similar individuals who went through traditional processes. But finding comparable groups is difficult. Participants in restorative justice are often self-selected or selected by practitioners, and they may differ from non-participants in important ways. Random assignment to restorative justice or traditional processing is the gold standard for evaluation, but it is often difficult to implement in practice.

The challenge of program diversity is equally significant. Restorative justice encompasses a wide range of programs with different goals, practices, and populations. A victim-offender dialogue program for first-time property offenders is very different from a family group conference program for serious violent offenders. Combining results across these diverse programs can obscure important differences and make it difficult to know what works for whom.

The challenge of variability among programs compounds this diversity. Even within the same program type, there can be substantial variability in referral criteria, facilitator competence, legislative frameworks, and outcome benchmarks. A program implemented in one jurisdiction with well-trained facilitators and strong community support may produce very different results from a similar program implemented elsewhere with less support and weaker facilitation.

The challenge of variable indicators is also significant. Studies use different measures of success—recidivism, victim satisfaction, offender accountability, community cohesion—and these measures are not always comparable. Some studies follow participants for one year, others for five. Some use official records of reoffending, others use self-reports. These differences make it difficult to synthesize results across studies.

The challenge of quantifying subjective experiences is perhaps the most difficult. Restorative justice aims to produce outcomes that are inherently subjective—healing, closure, empowerment, accountability. These experiences are real and important, but they are difficult to measure with the kind of precision that satisfies scientific standards. Researchers must develop valid and reliable measures of these subjective experiences, a task that is ongoing.

The challenge of assessing capacity enhancement adds another layer of complexity. Restorative justice aims to enhance community capacity, family capacity, and system capacity—abstract concepts that are difficult to define and measure. What does it mean for a community to have enhanced capacity? How do we know when it has happened? These are questions that resist simple answers.

The challenge of cost-effectiveness analysis is also significant. To know whether restorative justice is a good investment, we need to compare its costs and benefits with those of alternatives. This requires assigning dollar values to outcomes like victim satisfaction and community cohesion, a process that is inherently subjective and contested.

The psychological research on program evaluation emphasizes the importance of multiple methods and multiple measures. No single study can answer all questions; we need a body of research using diverse methods, examining diverse outcomes, and conducted in diverse settings. This research must include rigorous quantitative studies, but it must also include qualitative research that captures the richness of participant experience and the complexity of program implementation.

The theological response to evaluation challenges is grounded in the biblical call to wisdom. The book of Proverbs is filled with exhortations to seek wisdom, to learn from experience, to test and discern. Evaluation is a form of wisdom-seeking, an attempt to learn from what has been done so that we can do better in the future. It requires humility, recognizing that our knowledge is always partial and provisional. It requires patience, recognizing that learning takes time. And it requires commitment, recognizing that the work of evaluation is never complete.

Addressing evaluation challenges requires multiple strategies. First, researchers must use rigorous methods, including randomized controlled trials when possible and well-designed quasi-experimental studies when not. Second, researchers must attend to program diversity, examining not only whether restorative justice works but for whom and under what conditions. Third, researchers must develop and validate measures of the subjective outcomes that restorative justice aims to produce, including victim healing, offender accountability, and community cohesion. Fourth, researchers must conduct cost-effectiveness analyses that capture the full range of benefits and costs. Fifth, researchers must include qualitative methods that capture the richness of participant experience and the complexity of program implementation.

The Role of Key Stakeholders

Existing evaluations have focused primarily on the experiences of victims and offenders, while offering less insight into the perspectives of other key stakeholders. Politicians, senior law enforcement officials, and criminal justice personnel have a substantial impact on the development, implementation, and overall success of restorative justice processes, yet their perspectives are rarely studied.

Politicians shape the legislative and funding environment for restorative justice. Their support or opposition can determine whether programs are established, whether they receive adequate resources, and whether they can operate effectively. Understanding their perspectives—their concerns, their priorities, their sources of information—is essential for advocates seeking to build political support.

Law enforcement officials are often the first point of contact between young offenders and the justice system. Their decisions about arrest, diversion, and referral shape which cases enter the restorative justice pipeline. Understanding their perspectives on restorative justice—their trust in the process, their willingness to refer cases, their concerns about safety and accountability—is essential for building effective partnerships.

Judges, prosecutors, and probation officers also play crucial roles. Judges may order restorative justice as a disposition or may approve agreements reached through restorative processes. Prosecutors may refer cases to restorative justice or may oppose such referrals. Probation officers may supervise the implementation of restorative agreements or may be responsible for reporting on compliance. Understanding the perspectives of these actors is essential for integrating restorative justice into the broader justice system.

The role of facilitators in the success of restorative practices has also received insufficient attention. Facilitators are the ones who actually conduct restorative processes, and their training, personality, style, and experience significantly influence outcomes. A skilled facilitator can create conditions for healing and accountability even in challenging cases; an unskilled facilitator can undermine even the best-designed program. Research on facilitator characteristics and their relationship to outcomes is needed to guide training and selection.

The theological response to these gaps is grounded in the biblical understanding that we are members one of another. The work of restorative justice involves many actors—victims, offenders, families, communities, politicians, law enforcement, judges, facilitators—and the perspectives of all are important. Understanding these perspectives is not merely a matter of research efficiency but of respect for the diverse contributions that each makes to the work of restoration.

Addressing these gaps requires research that includes multiple stakeholder perspectives. Studies should examine the views of politicians, law enforcement officials, judges, prosecutors, probation officers, and facilitators, exploring their understanding of restorative justice, their support for it, their concerns about it, and their suggestions for improvement. This research should use both quantitative methods, such as surveys, and qualitative methods, such as interviews and focus groups, to capture the full range of perspectives.

The Path Forward

The challenges and criticisms we have explored in this chapter are real and significant. They remind us that restorative justice is not a perfect solution but a human practice, subject to all the limitations and possibilities that attend any human endeavor. They call us to humility, to ongoing learning, to the recognition that we do not have all the answers and must remain open to critique and correction. They point us toward the work that remains to be done—the work of refining our practices, addressing our limitations, and building restorative justice programs that are as fair, effective, and safe as humanly possible.

But these challenges are not arguments against restorative justice. They are arguments for doing it well. The alternative—continuing with traditional punitive approaches that have failed for centuries—is not acceptable. Those approaches have their own challenges and criticisms, their own failures and limitations. They have produced mass incarceration, racial disparities, high recidivism rates, and widespread dissatisfaction among victims. They have not made our communities safer or our young people better. The question is not whether restorative justice is perfect but whether it is better than the alternatives, and on that question the evidence is clear.

The path forward requires honest acknowledgment of challenges, rigorous attention to quality, and humble openness to learning. It requires investment in training, evaluation, and continuous improvement. It requires collaboration across disciplines and sectors, bringing the best of theology, philosophy, psychology, and law to bear on the work of restoration. And it requires patience, recognizing that the work of transformation—of individuals, of systems, of communities—takes time.

The theological virtues of faith, hope, and love are essential for this journey. Faith that restoration is possible, even when evidence is incomplete. Hope that our efforts will bear fruit, even when challenges seem overwhelming. Love that sustains us in the difficult work of accompanying victims and offenders through the pain of encounter and the possibility of healing. These virtues, grounded in the character of a God who is always working to restore what is broken, sustain us for the long journey ahead.

As we continue our exploration of restorative justice for juveniles, we will examine the legal frameworks that support restorative practice, the case studies that illustrate its power, the international perspectives that broaden our vision, and the future directions that invite our imagination and commitment. Throughout this journey, we will carry with us the challenges we have explored in this chapter, using them not as reasons for discouragement but as invitations to greater excellence. The work of restoration is never complete, but every step forward is a step toward justice that heals.

CHAPTER 10

LEGAL FRAMEWORK

The legal framework for implementing restorative justice for juveniles is not merely a matter of bureaucratic procedure or legislative technicality; it is the essential architecture that determines whether restorative practices can flourish or wither, whether they will be integrated meaningfully into the justice system or marginalized as peripheral experiments, whether they will serve all young people equitably or only those who happen to live in communities with supportive laws and policies. The legal framework is the bridge between the vision of restorative justice—with its profound principles of accountability, empathy, and community involvement—and the reality of its daily practice in courtrooms, probation offices, and community centers across the nation. Without a sound legal framework, even the most passionate advocates and skilled practitioners cannot sustain restorative justice over time; with such a framework, restorative practices can become not merely an alternative but a primary way of responding to juvenile offending.

The relationship between restorative justice and the legal system has been complex and sometimes contested. Restorative justice emerged in part as a critique of formal legal systems, which were seen as alienating, adversarial, and inadequate to address the real needs of victims, offenders, and communities. Early restorative practitioners often operated outside the formal system, creating alternative processes that bypassed courts and lawyers altogether. This independence allowed for innovation and fidelity to restorative principles, but it also limited the reach and sustainability of restorative practices. Programs that depended on the goodwill of individual judges or prosecutors could disappear when those individuals left their positions. Programs that lacked formal recognition could not accept referrals from courts or access public funding. The lesson learned over decades of practice is that restorative justice needs the law, even as it critiques the law's limitations.

The theological foundations of this relationship between restorative justice and law are deep and complex. The Hebrew scriptures present law as a gift from God, a means of ordering community life in ways that reflect divine justice and mercy. The Torah is not merely a list of rules but a teaching, a guidance for living in right relationship with God and neighbor. The psalmist celebrates the law: "Oh, how I love your law! I meditate on it all day long. Your commands are always with me and make me wiser than my enemies." Yet the prophets also critique the law when it becomes divorced from justice, when it is used to oppress rather than liberate. Amos condemns those who "turn justice into bitterness and cast righteousness to the ground," even as they observe religious rituals. The law is good, but it must be animated by the spirit of justice and mercy.

Jesus embodies this complex relationship with law. He declares that he has not come to abolish the law but to fulfill it, yet he also challenges interpretations of the law that have lost sight of its purpose. He heals on the Sabbath, challenging a rigidity that has forgotten that the Sabbath was made for people, not people for the Sabbath. He summarizes the entire law in the command to love God and love neighbor, insisting that love is the fulfillment of law. The apostle Paul wrestles with the relationship between law and grace, concluding that the law is holy, righteous, and good, but that it cannot save; salvation comes through faith in Christ. The law has a role, but it is not the final word.

The philosophical foundations of legal frameworks for restorative justice draw on traditions of thought that emphasize the rule of law, due process, and the protection of rights. The liberal tradition, from John Locke to John Rawls, insists that law must be general, public, and prospective, applying equally to all and known in advance. It must protect fundamental rights and liberties, ensuring that no one is subject to arbitrary power. These principles are essential for restorative justice as well. Restorative processes must operate within a framework that protects the rights of all participants, ensures fairness and consistency, and provides accountability for those who would abuse their power.

The legal framework for restorative justice must address multiple dimensions simultaneously. It must authorize restorative practices, giving them legal recognition and legitimacy. It must regulate restorative practices, ensuring that they meet standards of quality and fairness. It must integrate restorative practices with existing legal institutions, creating pathways for referral and mechanisms for enforcement. And it must protect restorative practices from co-optation, ensuring that they remain true to their restorative character even as they operate within systems shaped by very different assumptions.

Let us now examine the key elements of a legal framework for juvenile restorative justice, exploring each in depth and considering how they contribute to the overall goal of repairing harm, rebuilding lives, and restoring our youth.

1. Legislation and Policy

The foundation of any legal framework for restorative justice is legislation or formal policy that explicitly recognizes and supports restorative practices. This legislation serves multiple functions: it declares the legitimacy of restorative justice, defines its scope and purpose, establishes standards for practice, and provides authority for funding and implementation.

Legislation should begin by articulating the principles and purposes of restorative justice for juveniles. This statement of purpose is not merely rhetorical; it guides interpretation and implementation, ensuring that all aspects of the framework are aligned with restorative values. The legislation might declare that the purpose of restorative justice is to repair harm caused by juvenile offending, to hold young offenders accountable in meaningful ways, to empower victims and give them voice, to involve the community in the resolution process, and to promote the rehabilitation and reintegration of young offenders. This statement of purpose provides a touchstone against which all subsequent provisions can be measured.

The legislation should define the scope of restorative justice, specifying the types of cases for which restorative processes are available. This definition may be broad, allowing restorative justice for a wide range of offenses, or narrow, limiting it to less serious cases. It may include criteria related to offense severity, offender age and history, victim preferences, and other factors. The definition should be clear enough to guide practice but flexible enough to allow for discretion and adaptation.

The legislation should also define the types of restorative practices that are authorized. This may include victim-offender dialogues, restorative circles, family group conferences, and other approaches. The definitions should be broad enough to encompass diverse practices while providing enough specificity to distinguish restorative justice from other interventions. The legislation may also establish standards for practice, including requirements for facilitator training, program evaluation, and participant protections.

The legislation should address the relationship between restorative justice and traditional court proceedings. It may authorize restorative justice as a diversion option, allowing cases to be diverted from the formal system before charges are filed. It may authorize restorative justice as a disposition option, allowing courts to order restorative processes as part of a sentence. It may authorize restorative justice as an adjunct to court proceedings, allowing restorative processes to occur alongside traditional processing. The legislation should specify how restorative agreements are to be handled—whether they are submitted to the court for approval, whether they become part of the court record, whether they are enforceable through the court system.

The legislation should include provisions for confidentiality, protecting information shared during restorative processes from disclosure in other proceedings. This confidentiality is essential for creating the safe space that restorative justice requires; participants must be able to speak openly without fear that their words will be used against them later. The legislation should specify the scope of confidentiality, any exceptions (such as for threats of future harm), and the consequences for violations.

The legislation should address the rights of participants, including victims and offenders. Victims should have the right to information about restorative justice, the right to choose whether to participate, the right to support during the process, and the right to be heard in the development of agreements. Offenders should have the right to legal counsel, the right to understand the consequences of participation, the right to refuse participation without negative repercussions, and the right to a fair process. These rights protections ensure that restorative justice operates within the framework of due process and respect for human dignity.

The legislation should establish mechanisms for funding and oversight. Restorative justice programs need resources to operate—for facilitator salaries, training, facilities, and evaluation. The legislation should identify funding sources and establish procedures for allocating resources. It should also establish oversight mechanisms, such as advisory boards or regulatory agencies, to monitor program quality and compliance with standards.

The theological significance of legislation for restorative justice is profound. The giving of the law at Sinai was a foundational moment in the history of Israel, establishing the covenant community and providing guidance for life together. The law was not an end in itself but a means of shaping a people who would embody God's justice and mercy in the world. Restorative justice legislation, at its best, serves a similar function. It provides the structure within which restorative practices can flourish, guiding practitioners and protecting participants, while leaving room for the spirit of restoration to animate the letter of the law.

2. Referral Mechanisms

A critical aspect of any legal framework is the establishment of clear referral mechanisms for cases that are appropriate for restorative justice processes. Without effective referral pathways, even the best-designed restorative programs will remain empty shells, unable to reach the young people and victims they are designed to serve.

Referral mechanisms should involve collaboration among multiple stakeholders: law enforcement officers who make initial contact with young offenders, prosecutors who make charging decisions, probation officers who supervise young people in the community, judges who make disposition determinations, and school officials who address behavioral issues in educational settings. Each of these actors has the potential to identify cases that might be appropriate for restorative justice and to initiate the referral process.

The legal framework should specify who may make referrals, at what stages of the justice process referrals may occur, and what criteria should guide referral decisions. It may authorize law enforcement officers to divert cases to restorative justice at the point of arrest, before charges are filed. It may authorize prosecutors to refer cases after charges are filed but before adjudication. It may authorize judges to order restorative justice as a condition of probation or as part of a deferred adjudication agreement. It may authorize probation officers to refer cases for restorative justice as part of ongoing supervision.

The criteria for referral should be clear enough to guide decision-making but flexible enough to allow for discretion. Typical criteria might include: the offense is nonviolent or moderately serious; the offender acknowledges responsibility; the victim is willing to participate; the offender has no history of violent offending; the case is suitable for restorative processes given the relationships and circumstances involved. These criteria should be applied consistently, with attention to avoiding disparities based on race, class, or other irrelevant factors.

The referral mechanism should include a screening process to ensure that cases referred for restorative justice are indeed appropriate. This screening may be conducted by program staff, who assess the readiness of participants, the nature of the offense, and the potential for meaningful restorative encounter. Cases that are not appropriate should be referred back to the traditional justice system for processing.

The referral mechanism should also include provisions for informing participants about restorative justice and obtaining their consent. Victims and offenders need clear information about what restorative justice entails, what their rights are, what alternatives exist, and what the consequences of participation may be. This information should be provided in language they can understand, with opportunities to ask questions and receive answers. Consent should be documented and should be revocable at any time.

The theological significance of referral mechanisms lies in the biblical theme of invitation. Throughout scripture, God invites people into relationship, into covenant, into new ways of living. The invitation is extended, but it is not coerced; people are free to accept or decline. Restorative justice referrals are invitations—to victims to participate in their own healing, to offenders to take responsibility and make amends, to communities to engage in the work of restoration. The legal framework must ensure that these invitations are extended genuinely, with respect for the freedom of those invited.

3. Informed Consent

Informed consent is the cornerstone of ethical restorative practice. Restorative justice depends on the voluntary participation of all parties; without genuine consent, restorative processes become coercive, and their potential for healing and accountability is undermined. The legal framework must establish clear requirements for informed consent and ensure that these requirements are met in every case.

Informed consent requires that participants have adequate information about the restorative process. They need to understand what will happen, who will be present, how long the process may take, what kinds of outcomes are possible, and what will happen if an agreement is reached or if it is not. They need to understand their rights, including the right to withdraw at any time. They need to understand the alternatives to restorative justice and the consequences of choosing those alternatives. This information should be provided in a form that is accessible, given the participant's age, language, education, and circumstances.

Informed consent requires that participants have the capacity to make decisions about their participation. For young offenders, capacity may be affected by age, developmental stage, cognitive ability, and emotional state. Facilitators must assess capacity and ensure that participants are able to understand the information provided and make decisions based on that understanding. When capacity is limited, additional supports may be needed, such as involvement of parents or guardians, or the process may not be appropriate.

Informed consent requires that participation be voluntary, free from coercion or undue influence. Victims should not feel pressured to participate by expectations that they "should" forgive or by threats that the offender will receive harsher treatment if they do not participate. Offenders should not feel pressured to participate by threats of worse consequences if they decline. Both should understand that they have the right to say no, and that saying no will not be held against them.

The legal framework should specify the process for obtaining informed consent, including who is responsible for providing information, what information must be provided, how consent should be documented, and how participants can revoke consent. It should also address special considerations for minors, including the role of parents or guardians in the consent process. Some jurisdictions require parental consent for minors to participate in restorative justice; others allow mature minors to consent on their own behalf. The framework should balance respect for young people's developing autonomy with the need for protection and guidance.

The psychological research on decision-making emphasizes the importance of comprehension and voluntariness. People cannot make good decisions if they do not understand their options; they cannot make free decisions if they are under pressure. Adolescents are particularly vulnerable to coercion and may have difficulty understanding complex information, especially when they are stressed or anxious. Facilitators must be attentive to these vulnerabilities and take steps to ensure that consent is truly informed and voluntary.

The theological significance of informed consent lies in the biblical understanding of human dignity and freedom. God created human beings with the capacity to choose, and throughout scripture, God respects that capacity. The covenant at Sinai was offered to Israel, not imposed; the people were invited to accept it, and they did. Jesus invited people to follow him; he did not compel them. Restorative justice, by requiring informed consent, honors this dignity and freedom. It treats participants not as objects to be processed but as subjects to be respected, capable of making their own decisions about their own lives.

4. Rights Protections

The legal framework for restorative justice must protect the rights of all participants. Victims have rights to information, participation, and respect. Offenders have rights to due process, legal representation, and fair treatment. Both have rights to safety, confidentiality, and freedom from discrimination. Protecting these rights is not merely a legal requirement but an essential component of restorative practice; processes that violate rights cannot produce genuine healing or accountability.

For victims, rights protections include the right to receive information about restorative justice, the right to choose whether to participate, the right to withdraw at any time, the right to support during the process, the right to be heard in the development of agreements, and the right to be treated with dignity and respect throughout. Victims should also have the right to be informed about the outcome of the process and about any follow-up actions. These rights recognize that victims are not merely witnesses to someone else's process but central participants in their own healing.

For offenders, rights protections include the right to legal counsel, the right to understand the consequences of participation, the right to refuse participation without negative repercussions, the right to a fair process, and the right to be treated with dignity and respect. Offenders should also have the right to have their agreements reviewed by counsel before signing, and the right to challenge agreements that are unreasonable or that they did not freely accept. These rights recognize that offenders retain their humanity and their legal rights even as they are held accountable for their actions.

The legal framework should also protect against discrimination. Restorative justice programs must be accessible to all, regardless of race, ethnicity, national origin, religion, gender, sexual orientation, disability, or socioeconomic status. Programs should collect data on participant demographics and outcomes to monitor for disparities and should take corrective action when disparities are found. The framework should prohibit discrimination in referral, participation, and treatment.

The framework should address the relationship between restorative justice and the constitutional rights of participants. In the United States, this includes rights under the Fourth, Fifth, Sixth, and Fourteenth Amendments, among others. Restorative processes must not violate these rights, and participants must not be required to waive them as a condition of participation. The framework should specify how restorative justice interfaces with rights to counsel, protection against self-incrimination, and other constitutional protections.

The psychological research on procedural justice, conducted by Tom Tyler and his colleagues, demonstrates that people's satisfaction with legal processes depends heavily on their perception that the process is fair and that their rights are respected. Participants who feel that they have been treated fairly, that their voice has been heard, and that their rights have been protected are more likely to accept outcomes and comply with agreements, regardless of whether those outcomes are favorable to them. Rights protections are not merely legal formalities but essential components of effective practice.

The theological significance of rights protections lies in the biblical affirmation of human dignity. Every person is created in the image of God, and this image confers a dignity that must be respected by all human institutions. The law, in the biblical vision, is a means of protecting this dignity, ensuring that the vulnerable are not exploited, the powerless are not oppressed, and the voiceless are heard. Rights protections in restorative justice are a practical expression of this biblical commitment. They ensure that even in the context of accountability for harm, the dignity of every person is honored.

5. Confidentiality

Confidentiality is essential to restorative justice. Participants must be able to speak openly and honestly without fear that their words will be used against them in other proceedings. Victims must be able to express their pain, anger, and fear without worrying that their expressions will be taken out of context. Offenders must be able to acknowledge responsibility and express remorse without fear that their admissions will be used to enhance punishment. The legal framework must establish clear rules for confidentiality and provide strong protections for information shared in restorative processes.

The scope of confidentiality should be broad, covering all communications made during restorative processes, including verbal statements, written materials, and nonverbal communications. It should apply to all participants, including victims, offenders, supporters, facilitators, and any observers. It should extend beyond the formal process to include preparation sessions, follow-up meetings, and any related communications.

There should be exceptions to confidentiality for situations involving threats of future harm. If a participant discloses an intent to cause serious harm to themselves or others, facilitators may have a duty to report this threat to appropriate authorities. Similarly, if a participant discloses ongoing abuse of a child or vulnerable adult, facilitators may be required by law to report this abuse. These exceptions should be clearly stated in advance so that participants understand the limits of confidentiality.

The legal framework should specify how confidentiality is to be protected. This may include provisions that communications in restorative processes are not admissible in subsequent legal proceedings, that facilitators cannot be compelled to testify about what was said, and that records of restorative processes are not subject to disclosure except under limited circumstances. These protections should be strong enough to create the safe space that restorative justice requires.

The framework should also address the relationship between confidentiality and the rights of participants. Victims and offenders should have the right to share their own experiences of the restorative process with others, including family members, therapists, and support persons. They should not be prohibited from talking about their own participation, even as they are protected from having their words used against them.

The psychological research on self-disclosure emphasizes the importance of safety for honest communication. People cannot be expected to share vulnerable feelings and experiences if they fear that their disclosures will be used against them. The confidentiality protections in restorative justice create the conditions for this safety, allowing participants to speak openly and honestly without fear of negative consequences.

The theological significance of confidentiality lies in the biblical understanding of confession and forgiveness. The practice of confession, in both Jewish and Christian traditions, has long been accompanied by expectations of confidentiality. The one who confesses must be able to speak honestly without fear that their words will be used against them. The one who hears confession must hold what is shared in sacred trust. Restorative justice, with its emphasis on honest acknowledgment of harm, participates in this tradition. Confidentiality is the practical expression of the sacred trust that makes honest encounter possible.

6. Documentation and Records

The legal framework must specify requirements for documentation and record-keeping in restorative justice cases. Proper documentation serves multiple purposes: it provides a record of what was agreed, it enables monitoring and enforcement of agreements, it supports evaluation and research, and it protects the rights of participants by creating an objective record of the process.

Documentation should include basic information about the case: the names of participants, the date and location of restorative processes, the nature of the offense, and any relevant background information. It should include a record of the agreement reached, specifying what the offender has agreed to do, by when, and with what consequences for non-compliance. It should include documentation of consent, showing that participants agreed to participate voluntarily and with adequate information.

The framework should address who is responsible for creating and maintaining records, how long records should be kept, who has access to them, and how they are to be protected. Records should be maintained in a secure manner, with access limited to those who need it for legitimate purposes. Participants should have the right to review their own records and to request corrections if errors are found.

The framework should also address the relationship between restorative justice records and other justice system records. In some jurisdictions, restorative agreements become part of the court record and are accessible to judges, prosecutors, and probation officers. In others, they are maintained separately and are not part of the official record. The framework should specify how restorative records are to be treated and should ensure that participants understand this treatment before they agree to participate.

The psychological research on memory and perception emphasizes the fallibility of human recollection. People remember events differently, and memories can change over time. Written records provide an objective account that can be referred to when memories differ or when questions arise about what was agreed. They protect both victims and offenders by creating a clear record of commitments and expectations.

The theological significance of documentation lies in the biblical emphasis on witness and testimony. The law required two or three witnesses to establish a matter, recognizing the importance of reliable testimony. The prophets served as witnesses to God's covenant, calling the people to remember what they had promised. Documentation in restorative justice serves a similar function. It bears witness to what was said and agreed, providing a record that can be referred to in times of doubt or disagreement.

7. Enforceability

Agreements reached through restorative processes must be enforceable if they are to have meaning. An agreement that cannot be enforced is merely a statement of intent, not a binding commitment. The legal framework must establish mechanisms for enforcing restorative agreements and for addressing non-compliance.

Enforceability begins with clarity. Agreements should be written in clear, specific language, stating exactly what the offender has agreed to do, by when, and with what consequences for non-compliance. Vague agreements—"the offender will make things right"—are difficult to enforce; specific agreements—"the offender will complete 40 hours of community service at the local food bank within 90 days"—are much easier to monitor and enforce.

The framework should specify who is responsible for monitoring compliance with agreements. This may be the restorative justice program, a probation officer, or another designated entity. The monitor should have the authority to check on progress, to receive reports of compliance or non-compliance, and to take appropriate action when problems arise.

The framework should specify what happens when an offender fails to comply with an agreement. Options may include: returning to restorative process to revise the agreement, referral back to court for traditional processing, imposition of sanctions through the restorative program, or other consequences. The consequences for non-compliance should be clearly stated in advance so that offenders understand what will happen if they do not fulfill their commitments.

The framework should also address what happens when an offender completes the agreement successfully. This may include dismissal of charges, reduction of sentence, positive reports to the court, or other benefits. Successful completion should be recognized and celebrated, reinforcing the positive outcomes that restorative justice can achieve.

The psychological research on commitment and behavior change emphasizes the importance of follow-through. People are more likely to complete commitments when they know that their progress will be monitored and that there will be consequences for failure. The enforceability provisions in restorative justice provide this structure, supporting offenders in following through on their commitments.

The theological significance of enforceability lies in the biblical understanding of covenant. The covenant between God and Israel was not merely a statement of intent but a binding agreement, with blessings for obedience and consequences for disobedience. The prophets called Israel to account when they violated the covenant, reminding them of their commitments and the consequences of failing to keep them. Enforceability in restorative justice is a reflection of this covenantal understanding. Agreements are not optional; they are commitments that must be honored. And when they are honored, they bring blessings—restoration for victims, accountability for offenders, and healing for communities.

8. Training and Accreditation

The quality of restorative justice depends heavily on the skill and integrity of its practitioners. Facilitators must be trained in the principles and practices of restorative justice, skilled in managing complex emotional dynamics, knowledgeable about the legal framework within which they operate, and committed to ethical practice. The legal framework should establish requirements for training and accreditation to ensure that restorative processes are conducted professionally and ethically.

Training requirements should cover multiple domains: the theory and principles of restorative justice, the specific practices used in the program (dialogues, circles, conferences), the dynamics of trauma and its effects, communication and facilitation skills, cultural competence, legal and ethical issues, and self-care for practitioners. Training should include both didactic instruction and supervised practice, with opportunities for feedback and reflection.

Accreditation requirements should ensure that facilitators have demonstrated competence before they are allowed to practice independently. This may include completion of approved training, observation of practice by experienced facilitators, evaluation of skills, and commitment to a code of ethics. Accreditation should be renewed periodically, with requirements for continuing education and ongoing skill development.

The framework should also address training and accreditation for other roles in restorative justice, including program administrators, evaluators, and trainers. Each of these roles requires specific knowledge and skills, and the framework should ensure that those filling them are adequately prepared.

The psychological research on expertise and skill development emphasizes the importance of deliberate practice and ongoing learning. Skilled facilitators are not born but made, through extensive training, supervised experience, and continuous reflection. The training and accreditation requirements in the legal framework support this development, ensuring that facilitators have the opportunity to become truly skilled at their craft.

The theological significance of training and accreditation lies in the biblical understanding of calling and preparation. Throughout scripture, God calls people to specific tasks and prepares them for those tasks through experience, teaching, and spiritual formation. Moses was prepared in the desert before leading Israel. The disciples were trained by Jesus before being sent out to teach and heal. The apostles were formed by the Spirit before establishing the church. Training and accreditation in restorative justice are contemporary forms of this preparation, ensuring that those who are called to this work are equipped to do it well.

9. Evaluation and Oversight

Restorative justice programs must be subject to ongoing evaluation and oversight to ensure that they are achieving their goals, adhering to established standards, and serving participants well. The legal framework should establish mechanisms for evaluation and oversight and should require programs to participate in these processes.

Evaluation should assess multiple dimensions of program functioning: participant satisfaction, completion rates, recidivism outcomes, victim healing, offender accountability, community engagement, and cost-effectiveness. Evaluations should use rigorous methods, including comparison groups when possible, and should be conducted by qualified evaluators who are independent of program operations.

Oversight should ensure that programs are complying with legal requirements, ethical standards, and program guidelines. This may include regular site visits, review of records, observation of restorative processes, and investigation of complaints. Oversight bodies should have the authority to require corrective action when problems are identified and to suspend or terminate programs that fail to meet standards.

The framework should also establish mechanisms for ongoing learning and improvement. Programs should be required to use evaluation findings to refine their practices and to share lessons learned with other programs. The field of restorative justice is still developing, and continuous learning is essential for progress.

The psychological research on program evaluation emphasizes the importance of using data to guide improvement. Programs that collect data, analyze it, and use it to make adjustments are more likely to achieve positive outcomes than those that operate on intuition alone. The evaluation requirements in the legal framework support this data-driven approach to practice.

The theological significance of evaluation and oversight lies in the biblical call to accountability. The prophets held kings and priests accountable for their actions, calling them to account when they failed to live up to their responsibilities. Jesus taught that much is required of those to whom much is given. Evaluation and oversight in restorative justice are forms of this accountability, ensuring that programs and practitioners are faithful to their calling and responsible in their work.

10. Community Collaboration

Restorative justice is inherently collaborative, involving not only victims and offenders but also families, supporters, and community members. The legal framework should encourage and support this collaboration, recognizing that restorative justice is most effective when it is deeply embedded in community life.

The framework may encourage collaboration by requiring programs to establish advisory boards that include community representatives, by providing funding for community-based organizations to operate restorative programs, by creating mechanisms for community input into program design and evaluation, and by supporting partnerships between justice agencies and community groups.

The framework may also require collaboration by specifying that restorative processes must include community participants, by establishing standards for community representation, and by requiring programs to demonstrate community support as a condition of funding or accreditation.

The psychological research on community engagement emphasizes the importance of local ownership and participation. Programs that are designed and implemented with community input are more likely to be accepted and sustained than those that are imposed from outside. Community members who participate in restorative processes often become advocates for restorative justice, spreading the word and building support.

The theological significance of community collaboration lies in the biblical understanding of the people of God as a community. Israel was not merely a collection of individuals but a people, bound together by covenant and called to embody God's justice and mercy in their life together. The early church understood itself as a body, each member belonging to all the others. Community collaboration in restorative justice is an expression of this communal identity, recognizing that the work of restoration belongs to all and that all are needed for its success.

The Integration of Restorative Justice into the Legal System

Incorporating restorative justice into the legal framework for juvenile justice allows for a more balanced and comprehensive approach to addressing juvenile delinquency. It complements existing punitive measures with a focus on healing, rehabilitation, and community involvement, ultimately contributing to the well-being of young offenders and the communities they are part of.

This integration is not without challenges. Restorative justice and traditional legal systems operate on different assumptions and values. The legal system is adversarial, focused on determining guilt and imposing punishment. Restorative justice is collaborative, focused on repairing harm and restoring relationships. Integrating these two approaches requires careful attention to the points of tension and the development of practices that honor both sets of values.

But the integration is also full of promise. When restorative justice is embedded in a supportive legal framework, it can reach more young people, access more resources, and achieve more lasting change. It can influence the broader legal system, introducing restorative values and practices into traditional proceedings. It can build bridges between the justice system and communities, increasing trust and legitimacy. And it can demonstrate that justice can be done in ways that heal rather than hurt, that restore rather than destroy.

The theological vision that undergirds this integration is the vision of *shalom*—that comprehensive well-being, right relationship, and flourishing for all creation that is the goal of God's restorative work. The law, in this vision, is not an end in itself but a means to *shalom*. It provides structure and guidance, protection and accountability, but it is always in service of the larger goal of restoration. Restorative justice, integrated into the legal framework, is a practical expression of this vision. It uses the structures of law to create the conditions for healing, and it uses the practices of restoration to infuse law with the spirit of *shalom*.

As we continue our journey through the principles and practices of restorative justice, we will explore the case studies that bring these legal frameworks to life, the international perspectives that broaden our vision, and the future directions that invite our imagination and commitment. But for now, let us appreciate the importance of the legal framework itself—the architecture that makes restorative justice possible, the structure that supports its practice, the protection that ensures its integrity. This framework is not the end but the means; not the destination but the path. And it is a path that leads toward justice that heals.

CHAPTER 11

CASE STUDIES

Case studies hold a pivotal and irreplaceable role in elucidating the effectiveness and real-world impact of restorative justice in juvenile cases. While statistics, meta-analyses, and theoretical frameworks provide essential knowledge about what works and why, it is the living stories of real people—young offenders grappling with the consequences of their actions, victims navigating the painful aftermath of crime, communities struggling to heal and rebuild—that bring restorative justice to life in all its complexity and power. These real-life narratives serve as compelling examples of how restorative practices can transform lives and communities, offering hope and inspiration to practitioners, policymakers, and the public alike. In this chapter, we will explore several case studies in depth, drawing out the theological, philosophical, psychological, and legal dimensions that make them so instructive.

The power of case studies lies in their concreteness. They show us not abstract principles but embodied practices, not general trends but specific human beings making choices, experiencing change, and living with consequences. They remind us that restorative justice is not a formula to be applied mechanically but a living practice that must be adapted to the unique circumstances of each case, each person, each community. They reveal the complexity of real-world situations, where multiple factors interact in unpredictable ways and where outcomes depend on the skill of facilitators, the readiness of participants, and the support of communities. And they inspire us by demonstrating that change is possible, that healing can occur, that even the most difficult situations can be transformed through genuine encounter and committed effort.

The theological significance of case studies is profound. The scriptures themselves are largely composed of stories—narratives of human beings encountering God, failing and being restored, struggling and being transformed. The stories of Abraham and Sarah, of Moses and Miriam, of David and Bathsheba, of Peter and Paul—these are not merely illustrations of abstract truths but living testimonies to the ways God works in and through human lives. Jesus taught primarily through parables, stories that invited listeners to enter into another world and see their own lives differently. Case studies in restorative justice participate in this tradition of storytelling, bearing witness to the transformative power of encounter and the possibility of new beginnings.

The philosophical significance of case studies lies in their ability to capture the particularity and complexity of human experience. The philosophical tradition has often privileged universal principles over particular instances, seeking knowledge that applies everywhere and always. But thinkers like

Aristotle recognized the importance of practical wisdom (*phronesis*), the kind of knowledge that can only be gained through engagement with particular situations and that enables wise judgment in concrete circumstances. Case studies are vehicles for developing practical wisdom, allowing us to learn from the experiences of others and to apply those lessons in our own contexts.

The psychological significance of case studies lies in their ability to illuminate the inner dynamics of change. Quantitative research can tell us that restorative justice reduces recidivism, but it cannot tell us what that reduction feels like from the inside—how a young person experiences the shift from denial to acknowledgment, from shame to guilt, from isolation to connection. Case studies can capture these subjective dimensions, providing insight into the mechanisms of change that complement and enrich statistical findings.

The legal significance of case studies lies in their ability to illustrate how legal frameworks operate in practice. Laws and policies establish the structures within which restorative justice operates, but they cannot determine how those structures will be used, how discretion will be exercised, how conflicts will be resolved. Case studies show us the law in action, revealing both its possibilities and its limitations and providing guidance for those seeking to improve legal frameworks.

Let us now turn to several case studies that illustrate the power and potential of restorative justice for juveniles. Each case is real, though names and identifying details have been changed to protect privacy. Each illustrates different aspects of restorative practice and different pathways to healing and accountability.

Case Study One: The Peacemaking Circle in a School Setting

The Context

Alex was a fourteen-year-old student at Westlake Middle School, a diverse urban school serving approximately eight hundred students in grades six through eight. For much of the school year, Alex had been a source of concern for teachers and administrators. He was frequently involved in conflicts with other students, sometimes escalating to pushing and shoving in the hallways. He was disruptive in class, talking back to teachers, refusing to complete assignments, and distracting other students. He had been suspended twice already, and the school's discipline committee was considering recommending expulsion.

The school, like many across the country, had traditionally responded to behavioral issues with exclusionary discipline—suspensions, expulsions, referrals to law enforcement. But these approaches had not worked for Alex; each suspension seemed to make him more angry and more alienated, and his behavior worsened rather than improved. Frustrated by the failure of traditional approaches, the school had recently begun implementing restorative practices, and the principal decided that Alex's case might be appropriate for a restorative intervention.

The Restorative Process

The school's restorative justice coordinator, Ms. Rodriguez, met separately with Alex, his mother, his teachers, and several of the students who had been involved in conflicts with him. These preparation meetings were essential for understanding the situation from multiple perspectives and for determining whether restorative processes were appropriate.

What emerged from these meetings was a more complex picture than the discipline referrals suggested. Alex's mother worked two jobs and was rarely home; his father was absent. Alex had been diagnosed with ADHD but was not receiving any treatment or support. He had been bullied in elementary school and had learned to respond to perceived threats with aggression. The conflicts at school were often triggered by other students teasing him about his clothes, his family situation, or his academic struggles. Alex's disruptive behavior in class was partly a manifestation of his untreated ADHD and partly a response to feeling overwhelmed and unsupported.

Ms. Rodriguez also learned that several of Alex's classmates were interested in helping. They were tired of the conflicts and wanted the school to be a safer, more positive place. Some of them had been involved in teasing Alex and felt guilty about their role in the conflicts. They were open to participating in a restorative process.

With preparation complete, Ms. Rodriguez convened a peacemaking circle. In addition to Alex, the circle included his mother, three of his teachers, five students who had been involved in conflicts with him, the school principal, and a community volunteer who had been trained as a circle keeper. The circle was arranged with chairs in a circular formation, and a talking piece—a smooth stone that had been passed down through several restorative circles—was placed in the center.

Ms. Rodriguez opened the circle by explaining the process and the guidelines: speak from the heart, listen with respect, wait for the talking piece to come to you. She then invited participants to introduce themselves and share why they had come. One by one, each person spoke, and the circle began to take shape as a space of honesty and care.

When the talking piece came to Alex, he was initially reluctant to speak. He stared at the floor, his body tense. But as others shared their hopes for the circle—their desire for the conflicts to end, their care for Alex, their own feelings of frustration and sadness—he began to relax. When he finally spoke, his voice was quiet but clear: "I'm tired of all the fighting. I don't even know why it starts half the time. I just get so angry, and I can't stop."

The students who had been involved in conflicts with Alex spoke next. One admitted that he had teased Alex about his clothes and apologized. Another said she had spread rumors about Alex and was sorry. A third said he had seen others picking on Alex and had done nothing to stop it. The teachers spoke about their frustration with the disruptions but also their concern for Alex and their desire to see him succeed. Alex's mother spoke about her struggles to support him alone, her worry about his future, and her hope that this circle could make a difference.

As the circle continued, the conversation deepened. Alex began to understand that his behavior affected not only himself but also his classmates, his teachers, his mother. The other students began to understand that their teasing and exclusion had contributed to Alex's anger and isolation. The teachers began to understand that their disciplinary responses had sometimes made things worse. The principal began to understand that the school's culture needed to change.

The circle then turned to the question of what should happen next. What could Alex do to make amends for the harm he had caused? What could the school do to support Alex and prevent future conflicts? What could the other students do to create a more positive school environment?

The group developed a plan together. Alex agreed to participate in conflict resolution training and to help organize anti-bullying workshops for younger students. The school agreed to provide Alex with a mentor, a community volunteer who would meet with him weekly for support and guidance. The students agreed to form a peer support group that would watch out for students who were being bullied and intervene when they saw conflicts developing. The teachers agreed to receive training in restorative practices and to use circles in their classrooms to build community and address conflicts early.

The Outcome

The impact of the circle was profound and lasting. Alex completed the conflict resolution training and threw himself into organizing the anti-bullying workshops. He discovered that he had a gift for connecting with younger students, who looked up to him and listened when he spoke about his experiences. His relationship with his mentor became a source of stability and support; for the first time in years, he had an adult who was consistently there for him.

The school saw a significant reduction in disciplinary incidents involving Alex. He was not suspended again, and his teachers reported that his classroom behavior had improved dramatically. His grades improved, and he began to talk about going to college—something he had never considered before.

The peer support group became an important part of the school's culture. Students who had once been bystanders to bullying became active interveners, and the climate of the school shifted toward greater inclusion and respect. The teachers who received restorative training began using circles in their classrooms, and conflicts that once would have escalated to the principal's office were resolved at the classroom level.

Perhaps most significantly, Alex became an advocate for positive change in his school community. He spoke at school assemblies about his experience, encouraging other students to seek help when they were struggling and to treat one another with respect. He volunteered to mentor younger students who were having difficulties, drawing on his own experience to offer guidance and support. The young man who had been on the verge of expulsion became a leader, a role model, a source of hope for others.

Reflections on the Case

The Alex case illustrates several key principles of restorative justice. First, it demonstrates the importance of addressing underlying causes rather than merely punishing surface behaviors. Alex's disruptive behavior was not random or meaningless; it was a response to multiple factors—untreated ADHD, family stress, peer bullying, academic frustration—that needed to be understood and addressed. The circle provided a space where these factors could be explored and where a plan could be developed that addressed them holistically.

Second, the case illustrates the power of including all affected parties in the resolution process. The circle included not only Alex but also his mother, his teachers, the students he had conflicted with, and the school principal. Each of these participants had a piece of the truth about what was happening, and each had a role to play in creating a solution. The agreement that emerged was not imposed by authorities but developed collaboratively, and this collaborative process gave it legitimacy and power.

Third, the case illustrates the transformative potential of empathy. As Alex heard from the students who had teased him, from the teachers who had struggled with him, from his mother who worried about him, he began to understand his behavior in a new light. He saw that his actions affected others in ways he had not considered, and this understanding opened him to change. The other students, in turn, began to understand that their behavior had contributed to the problem, and this understanding led them to take responsibility and commit to doing better.

The theological dimensions of this case are rich. The circle process echoes the biblical practice of communal discernment, where the community gathers to address problems and seek God's guidance together. The inclusion of all affected parties reflects the biblical understanding that we are members one of another, that the suffering of one affects all, and that healing requires the participation of all. The transformation of Alex from problem to leader, from source of conflict to agent of peace, echoes the biblical theme of redemption—the possibility that even those who have caused harm can become sources of healing.

The psychological dimensions are equally significant. The circle created conditions for guilt rather than shame, allowing Alex to feel bad about what he had done without feeling bad about who he was. This distinction, crucial for change, was made possible by the respectful way he was treated throughout the process. The circle also provided opportunities for perspective-taking, helping Alex and the other students understand each other's experiences in new ways. This perspective-taking fostered empathy, and empathy fostered change.

The legal dimensions of the case are noteworthy as well. The school's decision to use restorative justice rather than expulsion was consistent with emerging legal frameworks that encourage alternatives to exclusionary discipline. Research has shown that exclusionary discipline is ineffective and disproportionately affects students of color and students with disabilities. By choosing restorative justice, the school not only helped Alex but also contributed to a broader movement toward more equitable and effective school discipline practices.

Case Study Two: Victim-Offender Dialogue in a Youth Offender Case

The Context

Sarah was sixteen years old when she was arrested for shoplifting from a local convenience store. She had taken several items—cosmetics, snacks, a small electronic device—with a total value of approximately seventy-five dollars. The store owner, Mr. Chen, had watched her on his security cameras and called the police. Sarah was detained, cited, and released to her mother.

This was Sarah's first offense. She was a junior at the local high school, a good student who had never been in trouble before. Her mother was bewildered and distressed, unable to understand why Sarah would do such a thing. Sarah herself was ashamed and frightened, afraid of what would happen to her and worried about how this would affect her future.

The case was referred to the county's juvenile diversion program, which offered first-time offenders an alternative to formal court processing. The diversion coordinator, after meeting with Sarah and her mother, determined that she was a good candidate for restorative justice. She contacted Mr. Chen to ask whether he would be willing to participate in a victim-offender dialogue.

Mr. Chen was initially hesitant. He was angry about the theft and frustrated by what he saw as a lack of consequences for young offenders. But as he thought about it, he remembered his own youth, the mistakes he had made, the second chances he had been given. He agreed to meet with Sarah, hoping that the experience might help her learn something that court proceedings could not teach.

The Restorative Process

The dialogue was facilitated by Ms. Thompson, a trained restorative justice practitioner with years of experience in victim-offender mediation. She met separately with Sarah and Mr. Chen before the joint session, preparing them for the encounter and exploring what they hoped to gain from it.

In her meeting with Sarah, Ms. Thompson learned more about the circumstances of the offense. Sarah's family was struggling financially; her mother had been laid off from her job, and money was tight. Sarah had felt pressure to keep up with her friends, who always seemed to have new clothes and gadgets. The shoplifting had been a desperate attempt to have something nice without asking her mother for money she didn't have. Sarah was deeply ashamed of what she had done and terrified of what would happen next.

In her meeting with Mr. Chen, Ms. Thompson learned about the impact of the theft. The store was a small family business, and every loss hurt. Mr. Chen worked long hours and worried constantly about theft, which was a growing problem in the neighborhood. He felt that young people today had no respect for others' property and no understanding of how hard small business owners worked. But he also expressed concern for Sarah, wondering what would lead a young person to do such a thing.

When the joint session began, Ms. Thompson created a safe and structured space for dialogue. She reviewed the guidelines—speak honestly, listen respectfully, take turns—and ensured that both Sarah and Mr. Chen understood the process.

Mr. Chen spoke first, as is typical in victim-offender dialogues. He described the moment he saw Sarah on his security cameras, the feeling of violation, the anger that rose up in him. He talked about the hours of work it took to earn seventy-five dollars, the sleepless nights worrying about his business, the sense that his community was becoming less safe. His voice was calm but his words carried the weight of genuine hurt.

Sarah listened, her eyes downcast, tears streaming down her face. When it was her turn to speak, her voice was barely audible. She apologized to Mr. Chen, explaining that she had never done anything like this before, that her family was struggling, that she had made a terrible mistake. She told him about the shame she felt, the fear of what would happen to her, the realization that she had hurt someone who had done nothing to her.

Mr. Chen listened. He saw Sarah's tears, heard the genuine remorse in her voice, understood something of her circumstances. He asked her a few questions—about her family, her school, her hopes for the future—and she answered honestly. By the end of her account, his anger had softened into something like compassion.

The dialogue then turned to the question of what should happen next. Ms. Thompson facilitated a conversation about restitution, helping Sarah and Mr. Chen develop a plan that would address the harm while also supporting Sarah's growth. They agreed that Sarah would complete forty hours of community service at a local food bank, write a letter of apology to Mr. Chen, and meet with him again in three months to report on her progress.

The Outcome

Sarah completed her community service with dedication, arriving early and staying late, earning the respect of the food bank staff. She wrote a heartfelt letter to Mr. Chen, expressing her remorse and her commitment to doing better. At their follow-up meeting, she reported on her progress and thanked him for giving her a second chance.

Mr. Chen, for his part, found the experience transformative. He had expected to feel satisfied if Sarah completed her obligations, but he was surprised to find that he felt something more—a sense of connection to a young person he might otherwise have written off. He began to think differently about the young people in his neighborhood, seeing them not as threats but as potential contributors to the community. He even started a small program at his store, hiring local teenagers for part-time work and mentoring them in business skills.

Sarah did not reoffend. She finished high school with good grades and went on to community college, where she studied business. She often thought about her encounter with Mr. Chen, about the lesson she had learned, about the second chance she had been given. She became an advocate for restorative justice, speaking to youth groups about her experience and encouraging other young people to learn from their mistakes rather than being defined by them.

Reflections on the Case

The Sarah case illustrates several key aspects of restorative justice. First, it demonstrates the importance of victim participation and empowerment. Mr. Chen was not merely a witness to someone else's process; he was a central participant whose voice shaped the outcome. He had the opportunity to express his feelings, to ask questions, to participate in developing the restitution plan. This participation was healing for him, allowing him to move from anger to compassion and to find meaning in the experience.

Second, the case illustrates the power of direct encounter to foster empathy and understanding. Sarah heard directly from Mr. Chen about the impact of her actions, and this direct encounter was far more powerful than any abstract lesson about the consequences of shoplifting. Mr. Chen saw Sarah's genuine remorse and understood something of her circumstances, and this understanding softened his anger and opened him to compassion. The mutual recognition that occurred in their dialogue was the foundation for everything that followed.

Third, the case illustrates the importance of addressing the underlying causes of offending. Sarah's shoplifting was not random or meaningless; it was connected to her family's financial struggles, her desire to fit in with peers, her sense of shame about her circumstances. The restorative process did not ignore these factors but created space for them to be acknowledged and addressed. Sarah's community service and her follow-up meeting with Mr. Chen were not merely punishments but opportunities for growth and change.

The theological dimensions of this case are profound. The encounter between Sarah and Mr. Chen echoes the biblical theme of reconciliation, the healing of relationships torn by wrongdoing. Sarah's confession and apology, Mr. Chen's willingness to listen and to offer a second chance—these are the stuff of which reconciliation is made. The story echoes the parable of the prodigal son, where a wayward child is welcomed home not with punishment but with celebration. Sarah, like the prodigal, was given the opportunity to return, to make amends, to begin again.

The psychological dimensions are equally significant. Sarah experienced guilt rather than shame; she felt bad about what she had done without feeling bad about who she was. This distinction, crucial for change, was made possible by Mr. Chen's respectful treatment and by the restorative process that distinguished clearly between the person and the behavior. The dialogue also provided opportunities for perspective-taking, helping Sarah understand the impact of her actions in concrete and personal terms. This understanding, in turn, fostered empathy and motivated change.

The legal dimensions of the case illustrate the importance of diversion programs that offer alternatives to formal court processing. Sarah's case was handled through the juvenile diversion program, which saved her from the stigma and consequences of a formal record while still holding her accountable. The legal framework that authorized this diversion and supported restorative justice was essential to the positive outcome.

Case Study Three: Community Conference for a Group of Juvenile Offenders

The Context

The Jefferson Heights neighborhood had been struggling with youth crime for years. A group of about a dozen teenagers, loosely affiliated with a local gang, had been responsible for a series of property crimes, vandalism, and minor assaults. Residents were frightened and angry; they felt unsafe in their own neighborhood and frustrated by what they saw as the failure of the justice system to address the problem.

The situation came to a head when the group vandalized a community center, spray-painting gang symbols on the walls and breaking windows. The damage was extensive, and the sense of violation was profound. The community center was more than just a building; it was a gathering place, a safe space for children and families, a symbol of the neighborhood's resilience. The vandalism felt like an attack on the community itself.

The police arrested several of the young people involved, but the arrests did little to address the underlying problem. The community remained frightened, the young people remained alienated, and tensions continued to simmer. It was at this point that a coalition of community organizations, faith leaders, and law enforcement decided to try something different: a restorative justice community conference.

The Restorative Process

The conference was planned over several weeks, with extensive preparation involving all stakeholders. The restorative justice facilitator, a community organizer named Reverend Johnson, met separately with each of the young offenders and their families, with victims of the crimes, with community residents, and with representatives from law enforcement and social services. These preparation meetings were essential for building trust, assessing readiness, and ensuring that all voices would be heard.

The young offenders, a group of boys aged fourteen to seventeen, were initially resistant. They were angry at the police, distrustful of adults, and skeptical that any process could make a difference. But as they met with Reverend Johnson, they began to open up. They talked about their lives—the poverty, the violence, the lack of opportunities. They talked about their reasons for joining the gang—the sense of belonging, the protection, the excitement. They talked about their regrets—the people they had hurt, the trouble they had caused, the futures they were throwing away.

The victims, too, had stories to tell. The director of the community center spoke about the hours of work it took to repair the damage, the fear that had gripped the neighborhood, the children who were afraid to play outside. A shopkeeper whose store had been broken into multiple times spoke about the financial losses, the sleepless nights, the sense of being under siege. An elderly woman whose car had been vandalized spoke about her fear of leaving her home, her isolation, her longing for the neighborhood she remembered from her youth.

The community residents had their own concerns. They wanted to feel safe in their homes, to be able to walk the streets without fear, to trust that their children could play outside without danger. They were angry at the young people who had caused so much harm, but they were also concerned about them, worried about what would become of these boys if something didn't change.

When the conference convened, it was held in the community center itself, surrounded by the very walls that had been vandalized. The room was filled—more than fifty people, seated in a large circle. Reverend Johnson opened with a prayer, invoking the community's faith traditions and asking for wisdom and courage for all present.

The conference followed a structured format. First, the victims spoke, each describing the impact of the crimes on their lives. The director of the community center spoke about the sense of violation, the hours of work, the children who were afraid. The shopkeeper spoke about the financial losses, the sleepless nights, the anger that consumed him. The elderly woman spoke about her fear, her isolation, her longing for peace.

Then the young offenders spoke. One by one, they stood and addressed the community. They acknowledged what they had done, expressed remorse, and answered questions from victims and residents. They talked about their lives, their struggles, their reasons for joining the gang. They spoke of their shame and their desire to change.

The community members responded. Some expressed anger and demanded accountability. Others expressed concern and offered support. Still others shared their own experiences—of growing up in the neighborhood, of making mistakes, of finding their way. The conversation was intense, emotional, and sometimes difficult, but through it all, Reverend Johnson maintained a safe and respectful space.

Finally, the group turned to the question of what should happen next. What could the young offenders do to make amends? What could the community do to support them? What needed to change to prevent future crimes?

The agreement that emerged was comprehensive and collaborative. The young offenders agreed to participate in a community cleanup project, repairing the damage they had caused and improving the neighborhood. They agreed to attend conflict resolution workshops and to engage with mentors who would support them in leaving the gang. They agreed to meet regularly with a community accountability board that would monitor their progress and provide ongoing support.

The community, for its part, agreed to create new opportunities for young people—a youth center with evening hours, a job training program, a mentorship initiative. They agreed to work with law enforcement to address the underlying causes of crime, not just its symptoms. And they agreed to welcome the young offenders back into the community, treating them not as outcasts but as young people who had made mistakes and were working to make things right.

The Outcome

The impact of the conference was transformative, both for the young offenders and for the community. The community cleanup project brought the young people together with residents who had been victims of their crimes, and the shared work of repair became a bridge to relationship. The conflict resolution workshops gave them skills they had never learned, and the mentors provided support and guidance that many had never received.

Over time, the neighborhood began to change. Youth crime decreased significantly, and the sense of fear that had gripped the community began to lift. The youth center became a hub of positive activity, offering programs and opportunities that kept young people engaged and out of trouble. The job training program helped several of the young offenders find employment, giving them a stake in the community and a reason to stay out of gangs.

The young offenders themselves were transformed. Several left the gang and became advocates for peace in the neighborhood. One became a youth worker, using his experience to help other young people avoid the mistakes he had made. Another started a small business, employing other young people and contributing to the local economy. All of them spoke of the conference as a turning point, the moment when they realized that the community cared about them and that they had something to contribute.

Reflections on the Case

The Jefferson Heights case illustrates the power of restorative justice to address not only individual offenses but the underlying conditions that produce them. The young people in this case were not simply "bad kids" who needed to be punished; they were young people whose lives had been shaped by poverty, violence, and lack of opportunity. The conference created space for these realities to be acknowledged and for a response that addressed them.

The case also illustrates the importance of community involvement in restorative justice. The conference was not just about the young offenders and their victims; it was about the entire community, which had been harmed by the crimes and which had a role to play in creating solutions. The agreement that emerged was not imposed by authorities but developed collaboratively, and this collaborative process gave it legitimacy and power.

The case illustrates the potential of restorative justice to transform communities, not just individuals. The neighborhood that emerged from this process was different from the one that entered it—safer, more connected, more hopeful. The relationships that were built across lines of conflict became resources for addressing future challenges. The sense of collective efficacy that was strengthened through the process became a protective factor against future crime.

The theological dimensions of this case are profound. The conference echoed the biblical practice of communal lament and restoration, where the community gathers to acknowledge its brokenness and seek God's healing. The inclusion of all voices—victims, offenders, community members—reflected the biblical understanding that all are affected by sin and all are called to participate in restoration. The transformation of the young offenders from sources of harm to agents of healing echoed the biblical theme of redemption—the possibility that even those who have caused great harm can become instruments of peace.

The psychological dimensions are equally significant. The conference created conditions for the young offenders to experience guilt rather than shame, to acknowledge their wrongdoing without being defined by it. The presence of supportive community members provided a sense of belonging that many of them had never experienced, and this belonging became a foundation for change. The opportunity to make amends through meaningful work provided a pathway to redemption that passive punishment could never offer.

The legal dimensions of the case illustrate the importance of collaboration between justice agencies and community organizations. The conference was made possible by a coalition that included law enforcement, social services, faith communities, and neighborhood groups. This collaboration ensured that the response was comprehensive, addressing not only the immediate offenses but the underlying conditions that produced them.

The Power of Case Studies

These three case studies—Alex in the school peacemaking circle, Sarah in the victim-offender dialogue, and the Jefferson Heights community conference—illustrate the diverse ways that restorative justice can be applied and the profound outcomes it can achieve. Each case is unique, shaped by the particular individuals, relationships, and circumstances involved. Yet each also reveals common themes that run through all restorative practice.

First, these cases demonstrate the importance of addressing underlying causes rather than merely punishing surface behaviors. Alex's disruptive behavior was connected to untreated ADHD, family stress, and peer bullying. Sarah's shoplifting was connected to family financial struggles and peer pressure. The Jefferson Heights young offenders' crimes were connected to poverty, violence, and lack of opportunity.

Restorative processes created space for these underlying factors to be acknowledged and addressed, making genuine change possible.

Second, these cases demonstrate the power of direct encounter to foster empathy and understanding. Alex heard from classmates about the impact of his behavior. Sarah heard from Mr. Chen about the impact of her theft. The Jefferson Heights young offenders heard from victims about the impact of their crimes. This direct encounter was far more powerful than any abstract lesson, creating understanding that could not be achieved through punishment alone.

Third, these cases demonstrate the importance of involving all affected parties in the resolution process. Alex's circle included classmates, teachers, and family. Sarah's dialogue included Mr. Chen and her mother. The Jefferson Heights conference included victims, community members, and service providers. This inclusive approach ensured that all voices were heard, all perspectives considered, and all needs addressed.

Fourth, these cases demonstrate the potential of restorative justice to transform not only individuals but relationships and communities. Alex became an advocate for positive change in his school. Sarah's encounter with Mr. Chen led to a broader community initiative. The Jefferson Heights conference led to lasting changes in the neighborhood. Restorative justice, at its best, creates ripple effects that extend far beyond the immediate case.

The theological significance of these case studies lies in their witness to the possibility of redemption. Each of these young people could have been written off, defined by their worst actions, consigned to a future shaped by their past. Instead, they were given opportunities to acknowledge their wrongdoing, to make amends, to become something new. Their stories bear witness to the truth that no one is beyond redemption, that change is possible, that new beginnings are real.

The philosophical significance lies in their demonstration of practical wisdom. Each case required judgment, discernment, and adaptation to unique circumstances. There was no formula to be applied mechanically, no algorithm to determine the outcome. Skilled facilitators made countless judgments—about when to push and when to wait, about what questions to ask and what support to offer—and these judgments shaped the outcomes in ways that cannot be captured by general principles alone.

The psychological significance lies in their illumination of the mechanisms of change. These cases show us how guilt rather than shame, empathy rather than indifference, connection rather than isolation can be fostered through intentional practice. They show us that change is not magic but process, not mystery but method.

The legal significance lies in their demonstration of what is possible when legal frameworks support restorative practice. Each of these cases was made possible by laws, policies, and programs that authorized restorative justice, provided resources for its implementation, and protected the rights of participants. The legal framework was not the story but the stage on which the story could unfold.

As we continue our journey through the principles and practices of restorative justice, we will explore international perspectives that broaden our vision and future directions that invite our imagination and commitment. But for now, let us hold these case studies in our hearts—the stories of Alex and Sarah and the young people of Jefferson Heights. Let us remember their struggles and their transformations, their pain and their healing. And let us be inspired by the knowledge that similar transformations are possible in every community, for every young person, for every victim, for all of us.

CHAPTER 12

RESTORATIVE JUSTICE WORLDWIDE

Restorative justice practices have gained recognition and acceptance on a global scale, yet their implementation varies significantly across different countries and cultures, reflecting the rich diversity of human societies and the complex ways that justice is understood and practiced around the world. This global perspective is essential for anyone seeking to understand restorative justice fully, for it reveals both the universal resonance of restorative principles and the necessary adaptability of restorative practices to local contexts. While some nations have embraced restorative principles as a fundamental component of their justice systems, others are still in the early stages of adopting or experimenting with these practices, and still others have maintained restorative traditions for centuries, long before the term "restorative justice" was ever coined.

The global landscape of restorative justice is a tapestry woven from many threads—indigenous traditions that have practiced restorative approaches for millennia, national legal systems that have integrated restorative principles into formal law, grassroots movements that have developed innovative practices in response to local needs, and international instruments that have articulated standards and guidelines for restorative practice. Understanding this landscape requires attention to both commonalities and differences, to both the universal principles that unite restorative practitioners across cultures and the particular adaptations that make restorative justice work in specific contexts.

The theological significance of this global perspective is profound. The biblical vision is not limited to one nation or culture but encompasses "every nation, tribe, people and language." The story of Pentecost, when people from every nation heard the disciples speaking in their own languages, symbolizes the way the gospel transcends cultural boundaries while honoring cultural particularity. Restorative justice, like the gospel, speaks to universal human needs—the need for healing after harm, the need for accountability that transforms, the need for community that supports—while taking different forms in different cultural contexts. The global spread of restorative justice is a sign of its deep resonance with fundamental human values, a resonance that transcends the particularities of any single culture.

The philosophical significance of this global perspective lies in its challenge to cultural provincialism. Philosophers have long debated the relationship between universal principles and cultural particularity. Some have argued for universal standards of justice that apply everywhere and always; others have emphasized the cultural embeddedness of all values and practices. The global experience of restorative justice suggests a middle path: there are indeed universal principles—accountability, empathy, community involvement—that resonate across cultures, but these principles must be embodied in practices that are adapted to local contexts. This insight has implications far beyond restorative justice, touching on fundamental questions about the nature of justice, the relationship between the universal and the particular, and the possibilities for cross-cultural learning and exchange.

The psychological significance of this global perspective lies in its demonstration of the diverse ways that human beings can respond to harm and conflict. Psychological research has often been criticized for its reliance on Western samples and its assumption of universality. The global experience of restorative justice reveals that there are multiple pathways to healing and accountability, multiple ways of understanding and practicing justice. This diversity enriches our psychological understanding, challenging us to expand our conceptions of what is possible and to learn from cultures different from our own.

The legal significance of this global perspective lies in its implications for law reform and policy development. As countries around the world consider how to integrate restorative justice into their legal systems, they can learn from the experiences of others—both successes and failures. International instruments like the United Nations Basic Principles on the Use of Restorative Justice Programmes in Criminal Matters provide guidance, but they must be adapted to local legal traditions and constitutional frameworks. The global exchange of ideas and practices is essential for the continued development of restorative justice.

Let us now examine the global landscape of restorative justice for juveniles, exploring the varying levels of implementation across countries, the cultural factors that influence acceptance and effectiveness, the impact on key outcomes like recidivism and victim satisfaction, the role of community engagement and legal frameworks, and the challenges that persist. We will then examine in depth the experiences of several countries that have been at the forefront of restorative justice development, drawing lessons that can inform practice elsewhere.

1. Varying Levels of Implementation

The adoption and implementation of juvenile restorative justice practices differ dramatically from country to country, reflecting differences in legal traditions, cultural values, political will, and available resources. Some nations have well-established restorative justice programs integrated into their juvenile justice systems, with clear legal frameworks, dedicated funding, trained practitioners, and robust evaluation mechanisms. Others are just beginning to explore these approaches, with pilot programs, limited funding, and uncertain political support. Still others have maintained restorative traditions for centuries, practices that predate the modern restorative justice movement and continue to operate alongside or within formal legal systems.

New Zealand stands as perhaps the most notable example of comprehensive integration. The Children, Young Persons, and Their Families Act 1989 made family group conferencing the primary response to youth offending, fundamentally transforming the juvenile justice system. Under this model, most youth offenses are diverted from court to family group conferences, where the young person, their family, the victim, and relevant professionals come together to develop a plan for accountability and rehabilitation. The conference is facilitated by a youth justice coordinator, and the resulting plan must be agreed to by all parties. This approach has been remarkably successful, reducing the use of court processing and incarceration while maintaining accountability and improving outcomes for both victims and offenders.

Several Scandinavian countries have also integrated restorative principles extensively into their juvenile justice systems. Norway, Sweden, and Denmark emphasize rehabilitation over punishment, with youth justice systems focused on support, education, and therapeutic intervention rather than confinement. Restorative practices, including victim-offender mediation and family group conferences, are available in many jurisdictions and are used as alternatives to formal processing or as supplements to court-ordered dispositions. These countries benefit from strong welfare systems that provide the social supports necessary for rehabilitation, as well as cultural values that emphasize consensus, cooperation, and community responsibility.

In contrast, many countries in Asia and the Middle East have been slower to adopt restorative justice, though interest is growing. Traditional notions of justice in these regions often emphasize retribution, family honor, and social harmony in ways that can both support and hinder restorative approaches. In some contexts, traditional dispute resolution mechanisms—such as village elders, religious leaders, or community councils—have long practiced restorative approaches, and these traditions provide a foundation for modern restorative programs. In other contexts, formal legal systems are based on codes that emphasize punishment and deterrence, leaving little room for restorative alternatives.

The United States presents a mixed picture. Restorative justice programs exist in many jurisdictions, but they operate alongside a highly punitive juvenile justice system that has historically emphasized incarceration and control. Some states have embraced restorative justice, passing legislation that authorizes restorative practices and providing funding for programs. Others have been slower to adopt restorative approaches, and implementation is often uneven, with programs available in some communities but not others. The result is a patchwork of practices, with some young people having access to restorative justice and others facing traditional punishment for similar offenses.

The theological significance of these varying levels of implementation lies in the reminder that the kingdom of God is not fully realized in any human institution. Even the most advanced restorative justice systems are imperfect, limited by human fallibility and structural constraints. Yet every effort to implement restorative justice, no matter how partial or imperfect, is a sign of the kingdom, a glimpse of what is possible when human beings align their practices with God's restorative purposes. The diversity of implementation across countries is not a problem to be solved but a reality to be understood, a reminder that the work of restoration must be adapted to local circumstances and that progress will look different in different contexts.

2. Cultural Sensitivity and Acceptance

The effectiveness of restorative justice often depends critically on the cultural acceptance and appropriateness of these practices. In some cultures, restorative approaches align well with traditional dispute resolution mechanisms and community values, making them more effective and readily accepted. In other cultures, the introduction of restorative justice may face resistance or skepticism, requiring careful attention to cultural adaptation and community engagement.

In many indigenous cultures, restorative practices are not new but ancient. Maori communities in New Zealand, First Nations in Canada, Aboriginal and Torres Strait Islander peoples in Australia, Native American tribes in the United States—all have traditions of addressing harm through communal processes that emphasize healing, accountability, and restoration rather than punishment. These traditions provided models for modern restorative justice and continue to inform its development. When restorative programs are designed in partnership with indigenous communities and grounded in indigenous values, they can be highly effective, resonating with cultural understandings and building on existing strengths.

In some Asian cultures, restorative approaches resonate with Confucian values of harmony, relationship, and collective responsibility. The emphasis on maintaining social harmony and the importance of family and community in resolving conflicts provide fertile ground for restorative practices. Countries like Japan and South Korea have developed restorative programs that draw on these cultural values, emphasizing apology, forgiveness, and reintegration. However, these same cultural values can also create challenges, particularly when they pressure victims to forgive or offenders to apologize in ways that are not genuinely voluntary.

In many Western cultures, the individualistic values that dominate legal and social institutions can both support and hinder restorative justice. On one hand, the emphasis on individual rights and due process provides important protections for participants in restorative processes. On the other hand, the focus on individual autonomy can obscure the relational dimensions of harm and healing, making it difficult to engage communities in restorative processes. The challenge in Western contexts is to integrate restorative principles into legal frameworks that were designed for very different purposes.

The psychological research on cultural psychology, pioneered by scholars like Richard Shweder and Hazel Markus, demonstrates that cultural contexts shape fundamental aspects of human experience, including conceptions of self, relationships, and morality. In individualistic cultures, the self is understood as independent and autonomous; in collectivistic cultures, the self is understood as interdependent and embedded in relationships. These different conceptions have profound implications for how people experience harm, accountability, and healing. Restorative justice must be adapted to these different cultural contexts, drawing on local understandings while remaining faithful to restorative principles.

The theological significance of cultural sensitivity lies in the biblical affirmation of cultural diversity. The book of Revelation depicts a multitude from every nation, tribe, people, and language gathered around the throne of God, each bringing their unique gifts and perspectives. This diversity is not erased but celebrated. Restorative justice, at its best, honors this diversity, adapting its practices to local cultures while maintaining fidelity to restorative principles. The goal is not to impose a single model on all cultures but to support each culture in developing practices that embody restorative values in ways that are authentic and appropriate.

3. Impact on Recidivism

Research from around the world suggests that restorative justice programs can be effective in reducing recidivism among young offenders when properly implemented. However, the degree of effectiveness varies depending on the program's quality, duration, and the specific needs of the participants, as well as the broader context in which programs operate.

A meta-analysis by the Campbell Collaboration, an international research network that conducts systematic reviews of evidence, examined studies of restorative justice from multiple countries and found significant reductions in recidivism compared to traditional court processing. The effects were strongest for programs that involved face-to-face encounters between victims and offenders, that were well-implemented with trained facilitators, and that targeted moderate to serious offenses. The analysis also found that restorative justice was more effective for violent offenses than for property offenses, suggesting that the intensive engagement required by restorative processes is particularly valuable when harm has been most severe.

Studies from New Zealand have documented the effectiveness of family group conferencing in reducing recidivism. A longitudinal study following young people who participated in family group conferences found that they had significantly lower reoffending rates than those processed through court, even after controlling for offense severity and other factors. The study also found that conferences that resulted in agreements addressing underlying needs—such as education, employment, or substance abuse treatment—were particularly effective.

Research from Scandinavia has also shown positive results. A Swedish study of victim-offender mediation found that young people who participated in mediation had lower recidivism rates than those who did not, particularly when the mediation resulted in a written agreement. A Norwegian study found that restorative processes contributed to desistance by strengthening young people's connections to prosocial adults and community institutions.

The psychological mechanisms underlying these effects are consistent across cultures. Restorative justice reduces recidivism by addressing root causes, fostering genuine accountability, building social bonds, and reducing stigma. These mechanisms are universal, but their expression varies across cultures. In collectivistic cultures, the emphasis on social bonds may be particularly powerful; in individualistic cultures, the emphasis on personal accountability may be more salient.

The theological significance of reduced recidivism lies in its witness to the possibility of transformation. The God of the Bible is a God of new beginnings, of second chances, of redemption. Every young person who completes a restorative process and does not reoffend is a living testimony to this truth, a sign that the old has passed away and the new has come. The global evidence that restorative justice reduces recidivism is not merely a statistical finding but a theological affirmation: change is possible, redemption is real, new life can emerge from the ashes of old mistakes.

4. Victim Satisfaction

Restorative justice is consistently associated with higher levels of victim satisfaction compared to traditional punitive approaches across diverse cultural contexts. When victims feel heard, empowered, and involved in the resolution process, they are more likely to report a positive experience, regardless of the cultural setting.

A multinational study by the International Institute for Restorative Practices examined victim satisfaction across programs in multiple countries and found consistently high levels of satisfaction. Victims reported feeling that the process was fair, that their voice mattered, and that they had been treated with respect. They appreciated the opportunity to tell their story, to ask questions, and to participate in shaping the outcome. Many described the experience as healing, allowing them to move forward in ways that traditional court proceedings had not.

Research from Canada has documented particularly high levels of victim satisfaction among indigenous participants. For many indigenous victims, restorative processes grounded in traditional values and practices are more meaningful and healing than court proceedings that feel alien and imposed. The involvement of community elders, the use of circle processes, and the emphasis on relationship and reconciliation resonate with cultural values and produce outcomes that address not only material losses but spiritual and emotional wounds.

Studies from Australia have found similar patterns. Victims who participated in restorative conferences reported feeling more satisfied, more likely to feel that justice had been done, and more likely to recommend the process to others. These findings held across diverse cultural groups, though the specific factors that contributed to satisfaction varied. For some victims, the most important factor was receiving an apology; for others, it was having their questions answered; for still others, it was seeing the offender take concrete steps to make amends.

The psychological mechanisms underlying victim satisfaction are universal. Voice—the opportunity to tell one's story and be heard—is fundamental to human dignity across cultures.

Participation—the opportunity to have a say in decisions that affect one's life—is essential for psychological well-being. Respect—being treated with dignity and consideration—is a universal human need. Restorative justice provides these experiences, and victims respond positively regardless of cultural context.

The theological significance of victim satisfaction lies in the biblical emphasis on God's care for those who have been wronged. The psalmist cries out, "Hear my cry for help, my King and my God, for to you I pray." The prophets announce God's special concern for the vulnerable, the oppressed, the victimized. Jesus pronounces blessing on those who mourn and promises they will be comforted. Restorative justice, by attending to the needs of victims, by giving them voice and participation and healing, embodies this divine concern. The global evidence that victims are more satisfied with restorative justice than with traditional approaches is a sign that this approach aligns with deep truths about human dignity and divine care.

5. Community Engagement

The extent to which communities are engaged in restorative justice processes significantly influences their effectiveness across cultural contexts. In countries with strong community involvement, restorative programs tend to be more successful, drawing on local resources, building social capital, and creating sustainable supports for both victims and offenders.

In New Zealand, community engagement is built into the family group conference model. Extended family members, community elders, and other supporters participate actively in conferences, contributing to the development of plans and providing ongoing support for implementation. This engagement draws on Maori traditions of collective responsibility and has been essential to the model's success. Research has shown that conferences with strong family and community participation produce better outcomes, including lower recidivism and higher satisfaction.

In Canada, restorative justice programs in indigenous communities often involve extensive community engagement. Circle processes bring together victims, offenders, families, elders, and community members in collective dialogue and decision-making. These processes draw on indigenous traditions and have been effective in promoting healing, accountability, and community cohesion. The Truth and Reconciliation Commission's calls to action have emphasized the importance of such approaches in addressing the legacy of colonialism and reducing the overrepresentation of indigenous youth in the justice system.

In Scandinavian countries, community engagement takes different forms, reflecting different cultural values and social structures. The strong welfare state provides a foundation of social support that enables restorative processes to address underlying needs. Community organizations, schools, and social services collaborate with justice agencies to provide the resources that young people need to change. This collaborative approach, while less intensive than the family and community involvement in New Zealand or indigenous Canada, nonetheless reflects a commitment to collective responsibility for addressing youth offending.

The psychological research on social capital and collective efficacy, pioneered by scholars like Robert Putnam and Robert Sampson, demonstrates the importance of community engagement for public safety and individual well-being. Communities with strong social networks, high levels of trust, and shared expectations for behavior have lower crime rates and better outcomes for young people. Restorative justice, by engaging community members in addressing harm, builds these community capacities, creating virtuous cycles of increasing trust and cooperation.

The theological significance of community engagement lies in the biblical understanding of the people of God as a community of mutual care and responsibility. The early church shared their possessions, cared for the needy, bore one another's burdens. They were not merely individuals who happened to believe the same things but a community bound together by love. Restorative justice, by engaging communities in the work of restoration, participates in this vision, creating communities that are not merely collections of individuals but bodies, each member connected to all the others, each member responsible for all the others.

6. Legal Framework and Policy Support

The presence of a legal framework and policy support for restorative justice greatly affects its effectiveness across countries. Jurisdictions with well-defined legislation and policies that support restorative justice tend to have more successful implementation and higher levels of accountability than those where restorative justice operates in a legal vacuum.

New Zealand's Children, Young Persons, and Their Families Act 1989 provides a model of comprehensive legislative support. The act establishes family group conferencing as the primary response to youth offending, defines the roles and responsibilities of participants, sets standards for practice, and creates accountability mechanisms. This legislative framework has provided stability and legitimacy for restorative justice, enabling it to become deeply embedded in the juvenile justice system.

Several European countries have incorporated restorative justice into their legal frameworks through national legislation or European Union directives. The EU Directive on Victims' Rights, adopted in 2012, requires member states to ensure that victims have access to restorative justice services and that these services meet minimum quality standards. This directive has spurred the development of restorative justice programs across Europe and has encouraged the sharing of best practices among member states.

In Canada, restorative justice is supported by federal legislation and policy, as well as provincial initiatives. The Youth Criminal Justice Act, adopted in 2003, emphasizes the use of extrajudicial measures and sanctions, including restorative justice, as alternatives to court processing. The act encourages the involvement of victims, families, and communities in responding to youth offending and provides funding for restorative programs.

In the United States, the legal framework for restorative justice is more fragmented, with significant variation among states. Some states have passed comprehensive restorative justice legislation, establishing programs, funding, and standards. Others have more limited provisions, authorizing restorative practices in specific contexts or for specific offenses. Federal legislation, including the Juvenile Justice and Delinquency Prevention Act, encourages the use of restorative practices but leaves implementation to states and localities.

The theological significance of legal frameworks lies in the biblical understanding of law as a gift from God for ordering community life. The law is not an end in itself but a means of shaping a people who embody God's justice and mercy. Legal frameworks for restorative justice, at their best, serve this function, providing the structure within which restorative practices can flourish while leaving room for the spirit of restoration to animate the letter of the law.

7. Challenges and Barriers

Despite the global spread of restorative justice, significant challenges and barriers persist across countries and cultures. These challenges include resource limitations, lack of training, concerns about fairness, difficulties in engaging all parties, and resistance from traditional justice system actors.

Resource limitations are a universal challenge. Restorative justice programs require trained facilitators, adequate facilities, support services for victims and offenders, and evaluation systems. Many communities, particularly those with the highest crime rates and the greatest need for effective interventions, lack these resources. In developing countries, resource constraints are often severe, limiting the reach and quality of restorative programs.

Lack of training is another common challenge. Restorative justice requires skilled practitioners who understand the principles and practices of restorative justice, are competent in facilitation, and can work effectively with diverse populations. In many countries, training opportunities are limited, and practitioners learn on the job without adequate preparation. This can lead to inconsistent quality and negative outcomes that undermine confidence in restorative justice.

Concerns about fairness arise in many contexts. Critics worry that restorative justice may be applied inconsistently, that power imbalances may distort outcomes, that victims may be pressured to participate, and that offenders may not be genuinely accountable. These concerns are legitimate and must be addressed through careful program design, skilled facilitation, and ongoing evaluation.

Difficulties in engaging all parties are also common. Victims may be reluctant to participate, offenders may deny responsibility, families may be unavailable or unsupportive, and communities may be disengaged. Overcoming these difficulties requires outreach, education, and support that many programs struggle to provide.

Resistance from traditional justice system actors can be a significant barrier. Judges, prosecutors, and police officers who are accustomed to traditional approaches may be skeptical of restorative justice, reluctant to refer cases, or unsupportive of restorative outcomes. Building buy-in from these actors requires education, relationship-building, and demonstration of effectiveness.

The theological significance of these challenges lies in the reminder that the work of restoration is never complete and that human institutions are always imperfect. The prophets of Israel were relentless critics of injustice, even—perhaps especially—when it appeared in the guise of religious practice. The honest acknowledgment of challenges is itself a faithful practice, a recognition that we stand always in need of examination and reform. The challenges facing restorative justice are not arguments against it but invitations to greater excellence, to ongoing learning, to deeper commitment.

International Perspectives

Let us now examine in greater depth the experiences of several countries that have been at the forefront of restorative justice development, drawing lessons that can inform practice elsewhere.

New Zealand

New Zealand's family group conferencing model is perhaps the most influential restorative justice innovation in the world. Developed in partnership with Maori communities and enacted into law in 1989, the model has transformed the country's approach to youth offending and has been adapted for use in many other countries.

The family group conference is grounded in Maori traditions of collective decision-making and community responsibility. In traditional Maori society, conflicts and offenses were addressed through gatherings of extended family (*whanau*), sub-tribe (*hapu*), and tribe (*iwi*), where all affected parties would come together to discuss what had happened and what should be done to restore balance and harmony. The family group conference adapts these traditions to the modern legal context, bringing together the young person, their family, the victim, and relevant professionals to develop a plan for accountability and rehabilitation.

The conference process begins with a referral from the court or youth justice coordinator. The coordinator meets separately with the young person and family, the victim, and other participants to prepare them for the conference. The conference itself follows a structured format: the coordinator opens with an explanation of the process, the police youth justice officer presents the facts of the offense, the victim (or a representative) describes the impact of the offense, the family discusses the situation, and the group works together to develop a plan. The family then meets privately to develop a proposed plan, which is presented to the full group for discussion and approval. The plan, which may include apologies, restitution, community work, and other elements, is then submitted to the court for approval.

Research on family group conferencing has documented positive outcomes. Recidivism rates are lower for young people who participate in conferences than for those processed through court. Victims report higher levels of satisfaction than those whose cases go to court. Families report feeling more involved and supported. The model has been credited with reducing the use of court processing and incarceration while maintaining accountability and promoting rehabilitation.

The theological significance of the New Zealand model lies in its respect for indigenous wisdom and its recognition that God's truth can be found in many cultural traditions. The Maori values that underpin family group conferencing—community, relationship, restoration—resonate deeply with biblical values, even as they are expressed in distinct cultural forms. The partnership between Maori communities and the New Zealand justice system models the kind of cross-cultural collaboration that restorative justice requires.

Norway

Norway's juvenile justice system is grounded in principles of rehabilitation, normalization, and the least restrictive alternative. The country has one of the lowest youth incarceration rates in the world, emphasizing community-based responses and supportive interventions rather than confinement. This approach aligns closely with restorative principles, even when formal restorative justice programs are not used.

The Norwegian system is based on the Child Welfare Act, which gives primary responsibility for youth offending to the child welfare system rather than the criminal justice system. Young people who commit offenses are typically referred to child welfare services, which assess their needs and develop plans for support and intervention. These plans may include counseling, education, vocational training, and other services designed to address underlying issues and promote positive development.

Restorative justice programs, including victim-offender mediation, are available in many jurisdictions and are used as supplements to child welfare interventions or as alternatives to formal processing. The National Mediation Service, established in 1991, provides mediation services for both juvenile and adult cases, with a focus on facilitating dialogue between victims and offenders and developing agreements for restitution and repair.

Research on the Norwegian approach has documented positive outcomes. Youth crime rates are low, and recidivism rates for young people who receive child welfare interventions are lower than for those processed through the criminal justice system. Victims who participate in mediation report high levels of satisfaction. The emphasis on rehabilitation and support, rather than punishment and confinement, has produced a system that is both humane and effective.

The theological significance of the Norwegian model lies in its emphasis on human dignity and the possibility of change. The belief that every young person, regardless of what they have done, deserves support and opportunity reflects a deep conviction about the worth of every human being. This conviction is grounded in the biblical affirmation that every person is created in the image of God and that no one is beyond redemption.

Canada

Canada has integrated restorative justice practices into its juvenile justice system, with particular attention to the needs of indigenous youth. The overrepresentation of indigenous youth in the justice system has been a longstanding concern, and restorative justice has been seen as a promising approach to addressing this problem.

The Youth Criminal Justice Act, adopted in 2003, emphasizes the use of extrajudicial measures and sanctions, including restorative justice, as alternatives to court processing. The act requires that decision-makers consider the unique circumstances of indigenous young people and encourages the use of restorative approaches that are culturally appropriate. This has led to the development of numerous restorative programs in indigenous communities, drawing on traditional practices and values.

Circle sentencing, peacemaking circles, and other restorative practices have been used in many indigenous communities, often in partnership with the formal justice system. These practices bring together victims, offenders, families, elders, and community members in collective dialogue and decision-making. They emphasize healing, accountability, and restoration rather than punishment and have been effective in promoting positive outcomes for both victims and offenders.

Research on restorative justice in Canada has documented positive results. Recidivism rates are lower for indigenous young people who participate in restorative programs than for those processed through traditional courts. Victims report higher levels of satisfaction, and communities report increased trust and cohesion. The Truth and Reconciliation Commission has called for expanded use of restorative justice as part of the broader effort to address the legacy of colonialism and rebuild relationships between indigenous and non-indigenous peoples.

The theological significance of the Canadian experience lies in its witness to the power of restorative justice to address historical injustice. The overrepresentation of indigenous youth in the justice system is not an accident but a consequence of centuries of colonialism, oppression, and cultural destruction. Restorative justice, by honoring indigenous traditions and involving indigenous communities in the resolution process, contributes to the healing of these historical wounds. This is restorative justice at its deepest level—not merely addressing individual offenses but addressing the systemic injustices that shape who offends and who is punished.

Australia

Australia has developed restorative justice programs in various parts of its juvenile justice system, with particular attention to the needs of Aboriginal and Torres Strait Islander youth. Like Canada, Australia has struggled with the overrepresentation of indigenous young people in the justice system and has looked to restorative justice as a promising approach.

Family group conferencing, adapted from the New Zealand model, has been implemented in many Australian jurisdictions. These conferences bring together young offenders, their families, victims, and community members to develop plans for accountability and rehabilitation. In indigenous communities, conferences often incorporate traditional practices and involve elders and other community leaders.

Restorative justice programs in Australia have been evaluated with generally positive results. Studies have found that young people who participate in conferences have lower recidivism rates than those processed through court, particularly when conferences result in agreements that address underlying needs. Victims report higher levels of satisfaction, and communities report increased engagement and support.

However, challenges remain. Implementation has been uneven across jurisdictions, with some programs well-established and others struggling for resources and support. Concerns have been raised about the quality of facilitation, the consistency of referral practices, and the extent to which restorative programs are reaching the young people who need them most. Ongoing evaluation and improvement are needed to ensure that restorative justice fulfills its promise.

The theological significance of the Australian experience lies in its reminder that restorative justice is not a magic bullet but a human practice that requires ongoing attention and effort. The challenges that Australian programs face are not unique but universal, reflecting the difficulty of implementing any complex intervention in diverse and often under-resourced settings. The response to these challenges—ongoing evaluation, continuous improvement, and commitment to fidelity—is itself a form of faithfulness, a recognition that the work of restoration is never complete.

Lessons from the Global Experience

The global experience of restorative justice for juveniles offers several important lessons for practitioners, policymakers, and advocates.

First, restorative justice works. The evidence from multiple countries, using diverse research methods, consistently shows that restorative justice reduces recidivism, improves victim satisfaction, strengthens communities, and promotes accountability and rehabilitation. This evidence is robust enough to justify continued investment and expansion.

Second, context matters. The effectiveness of restorative justice depends on the cultural appropriateness of practices, the strength of legal frameworks, the level of community engagement, and the quality of implementation. What works in one context may not work in another without adaptation. The global experience underscores the importance of attending to local conditions and involving local communities in program design and implementation.

Third, indigenous wisdom is a gift. The restorative practices that have been developed in indigenous communities around the world—Maori family group conferences, First Nations circle processes, Aboriginal community justice programs—are not merely historical artifacts but living traditions that continue to inform and enrich restorative justice. Honoring these traditions and learning from them is essential for the continued development of restorative practice.

Fourth, legal frameworks matter. Countries with clear legislation and policy support for restorative justice have more successful implementation and more sustainable programs than those where restorative justice operates in a legal vacuum. Advocates should work for legal reform that authorizes, funds, and regulates restorative justice.

Fifth, challenges are universal but addressable. Resource limitations, training needs, fairness concerns, engagement difficulties, and resistance from traditional actors are challenges everywhere. They can be addressed through careful planning, ongoing evaluation, and commitment to quality.

The theological significance of these lessons lies in their witness to the universal and particular dimensions of God's work in the world. The universal principles of restorative justice—accountability, empathy, community involvement—reflect universal truths about human nature and divine purpose. The particular adaptations of restorative justice to diverse cultural contexts reflect the particularity of God's engagement with each people and place. Together, they reveal a God who is both universal and particular, both transcendent and immanent, both one and diverse.

The Future of Global Restorative Justice

As restorative justice continues to spread around the world, several trends are likely to shape its future development. The increasing exchange of ideas and practices across countries will enrich restorative justice, allowing practitioners to learn from one another and adapt successful approaches to new contexts. The growing evidence base will provide guidance for program design and implementation, helping to ensure that restorative justice is practiced with fidelity to its principles. The development of international standards, such as the United Nations Basic Principles, will provide a framework for quality and accountability.

At the same time, challenges will persist. Resource limitations will continue to constrain implementation in many countries. Cultural resistance will require ongoing attention and adaptation. The pull of punitive approaches, always present in political discourse, will require constant advocacy and education. The work of restorative justice is never done; it must be renewed in each generation, in each context, in each case.

The theological vision that sustains this work is the vision of the kingdom of God—that new order of reality that Jesus announced and embodied, in which the last are first, the lost are found, the broken are healed, and all things are made new. Restorative justice is not the kingdom, but it is a sign of the kingdom, a foretaste of what is possible when human beings align their practices with God's restorative purposes. The global spread of restorative justice is a sign that the kingdom is breaking in, that God's restorative work is advancing, that hope is alive in every nation, tribe, people, and language.

As we continue our journey through the principles and practices of restorative justice, we will explore future directions that invite our imagination and commitment. But for now, let us celebrate the global movement that is restorative justice, the diverse expressions of restorative practice around the world, the countless lives that have been transformed through restorative encounter. And let us commit ourselves to the ongoing work of learning, adapting, and spreading restorative justice, so that more young people, more victims, and more communities may experience the healing and hope that it offers.

CHAPTER 13

FUTURE DIRECTIONS

The future of restorative justice for juveniles holds exciting and transformative possibilities for expansion, refinement, and deepening impact. As we stand at the intersection of decades of 实践 experience, a growing body of empirical research, and increasing global recognition of restorative principles, we can glimpse horizons that were unimaginable when the modern restorative justice movement began in the 1970s. The journey ahead is not merely about doing more of the same but about evolving, adapting, and innovating in response to changing circumstances, emerging knowledge, and the enduring needs of young people, victims, and communities. In this chapter, we will explore the future directions that restorative justice for juveniles might take, drawing on the theological, philosophical, psychological, and legal foundations that have guided our journey thus far.

The future is not something that simply happens to us; it is something we actively create through our choices, our commitments, and our imagination. The shape of restorative justice in the decades to come will depend on the decisions made by practitioners, policymakers, advocates, and community members today. Will we settle for restorative justice as a marginal alternative, available to a fortunate few while the majority continue to experience punitive systems that have failed for centuries? Or will we work for restorative justice as the primary response to juvenile offending, integrated into the fabric of our legal systems and community institutions? Will we be content with practices that have proven effective, or will we continue to innovate, adapt, and improve? Will we reach only those who are easiest to serve, or will we extend restorative justice to the most challenging cases and the most marginalized communities? These questions, and many others, will shape the future of restorative justice.

The theological vision that animates this future-oriented thinking is the vision of the kingdom of God—that new order of reality that Jesus announced and embodied, in which the last are first, the lost are found, the broken are healed, and all things are made new. The kingdom is both already here and not yet fully realized; it breaks into the present in signs and glimpses, while we await its complete fulfillment. Restorative justice is a sign of the kingdom, a foretaste of what is possible when human beings align their practices with God's restorative purposes. The future directions we explore in this chapter are ways of opening ourselves more fully to the kingdom, of allowing its reality to shape our practices more completely, of participating more deeply in God's work of restoration.

The philosophical foundations of future-oriented thinking lie in traditions that emphasize possibility, creativity, and hope. The pragmatist tradition, with its emphasis on learning from experience and adapting practice based on results, provides a framework for continuous improvement. The existentialist tradition, with its emphasis on human freedom and the capacity to create meaning, reminds us that the future is not determined but chosen. The utopian tradition, with its visions of more just and humane societies, inspires us to imagine what might be possible and to work toward its realization. Restorative justice, in its future directions, draws on all of these traditions, combining rigorous evaluation with creative imagination, practical wisdom with visionary hope.

The psychological foundations of future-oriented thinking lie in research on hope, optimism, and human potential. Psychologists have documented the powerful effects of hope on human functioning—people who have hope cope better with adversity, persist longer in the face of challenges, and achieve more positive outcomes. Restorative justice, by its very nature, is a practice of hope—hope that change is possible, that healing can occur, that relationships can be restored. The future directions we explore are expressions of this hope, commitments to the possibility of a better way.

The legal foundations of future-oriented thinking lie in the ongoing development of laws and policies that support restorative justice. Law is not static but evolves in response to changing social conditions, emerging knowledge, and shifting values. The future of restorative justice will be shaped by legal reforms that authorize restorative practices, provide resources for their implementation, establish standards for quality, and protect the rights of participants. Advocates must continue to work for these reforms, building on the progress that has already been made.

Let us now explore the specific future directions that hold promise for the continued development of juvenile restorative justice.

1. Integration into Mainstream Juvenile Justice Systems

One of the most promising future directions is the further integration of restorative justice into existing juvenile justice systems. While restorative justice has often operated as a marginal alternative, available to a limited number of cases and dependent on the goodwill of individual judges or prosecutors, the future lies in making restorative justice a primary response to juvenile offending, embedded in the structure and culture of the justice system itself.

This integration involves multiple dimensions. First, it requires legislative and policy frameworks that authorize and support restorative justice. Laws should establish restorative justice as a legitimate option at all stages of the justice process—from diversion before charges are filed, to disposition after adjudication, to reentry after confinement. They should provide clear guidance on referral criteria, participant rights, facilitator qualifications, and agreement enforcement. They should allocate resources for program implementation, training, and evaluation.

Second, integration requires cultural change within justice system institutions. Judges, prosecutors, defense attorneys, probation officers, and law enforcement officials must understand restorative justice, value its principles, and support its practices. This requires education and training, but it also requires leadership from within the system—champions who model restorative approaches and advocate for their expansion. It requires building relationships between justice system actors and community-based restorative programs, creating pathways for collaboration and mutual support.

Third, integration requires that restorative justice be available to all young people who could benefit from it, not just those who happen to live in communities with well-established programs. This means expanding restorative programs geographically, ensuring that rural and underserved communities have access to restorative services. It means addressing disparities in access, ensuring that young people of color, indigenous youth, and other marginalized groups are not excluded from restorative justice. It means developing capacity in communities that have historically been underserved by the justice system.

The theological significance of integration lies in the biblical vision of *shalom*—that comprehensive well-being, right relationship, and flourishing for all creation that is the goal of God's restorative work. *Shalom* is not a marginal addition to the existing order but a transformation of that order from within. It is not a separate realm alongside the world but a new way of being in the world. Integrating restorative justice into mainstream systems is a way of allowing *shalom* to penetrate and transform the institutions that shape our collective life.

The psychological significance of integration lies in the message it sends to young people and communities. When restorative justice is marginal, it communicates that restorative approaches are optional, secondary, not quite legitimate. When restorative justice is integrated, it communicates that these approaches are valued, that accountability and healing matter, that the system believes in the possibility of change. This message itself can be healing, communicating respect and hope to those who come into contact with the system.

The legal significance of integration lies in the stability and sustainability it provides. Programs that depend on individual champions or temporary funding are vulnerable to changes in personnel or priorities. Programs that are embedded in legal frameworks and supported by dedicated funding can endure over time, providing consistent services and building trust with communities. Integration is essential for the long-term viability of restorative justice.

2. Early Intervention and Diversion Programs

Another crucial future direction is the expansion of restorative justice to include early intervention and diversion programs. The goal of these programs is to address minor offenses and conflicts at an early stage, before young people become deeply entrenched in the criminal justice system. By intervening early, restorative justice can prevent the escalation of problematic behavior, reduce the likelihood of further involvement in criminal activities, and spare young people the stigma and consequences of formal processing.

Early intervention programs operate at multiple levels. In schools, restorative practices can address conflicts, bullying, and behavioral issues before they escalate to law enforcement involvement. Classroom circles, peer mediation, and restorative conferences can resolve problems and repair harm while keeping students in school and out of the justice system. Research has shown that school-based restorative programs reduce suspensions, expulsions, and referrals to law enforcement, while improving school climate and academic outcomes.

In communities, early intervention programs can engage young people who are at risk of involvement in crime before they offend. Mentoring programs, youth development initiatives, and community-based activities can provide positive alternatives and supportive relationships that steer young people away from delinquency. When conflicts do arise, community-based restorative processes can address them without involving the formal justice system, preserving relationships and building community capacity.

Diversion programs operate at the point of arrest or referral, offering young people an alternative to formal court processing. Instead of being charged and prosecuted, young people who admit responsibility can participate in restorative processes that hold them accountable while addressing underlying needs. Successful completion of the restorative process results in the case being dismissed, avoiding the stigma and consequences of a formal record. Research has shown that diversion programs reduce recidivism and are more cost-effective than formal processing.

The theological significance of early intervention and diversion lies in the biblical emphasis on prevention and the value of every person. The prophets called Israel to "seek justice, rescue the oppressed, defend the orphan, plead for the widow"—actions that prevent suffering before it occurs. Jesus welcomed children and warned against causing them to stumble, emphasizing the importance of protecting the vulnerable. Early intervention and diversion are ways of living out this concern, preventing harm before it occurs and protecting young people from the damaging effects of justice system involvement.

The psychological significance of early intervention lies in developmental research showing that adolescence is a critical period for intervention. The brain is still developing, and young people are particularly responsive to both positive and negative influences. Early intervention can shape developmental trajectories, steering young people toward prosocial paths before problematic patterns become entrenched. Diversion can prevent the labeling and stigmatization that often follow formal processing, reducing the likelihood of continued offending.

The legal significance of early intervention and diversion lies in their alignment with the purposes of juvenile justice. The juvenile court was founded on the principle that young people are different from adults and that the system should focus on rehabilitation rather than punishment. Early intervention and diversion embody this principle, intervening in the least restrictive manner possible and reserving formal processing for cases where it is truly necessary.

3. Customization and Tailored Approaches

Future directions in restorative justice must include the customization and tailoring of practices to meet the unique needs of different communities, cultures, and populations. One size does not fit all in restorative justice; what works in one context may not work in another, and practices must be adapted to local circumstances, values, and traditions.

Customization is particularly important for indigenous youth, who have been historically overrepresented in justice systems and underserved by conventional approaches. Restorative practices that draw on indigenous traditions—such as circle processes, family group conferences, and peacemaking courts—have proven effective in engaging indigenous young people and communities. These practices honor indigenous values, involve indigenous elders and community members, and address the historical trauma that contributes to indigenous involvement in the justice system. Future directions should include the continued development and expansion of culturally grounded restorative practices, developed in partnership with indigenous communities and grounded in indigenous sovereignty.

Customization is also important for other marginalized populations, including youth of color, LGBTQ+ youth, youth with disabilities, and youth from immigrant and refugee communities. Each of these populations has unique experiences, needs, and strengths that should inform the design of restorative practices. This requires engaging with these communities, learning from their members, and adapting practices accordingly. It requires training facilitators in cultural competence and ensuring that programs are accessible to all.

Customization extends to individual young people as well. Restorative justice should be responsive to the unique circumstances of each case—the nature of the offense, the needs of the victim, the strengths and challenges of the offender, the resources of the community. This requires flexibility in practice, the ability to adapt processes to fit the situation, and the wisdom to know what adaptations are appropriate.

The theological significance of customization lies in the biblical affirmation of the dignity and uniqueness of every person. Each human being is created in the image of God, and that image is expressed differently in each person. The Psalms celebrate this diversity: "I praise you because I am fearfully and wonderfully made; your works are wonderful, I know that full well." Restorative justice, by tailoring practices to the unique needs of each person and community, honors this divine creativity, recognizing that God's image is reflected in infinite variety.

The psychological significance of customization lies in research on individual differences and treatment matching. People respond differently to interventions based on their personality, culture, history, and circumstances. Interventions that are matched to individual needs and characteristics are more effective than those that are applied uniformly. Restorative justice, by its nature, is individualized, but this individualization must be intentional and informed by knowledge of what works for whom.

The legal significance of customization lies in the principle of individualized justice that has always been central to the juvenile court. The founders of the juvenile court believed that each young person should be treated as an individual, with dispositions tailored to their unique needs and circumstances. Restorative justice, with its emphasis on customization, is deeply aligned with this principle and can help to realize it in practice.

4. Research and Evidence-Based Practices

The future of restorative justice depends on continued research and the development of evidence-based practices. While we know a great deal about what works, there is much we do not know, and ongoing research is essential for improving effectiveness, identifying best practices, and building the case for expanded implementation.

Research priorities for the future include: rigorous evaluations of restorative programs using randomized controlled trials and quasi-experimental designs; studies that examine the mechanisms through which restorative justice produces its effects, shedding light on why it works; research on what works for whom, identifying factors that moderate effectiveness; longitudinal studies that track outcomes over extended periods; cost-benefit analyses that document the economic case for restorative justice; and implementation research that identifies the conditions under which programs succeed or fail.

Research should also explore new applications of restorative justice, including for serious and violent offenses, for youth with complex needs, and in new settings such as residential facilities, foster care, and mental health systems. As restorative justice expands into new domains, research must keep pace, ensuring that practices are effective and that they do not cause unintended harm.

The development of evidence-based practices requires not only research but also mechanisms for translating research into practice. Practitioners need access to research findings, training in evidence-based approaches, and support for implementation. Programs need to be evaluated and to use evaluation findings for continuous improvement. The field needs standards for what constitutes evidence-based practice and mechanisms for disseminating best practices.

The theological significance of research and evidence-based practice lies in the biblical call to wisdom. The book of Proverbs is filled with exhortations to seek wisdom, to learn from experience, to test and discern. "The heart of the discerning acquires knowledge, for the ears of the wise seek it out." Research is a form of wisdom-seeking, an attempt to learn from what has been done so that we can do better in the future. Evidence-based practice is a way of honoring what we have learned, of ensuring that our practices are guided by knowledge rather than by habit or ideology.

The philosophical significance of research lies in the pragmatist commitment to learning from experience. Pragmatism, as developed by thinkers like John Dewey, holds that the truth of an idea is tested by its consequences. Restorative justice, from a pragmatist perspective, is validated by its outcomes. Research is the means by which we assess those outcomes and determine whether our practices are achieving their intended purposes.

The psychological significance of research lies in the commitment to scientific inquiry that has advanced our understanding of human behavior and change. Psychology has made tremendous progress through rigorous research, and restorative justice should be informed by this research. At the same time, research on restorative justice contributes to psychological knowledge, expanding our understanding of how people change and what promotes healing and accountability.

5. Technology and Accessibility

Technology offers significant opportunities for expanding the accessibility and reach of restorative justice. Online platforms and virtual conferencing can facilitate victim-offender dialogues, restorative circles, and conferences, making these processes available to participants who might otherwise be unable to participate due to geographical distance, transportation challenges, scheduling conflicts, or other barriers.

Virtual restorative processes have become more common in response to the COVID-19 pandemic, and the experience has demonstrated both possibilities and limitations. On the positive side, virtual processes can be convenient, accessible, and effective. Participants can join from their homes or other safe locations, reducing the logistical challenges of in-person meetings. Facilitators can work with participants across distances, making restorative justice available in underserved areas. Research on virtual restorative processes, while still limited, suggests that they can produce outcomes comparable to in-person processes when properly facilitated.

On the other hand, virtual processes have limitations. The technology may not be available or reliable for all participants. The lack of physical presence can reduce the sense of connection and make it harder to read nonverbal cues. The informality of virtual spaces can undermine the solemnity and significance of restorative encounters. Facilitators need training and support to conduct virtual processes effectively, and programs need to ensure that participants have access to the technology and support they need.

The future will likely see a hybrid approach, with in-person processes remaining the gold standard for serious cases while virtual processes are used for appropriate cases and to increase access. Technology may also be used to enhance in-person processes—for example, through video recordings that allow participants to review agreements, online platforms that support communication and follow-up, and data systems that track outcomes and support evaluation.

The theological significance of technology lies in the biblical call to use our gifts for the service of others. Technology is a gift of human creativity, a reflection of the image of God in which we are created. Like all gifts, it can be used for good or ill. Used wisely, technology can extend the reach of restorative justice, bringing healing and accountability to those who might otherwise be excluded. Used unwisely, it can create new forms of exclusion and undermine the relational core of restorative practice. The challenge is to use technology in ways that serve restorative values rather than distorting them.

The psychological significance of technology lies in research on communication and relationship in mediated contexts. Psychologists have studied how people connect through technology, identifying both the possibilities and limitations of virtual interaction. This research can inform the design of virtual restorative processes, helping facilitators create conditions for genuine encounter even when participants are not physically present.

The legal significance of technology lies in questions about jurisdiction, confidentiality, and enforceability in virtual contexts. When participants are in different states or countries, questions arise about which laws apply. When processes are conducted online, questions arise about how to protect confidentiality and ensure that communications are secure. When agreements are reached virtually, questions arise about how to document and enforce them. Legal frameworks must evolve to address these questions, providing guidance for virtual restorative processes.

6. Community Empowerment

The future of restorative justice lies in continuing to empower communities to take an active role in the resolution of juvenile offenses. Community empowerment is not merely about involving community members in processes designed by professionals but about supporting communities to develop and lead their own restorative initiatives, grounded in their own values and responsive to their own needs.

Community-led restorative initiatives take many forms. In some communities, neighborhood-based restorative justice programs are governed by community boards and staffed by community volunteers. These programs have deep roots in the community, understand local dynamics, and can respond in culturally appropriate ways. They build community capacity, strengthen social networks, and create sustainable structures for addressing conflict and harm.

In other communities, restorative practices are integrated into existing community institutions—schools, faith communities, youth organizations, cultural centers. These institutions have relationships with young people and families, credibility in the community, and resources that can support restorative work. By embedding restorative practices in these institutions, communities can create multiple pathways for young people to access restorative justice.

Community empowerment also involves supporting communities to address the root causes of juvenile delinquency. Restorative justice is most effective when it is part of a broader strategy that includes economic opportunity, educational support, mental health services, and other resources that address the conditions that produce crime. Communities that are empowered to address these conditions can prevent crime before it occurs, reducing the need for restorative interventions.

The theological significance of community empowerment lies in the biblical vision of a people called and empowered by God. Israel was not a collection of individuals ruled by a distant authority but a community called to embody God's justice and mercy in their life together. The early church understood itself as a body, each member gifted for the service of the whole. Community empowerment in restorative justice is an expression of this vision, recognizing that communities have gifts, wisdom, and resources for addressing their own problems and that the role of professionals is to support, not supplant, community capacity.

The psychological significance of community empowerment lies in research on collective efficacy and community resilience. Communities that have strong social networks, high levels of trust, and shared expectations for behavior are better able to address problems and support their members. Restorative justice, by empowering communities, builds these capacities, creating virtuous cycles of increasing trust and cooperation.

The legal significance of community empowerment lies in the principle of subsidiarity—the idea that decisions should be made at the most local level possible. This principle, rooted in Catholic social teaching and reflected in many legal systems, holds that higher-level authorities should support but not supplant the functions of lower-level communities. Community-led restorative justice embodies this principle, recognizing that communities are the primary agents of their own well-being and that the justice system should support, not replace, community capacity.

7. Restorative Education in Schools

The future of restorative justice includes the incorporation of restorative principles and practices into school curricula, educating young people about conflict resolution, empathy, and accountability from an early age. This preventive approach can contribute to a reduction in school-based conflicts and delinquent behavior, while also building the skills and values that support restorative justice throughout life.

Restorative education takes many forms. In elementary schools, students can learn about feelings, empathy, and peaceful conflict resolution through stories, games, and classroom discussions. They can practice using "I messages," listening actively, and solving problems collaboratively. These foundational skills prepare them for more complex restorative practices as they grow older.

In middle and high schools, students can learn about restorative justice more directly, studying its principles and practices, examining case studies, and participating in restorative processes. They can be trained as peer mediators, learning to facilitate restorative conversations between their classmates. They can participate in restorative circles that address issues in their school or community, learning to listen deeply, speak honestly, and work collaboratively.

Restorative education also involves teaching about the broader social context of conflict and crime—issues of inequality, injustice, and historical trauma that shape individual behavior and community dynamics. Students can learn about the ways that systemic factors contribute to delinquency and about the role of restorative justice in addressing both individual harm and systemic injustice. This critical consciousness prepares them to be active citizens who work for justice in their communities.

The theological significance of restorative education lies in the biblical emphasis on teaching and formation. The book of Deuteronomy instructs parents to teach their children diligently, talking about God's commands "when you sit at home and when you walk along the road, when you lie down and when you get up." The Proverbs are filled with teachings about wisdom, character, and right living. Restorative education is a form of this teaching, forming young people in the values and practices that make restorative justice possible.

The psychological significance of restorative education lies in research on social-emotional learning. Programs that teach skills like empathy, emotion regulation, and conflict resolution have been shown to improve academic outcomes, reduce behavioral problems, and promote positive development. Restorative education, by integrating these skills with restorative principles and practices, can amplify these effects, creating school environments that support both learning and well-being.

The legal significance of restorative education lies in its potential to reduce the flow of young people into the juvenile justice system. Schools that implement restorative practices have fewer suspensions, expulsions, and referrals to law enforcement. This reduces the number of young people who enter the justice system, alleviating pressure on courts and corrections while also sparing young people the damaging effects of system involvement.

8. Victim Services and Support

The future of restorative justice must include comprehensive victim services and support throughout the restorative process. While restorative justice has always emphasized victim participation and healing, the quality and availability of victim services vary widely across programs. Future developments should focus on ensuring that all victims have access to the support they need to participate meaningfully and to heal from the harm they have suffered.

Comprehensive victim services include preparation for restorative processes, accompaniment during encounters, and follow-up support afterward. Victims need to understand what restorative justice entails, what their rights are, and what to expect. They need opportunities to explore their hopes and fears, to develop coping strategies, and to make informed decisions about participation. During the restorative encounter, they need support from trained advocates who can help them feel safe and empowered. Afterward, they need follow-up to process their experience, address any ongoing needs, and celebrate their healing.

Victim services also include access to counseling, legal guidance, and practical resources. Many victims need professional support to address trauma, navigate the legal system, or meet basic needs that have been disrupted by the crime. Restorative justice programs should have relationships with service providers who can offer this support, and they should have mechanisms for connecting victims with these resources.

The theological significance of victim services lies in the biblical call to care for those who have been wronged. The prophets consistently speak of God's concern for the vulnerable—the orphan, the widow, the stranger. Jesus heals the sick, comforts the mourning, and welcomes the outcast. Comprehensive victim services are a way of living out this concern, ensuring that those who have been harmed receive the care and support they need.

The psychological significance of victim services lies in research on trauma and recovery. Victims need safety, support, and empowerment to heal from trauma. Comprehensive services provide these conditions, increasing the likelihood that restorative processes will be healing rather than retraumatizing. They also ensure that victims who choose not to participate in restorative processes still receive the support they need.

The legal significance of victim services lies in victims' rights legislation that has been enacted in many jurisdictions. These laws guarantee victims certain rights—to information, to participation, to protection, to restitution. Comprehensive victim services help programs fulfill these legal obligations, ensuring that victims' rights are respected and that programs are accountable.

9. International Collaboration and Exchange

The future of restorative justice depends on continued international collaboration and the exchange of best practices across countries and cultures. Restorative justice is a global movement, and practitioners around the world have much to learn from one another. By sharing experiences, research, and innovations, we can accelerate the development of restorative justice and ensure that it continues to evolve in response to changing conditions.

International collaboration takes many forms. Conferences and gatherings bring practitioners together to share ideas and build relationships. Research collaborations enable cross-national studies that examine the effectiveness of restorative justice in different contexts. Exchange programs allow practitioners to learn from programs in other countries and to bring new ideas home. Online platforms facilitate ongoing communication and resource sharing.

International collaboration also involves the development of common standards and principles that can guide practice across countries. The United Nations Basic Principles on the Use of Restorative Justice Programmes in Criminal Matters provide a framework that has been widely endorsed. Future work should build on these principles, developing more detailed guidance for specific aspects of practice and adapting them to diverse contexts.

The theological significance of international collaboration lies in the biblical vision of a global community united in God's love.

The book of Revelation depicts a multitude from every nation, tribe, people, and language gathered around the throne of God. This diversity is not erased but celebrated; each brings their unique gifts and perspectives to the worship of God. International collaboration in restorative justice is a foretaste of this vision, bringing together people from diverse cultures to share their gifts and learn from one another.

The philosophical significance of international collaboration lies in the recognition that truth is discovered through dialogue. No single culture has a monopoly on wisdom; each has insights that can enrich others. By engaging in genuine dialogue across cultures, we can deepen our understanding of restorative justice and develop practices that are both universally grounded and locally adapted.

The psychological significance of international collaboration lies in the opportunity to test the generalizability of research findings. What works in one cultural context may not work in another, and cross-national research can identify factors that moderate effectiveness. This knowledge can guide adaptation and ensure that restorative practices are appropriate for diverse populations.

10. Restorative Legislation and Policy Reform

The future of restorative justice depends on continued legislative and policy reform that strengthens and supports these practices. Clear legal frameworks can ensure consistency, fairness, and accountability, while also providing the resources and authority that programs need to operate effectively.

Restorative legislation should address multiple dimensions. It should authorize restorative justice at all stages of the justice process, from diversion to reentry. It should establish standards for practice, including requirements for facilitator training, participant protections, and agreement enforcement. It should provide funding for program implementation, evaluation, and research. It should create oversight mechanisms to ensure quality and accountability. And it should protect the rights of participants, ensuring that restorative processes are voluntary, fair, and respectful.

Policy reform should extend beyond the justice system to include education, child welfare, mental health, and other systems that intersect with juvenile justice. Restorative practices should be available in schools, foster care, residential treatment, and other settings where young people are served. Policies should support cross-system collaboration, ensuring that young people have access to restorative interventions regardless of where they are.

The theological significance of legislative and policy reform lies in the biblical call to establish justice. The prophets consistently call for laws and policies that protect the vulnerable and promote right relationship. "Learn to do right; seek justice. Defend the oppressed. Take up the cause of the fatherless; plead the case of the widow." Restorative legislation and policy reform are ways of responding to this call, creating structures that support restorative practice and protect those who participate.

The philosophical significance of legislative reform lies in the recognition that justice requires both good laws and good practices. Laws provide the framework within which practices operate; they can either enable or constrain restorative justice. Advocates must work for laws that enable restorative practice while protecting against abuse. This requires philosophical clarity about the purposes of restorative justice and the principles that should guide its implementation.

The legal significance of legislative reform is obvious: without supportive laws, restorative justice cannot achieve its full potential. Laws that authorize restorative justice, provide resources, establish standards, and protect rights are essential for the continued development of the field.

11. Cross-Sector Collaboration

The future of restorative justice depends on collaboration across sectors, including education, social services, mental health, and other systems that serve young people. Juvenile delinquency does not arise in a vacuum; it is connected to challenges in multiple domains—family instability, school failure, mental health issues, substance abuse, poverty, and community violence. Addressing these challenges requires collaboration across systems, with restorative justice as one component of a comprehensive response.

Cross-sector collaboration takes many forms. Schools, child welfare agencies, mental health providers, and juvenile justice programs can work together to identify young people at risk and to provide coordinated interventions. They can share information, coordinate services, and align their approaches to ensure that young people receive consistent support across systems. They can develop joint protocols for referral, case management, and follow-up, ensuring that young people do not fall through the cracks.

Restorative justice can serve as a unifying framework for cross-sector collaboration. Its principles of accountability, empathy, and community involvement apply across domains, and its practices can be adapted for use in multiple settings. By adopting restorative approaches across systems, communities can create a coherent response to juvenile offending that addresses both individual behavior and systemic conditions.

The theological significance of cross-sector collaboration lies in the biblical vision of *shalom*—that comprehensive well-being that encompasses all dimensions of life. *Shalom* is not merely the absence of conflict but the presence of justice, health, and flourishing in every domain. Cross-sector collaboration is a way of pursuing *shalom* holistically, recognizing that the well-being of young people depends on multiple factors and that no single system can address them alone.

The psychological significance of cross-sector collaboration lies in research on developmental contexts. Young people develop within multiple overlapping systems—family, school, peer group, community. Interventions that address only one of these contexts are less effective than those that address multiple contexts in an integrated way. Cross-sector collaboration enables this kind of comprehensive intervention, increasing the likelihood of positive outcomes.

The legal significance of cross-sector collaboration lies in the need for coordinated legal frameworks. When multiple systems are involved in a young person's life, questions arise about jurisdiction, confidentiality, and accountability. Clear legal frameworks can facilitate collaboration while protecting rights and ensuring appropriate oversight.

The Horizon of Hope

As we look toward the future of restorative justice for juveniles, we see a horizon bright with possibility. The directions we have explored in this chapter—integration into mainstream systems, early intervention and diversion, customization and tailored approaches, research and evidence-based practices, technology and accessibility, community empowerment, restorative education, victim services, international collaboration, legislative reform, and cross-sector collaboration—are not separate paths but interconnected dimensions of a comprehensive vision. Each supports and amplifies the others, creating a whole that is greater than the sum of its parts.

The realization of this vision will not be easy. It will require sustained effort, political will, and financial resources. It will require overcoming resistance from those invested in punitive approaches and skepticism from those who doubt that change is possible. It will require learning from failures and adapting to changing circumstances. It will require patience, persistence, and hope.

But the promise is great. A future in which restorative justice is fully integrated into juvenile justice systems, available to all young people who could benefit from it, and supported by research, law, and community commitment—this is a future worth working for. A future in which young people who cause harm are held accountable in ways that promote growth and healing, in which victims are supported and empowered, in which communities are strengthened and united—this is a future worth imagining.

The theological vision that sustains this hope is the vision of the kingdom of God—that new order of reality that is both already here and not yet fully realized. In the kingdom, the last are first, the lost are found, the broken are healed, and all things are made new. Restorative justice is a sign of the kingdom, a foretaste of what is possible when human beings align their practices with God's restorative purposes. The future directions we have explored are ways of opening ourselves more fully to the kingdom, of allowing its reality to shape our practices more completely, of participating more deeply in God's work of restoration.

As we continue our journey through the principles and practices of restorative justice, we will explore practical guidance for implementation and final reflections on the significance of this work. But for now, let us hold this vision of the future in our hearts—a future of healing, accountability, and restoration for all young people, all victims, all communities. And let us commit ourselves to the work of making that vision real.

CHAPTER 14

PRACTICAL GUIDANCE

The journey through the principles, practices, benefits, challenges, legal frameworks, case studies, international perspectives, and future directions of restorative justice for juveniles has prepared us for the most important question of all: How do we actually do this work? How do we translate the vision we have explored into concrete practice in our communities, our schools, our justice systems? How do we become agents of restoration in the lives of young people who have caused harm, victims who have suffered, and communities that have been wounded? This chapter provides practical guidance for individuals, professionals, and policymakers who are committed to implementing restorative justice programs for juveniles. It is a roadmap for the journey ahead, drawing on the wisdom of those who have gone before, the research that illuminates what works, and the theological, philosophical, and psychological foundations that give this work its depth and meaning.

The practical guidance that follows is not a rigid formula to be applied mechanically but a set of principles and considerations to be adapted to local circumstances. Every community is unique, with its own history, culture, resources, and challenges. What works in one context may not work in another without thoughtful adaptation. The key is to remain faithful to restorative principles while being flexible in their application, to hold fast to the vision while being open to learning and adjustment. This requires wisdom, humility, and commitment—qualities that are cultivated over time through practice, reflection, and ongoing engagement with the communities we serve.

The theological foundation for practical guidance lies in the biblical understanding of wisdom as both knowledge and practice. The book of Proverbs is filled with practical guidance for everyday life—how to manage money, how to resolve conflicts, how to treat others, how to live with integrity. This guidance is not merely technical but moral, grounded in the fear of the Lord and the pursuit of righteousness. The practical guidance for restorative justice is similarly grounded in the pursuit of *shalom*—that comprehensive well-being, right relationship, and flourishing for all creation that is the goal of God's restorative work. Every step we take in implementing restorative justice is a step toward *shalom*, a participation in God's work of restoration.

The philosophical foundation for practical guidance lies in the pragmatist tradition, which emphasizes learning from experience and adapting practice based on results. Pragmatism holds that the truth of an idea is tested by its consequences, and that we should continually evaluate our practices and adjust them based on what we learn. The practical guidance that follows is informed by decades of experience and research, but it is not the final word. As we implement restorative justice in new contexts and with new populations, we will learn more, and our practices will evolve. The key is to remain open to this learning, to treat our programs as experiments in restorative practice, and to use evaluation as a tool for continuous improvement.

The psychological foundation for practical guidance lies in research on behavior change, program implementation, and organizational development. We know that change is difficult, that programs often fail to achieve their intended effects when implementation is poor, and that organizations need support to adopt new practices effectively. The practical guidance that follows incorporates what we have learned about these dynamics, offering strategies for overcoming common challenges and increasing the likelihood of success.

The legal foundation for practical guidance lies in the recognition that restorative justice operates within legal frameworks that both enable and constrain practice. Practitioners must understand these frameworks, work within them, and advocate for their improvement. The guidance that follows addresses the legal dimensions of restorative practice, offering strategies for navigating legal requirements and building supportive legal frameworks.

Let us now turn to the practical guidance itself, organized by the audiences it addresses: individuals and community members, professionals and practitioners, and policymakers and government officials. Each has a crucial role to play in the implementation of restorative justice, and each requires different kinds of guidance.

For Individuals and Community Members

The work of restorative justice begins with each of us. Before we can implement programs or change policies, we must cultivate within ourselves the values, knowledge, and skills that restorative justice requires. Individuals and community members are the foundation on which all else is built; without their understanding, commitment, and participation, restorative justice cannot flourish.

1. Education and Training

The first step for individuals and community members is to educate themselves about restorative justice. This means more than reading a book or attending a single workshop; it means developing a deep understanding of restorative principles, practices, and values. It means learning about the research that demonstrates what works and why. It means understanding the experiences of victims, offenders, and communities who have participated in restorative processes. And it means reflecting on how restorative justice connects to one's own values, faith, and life experience.

Numerous organizations offer training and education in restorative justice. Some provide introductory workshops that cover the basics; others offer comprehensive certification programs that prepare participants to facilitate restorative processes. Online courses make training accessible to those who cannot attend in person. Books, articles, videos, and podcasts provide additional resources for learning. The key is to approach this education with an open mind and heart, ready to be challenged and transformed by what you learn.

For those who feel called to deeper engagement, becoming a trained facilitator or volunteer in an existing restorative program is a powerful next step. Facilitator training typically covers the principles and practices of restorative justice, communication and facilitation skills, the dynamics of trauma and conflict, and the ethical dimensions of restorative practice. It includes supervised practice and feedback, ensuring that trainees are prepared to facilitate restorative processes effectively. Volunteering in a program provides hands-on experience and the opportunity to learn from experienced practitioners.

The theological significance of education and training lies in the biblical call to grow in wisdom and understanding. The book of Proverbs exhorts us to "get wisdom, get understanding; do not forget my words or turn away from them." Jesus taught his disciples, preparing them for the work they would do. The early church devoted itself to the apostles' teaching, learning the way of Jesus together. Education and training in restorative justice are forms of this discipleship, preparing us to participate in God's work of restoration.

The psychological significance of education and training lies in research on skill development and expertise. Skilled practitioners are not born but made, through deliberate practice, feedback, and reflection. Training provides the foundation for this development, equipping individuals with the knowledge and skills they need to begin their journey toward expertise.

2. Advocacy and Support

Individuals and community members can also contribute to restorative justice through advocacy and support. This means speaking up for restorative justice in your community, letting others know about its benefits, and encouraging its adoption. It means supporting local organizations and initiatives that promote restorative justice, whether through volunteering, donating, or simply spreading the word.

Advocacy can take many forms. You can write letters to elected officials, urging them to support restorative justice legislation. You can speak at community meetings, sharing what you have learned about restorative justice and why it matters. You can talk with friends, neighbors, and colleagues, raising awareness and building support. You can use social media to share information and connect with others who care about restorative justice.

Support can also take many forms. You can volunteer with a restorative justice program, offering your time and skills. You can donate to organizations that provide restorative services. You can attend events and fundraisers, showing your support and encouraging others to do the same. You can simply be present, letting those who do this work know that they are not alone.

The theological significance of advocacy and support lies in the biblical call to speak up for justice. The prophets were advocates, speaking truth to power and calling God's people to faithfulness. Esther used her position to advocate for her people, risking her life to save them. Advocacy for restorative justice is a form of prophetic witness, speaking up for a different way of responding to harm and calling our communities to a more excellent way.

The psychological significance of advocacy lies in research on social movements and attitude change. Change happens when enough people speak up, when ideas spread through social networks, when new norms are established. Advocacy accelerates this process, building the political will and public support that restorative justice needs to thrive.

3. Community Engagement

Individuals and community members can engage with local institutions to encourage the adoption of restorative practices. Schools, community centers, faith communities, law enforcement agencies, and other organizations all have roles to play in creating a restorative community. By engaging with these institutions, you can help them understand restorative justice and support them in implementing restorative approaches.

In schools, you can advocate for restorative discipline policies, volunteer to support restorative circles, and help educate teachers and administrators about restorative practices. In faith communities, you can encourage the use of restorative approaches for addressing conflicts within the congregation and for engaging with the broader community. With law enforcement, you can build relationships and explore opportunities for collaboration, such as diversion programs that refer young people to restorative justice instead of formal processing.

Community engagement also means fostering dialogue and partnership among different groups and organizations. Restorative justice is most effective when it is part of a coordinated community response to youth offending, with multiple institutions working together in alignment. By building relationships and facilitating collaboration, you can help create this coordinated response.

The theological significance of community engagement lies in the biblical vision of *shalom*—that comprehensive well-being that encompasses all dimensions of community life. *Shalom* is not achieved by isolated individuals but by communities working together for the common good. Community engagement in restorative justice is a way of pursuing *shalom* collectively, recognizing that we all have a role to play in creating communities that are safe, just, and compassionate.

The psychological significance of community engagement lies in research on social capital and collective efficacy. Communities with strong networks of relationship and high levels of trust are better able to address problems and support their members. Community engagement builds these networks and this trust, creating the conditions for effective restorative practice.

4. Restorative Values

Individuals and community members can promote restorative values in their personal and community interactions. Restorative justice is not only a set of practices but a way of being in the world—a way of relating to others that emphasizes empathy, accountability, respect, and relationship. By embodying these values in our daily lives, we create a culture that supports restorative practice and makes it more likely to succeed.

Promoting restorative values means practicing empathy in our interactions with others, seeking to understand their perspectives and experiences. It means taking accountability for our own actions, acknowledging when we have caused harm and making amends. It means treating others with respect, honoring their dignity even when we disagree. It means investing in relationships, building connections that can sustain us through conflict and challenge.

It also means encouraging others to embrace these values. By modeling restorative behavior, we invite others to do the same. By naming and affirming restorative values when we see them, we reinforce their importance. By gently challenging behavior that violates these values, we create opportunities for growth and learning.

The theological significance of restorative values lies in their alignment with the character of God and the teachings of Jesus. God is described as compassionate, gracious, slow to anger, abounding in love and faithfulness. Jesus taught his followers to love their neighbors, to forgive one another, to seek reconciliation. Restorative values are a reflection of this divine character and a response to this teaching. By embodying them, we become more like the God we worship and more faithful to the way of Jesus.

The psychological significance of restorative values lies in research on moral development and character formation. Values are not merely abstract principles but internal guides that shape behavior. By cultivating restorative values, we strengthen these internal guides, making it more likely that we will act restoratively in challenging situations.

5. Victim and Offender Support

Individuals and community members can offer support and resources to victims and offenders who have gone through restorative processes. This support can be crucial for helping them reintegrate into the community and access the services they need to heal and grow.

For victims, support might include offering a listening ear, helping with practical needs, connecting them with counseling or other services, or simply letting them know that they are not alone. Victims often feel isolated after a crime, and community support can be a powerful antidote to this isolation. By showing up for victims, we communicate that they matter, that their suffering is seen, and that they have a place in the community.

For offenders, support might include mentorship, assistance with education or employment, help in accessing services, or simply consistent presence and encouragement. Young offenders often lack positive relationships with adults, and community support can fill this gap. By showing up for young people who have caused harm, we communicate that they are not defined by their worst actions, that they have value, and that they can change.

The theological significance of victim and offender support lies in the biblical call to bear one another's burdens. The apostle Paul writes, "Carry each other's burdens, and in this way you will fulfill the law of Christ." Supporting victims and offenders is a way of carrying their burdens, of sharing in their struggles, of walking with them on the journey toward healing and restoration.

The psychological significance of support lies in research on social support and well-being. People who have strong social support cope better with stress, recover more quickly from trauma, and are more likely to make positive changes. By offering support to victims and offenders, we contribute to their well-being and increase the likelihood of positive outcomes.

For Professionals and Practitioners

Professionals and practitioners are on the front lines of restorative justice, facilitating processes, supporting participants, and managing programs. Their skill, wisdom, and commitment are essential for the success of restorative justice. The following guidance is offered to support them in this crucial work.

1. Training and Certification

Professionals and practitioners should pursue formal training and certification in restorative justice practices. This training provides the foundation of knowledge and skills that restorative practice requires, ensuring that practitioners are prepared to facilitate processes effectively and ethically.

Training programs vary in length and intensity, from introductory workshops to comprehensive certification programs. The best programs include both didactic instruction and supervised practice, allowing trainees to learn through experience and receive feedback on their performance. They cover the principles and practices of restorative justice, communication and facilitation skills, the dynamics of trauma and conflict, cultural competence, ethical considerations, and self-care for practitioners.

Certification provides external validation of competence and commitment. It assures programs, participants, and referral sources that practitioners meet established standards. It also provides a framework for ongoing professional development, requiring continuing education and periodic recertification.

The theological significance of training and certification lies in the biblical understanding of calling and preparation. God calls people to specific tasks and prepares them for those tasks through experience, teaching, and formation. Training and certification are contemporary forms of this preparation, ensuring that those who are called to restorative work are equipped to do it well.

The psychological significance of training lies in research on expertise development. Expertise is not achieved through experience alone but through deliberate practice, feedback, and reflection. Training provides the structure for this development, accelerating the journey from novice to expert.

2. Collaboration

Professionals and practitioners should collaborate with other professionals to provide comprehensive support to young offenders and victims. Restorative justice does not operate in a vacuum; it is most effective when it is part of a coordinated response that addresses multiple dimensions of young people's lives.

Collaboration with social workers can ensure that young people have access to the services they need—counseling, substance abuse treatment, housing assistance, and more. Collaboration with counselors can support the healing of victims and offenders, addressing trauma and promoting mental health. Collaboration with educators can support young people's academic success and provide opportunities for positive engagement. Collaboration with probation officers can ensure that restorative agreements are monitored and enforced, and that young people receive consistent supervision and support.

Collaboration also means building relationships with other restorative practitioners, sharing experiences and learning from one another. No one has all the answers, and we all have much to learn from colleagues who are doing similar work in different contexts. By creating networks of mutual support and learning, we strengthen the entire field.

The theological significance of collaboration lies in the biblical image of the body, with each member contributing to the whole. Paul writes, "The body is a unit, though it is composed of many parts. And though its parts are many, they form one body." Collaboration in restorative justice is a way of living out this image, recognizing that we need one another and that our work is enriched by the contributions of others.

The psychological significance of collaboration lies in research on interdisciplinary teamwork and its benefits. Teams that include diverse perspectives and expertise are better able to address complex problems and achieve positive outcomes. Collaboration harnesses this diversity, bringing multiple resources to bear on the challenges that young people and victims face.

3. Cultural Competence

Professionals and practitioners should develop cultural competence to ensure that restorative justice processes are respectful and inclusive of diverse backgrounds and identities. Cultural competence is not a static achievement but an ongoing process of learning, reflection, and adaptation.

Cultural competence begins with self-awareness—understanding one's own cultural background, biases, and assumptions. It extends to knowledge about other cultures—their values, communication styles, conflict resolution practices, and historical experiences. It includes skills for working across cultures—the ability to listen deeply, to ask respectful questions, to adapt one's approach to fit cultural contexts. And it involves humility—the recognition that one never fully masters another culture and must always remain open to learning.

In restorative practice, cultural competence means adapting processes to fit the cultural contexts of participants. It means being aware of cultural differences in communication—some cultures value directness, others indirectness; some express emotion openly, others more reservedly. It means understanding how historical trauma—such as the legacy of colonialism for indigenous peoples—shapes participants' experiences and expectations. It means ensuring that processes are accessible to those with limited English proficiency, and that interpreters are used effectively when needed.

The theological significance of cultural competence lies in the biblical affirmation of cultural diversity. The book of Revelation depicts a multitude from every nation, tribe, people, and language gathered around the throne of God. This diversity is not erased but celebrated. Cultural competence in restorative justice honors this diversity, ensuring that people from all backgrounds can participate fully and authentically in restorative processes.

The psychological significance of cultural competence lies in research on cross-cultural communication and its challenges. Misunderstandings arising from cultural differences can undermine restorative processes, causing participants to feel unheard, disrespected, or misunderstood. Cultural competence reduces these risks, creating conditions for genuine encounter across cultural boundaries.

4. Assessment and Evaluation

Professionals and practitioners should establish mechanisms for assessing the effectiveness of their restorative justice programs. Assessment and evaluation are essential for learning what works, identifying areas for improvement, and demonstrating the impact of restorative practice to funders, policymakers, and the community.

Assessment begins with clear goals and objectives. What is your program trying to achieve? Reduced recidivism? Increased victim satisfaction? Stronger community connections? Improved offender accountability? Once goals are clear, you can identify indicators that measure progress toward them—recidivism rates, victim satisfaction surveys, participant feedback, completion rates for restitution agreements.

Data collection should be systematic and ongoing. Track who participates in your program, what processes are used, what agreements are reached, and what outcomes are achieved. Collect feedback from participants about their experiences—what was helpful, what was challenging, what could be improved. Use standardized measures when possible to allow comparison with other programs and with research benchmarks.

Evaluation should be used for learning and improvement, not just for reporting. Regularly review your data, looking for patterns and trends. Identify areas where outcomes are strong and areas where they could be improved. Experiment with changes to your practices and assess their impact. Share your findings with staff, board members, funders, and the community, inviting their input and support.

The theological significance of assessment and evaluation lies in the biblical call to test and discern. The apostle Paul writes, "Test everything; hold fast to what is good." Assessment and evaluation are forms of testing, helping us identify what is good and hold fast to it. They are also forms of stewardship, ensuring that we use the resources entrusted to us wisely and effectively.

The psychological significance of evaluation lies in research on feedback and improvement. Organizations that collect and use data are better able to learn and adapt than those that operate on intuition alone. Evaluation provides the feedback that programs need to improve, increasing their effectiveness over time.

5. Community Outreach

Professionals and practitioners should actively engage with the community to raise awareness of restorative justice benefits and principles. Community outreach builds understanding and support, which are essential for program sustainability and growth.

Outreach can take many forms. Presentations to community groups—faith communities, neighborhood associations, service clubs—can introduce restorative justice and explain how it works. Workshops and trainings can build skills and deepen understanding. Participation in community events can increase visibility and build relationships. Media engagement—op-eds, interviews, social media—can reach broader audiences and shape public discourse.

Outreach should be bidirectional—not just telling the community about restorative justice but listening to the community's concerns, questions, and ideas. Community members have valuable knowledge about local conditions, cultural dynamics, and what might work in their context. By listening to them, you can adapt your program to better serve the community and build the relationships that make collaboration possible.

The theological significance of community outreach lies in the biblical call to be a witness. Jesus told his followers, "You are the light of the world. A town built on a hill cannot be hidden." Community outreach is a way of letting our light shine, of bearing witness to the transformative power of restorative justice. It is also a way of honoring the community, treating its members as partners rather than passive recipients of services.

The psychological significance of outreach lies in research on attitude change and social norms. People are more likely to support restorative justice when they understand it, when they see it as aligned with their values, and when they know that others in their community support it. Outreach builds this understanding and this social support, creating conditions for program success.

For Policymakers and Government Officials

Policymakers and government officials have the power to create the conditions in which restorative justice can flourish. Through legislation, funding, and policy, they can authorize restorative practices, provide resources for their implementation, and ensure that they are available to all who could benefit from them. The following guidance is offered to support them in this crucial work.

1. Legislation and Policy Development

Policymakers should advocate for the development and implementation of legislation and policies that support restorative justice. Clear legal frameworks are essential for ensuring that restorative practices are authorized, funded, and accountable.

Legislation should define the scope of restorative justice, specifying the types of cases for which it is available and the stages of the justice process at which it may be used. It should establish standards for practice, including requirements for facilitator training, participant protections, and agreement enforcement. It should provide for funding of programs, training, and evaluation. It should create oversight mechanisms to ensure quality and accountability. And it should protect the rights of participants, ensuring that restorative processes are voluntary, fair, and respectful.

Policy development should be informed by research and best practices. What does the evidence show about what works? What have other jurisdictions done, and what can we learn from their successes and failures? How can we adapt successful approaches to our own context? Answering these questions requires engagement with researchers, practitioners, and community members.

The theological significance of legislation and policy development lies in the biblical call to establish justice. The prophets consistently call for laws and policies that protect the vulnerable and promote right relationship. "Learn to do right; seek justice. Defend the oppressed. Take up the cause of the fatherless; plead the case of the widow." Restorative legislation and policy are ways of responding to this call, creating structures that support restorative practice and protect those who participate.

The psychological significance of legislative support lies in research on program sustainability. Programs that operate without clear legal authorization are vulnerable to changes in leadership or priorities. Programs that are embedded in legislation have greater stability and are more likely to endure over time.

2. Resource Allocation

Policymakers should allocate resources to support the training of professionals and the establishment of restorative justice programs. Restorative justice requires investment—in people, in programs, in evaluation. Without adequate resources, even the best-designed programs cannot succeed.

Resource allocation should cover multiple areas. Funding for training ensures that facilitators and other practitioners have the skills they need. Funding for program operations supports staff salaries, facilities, and materials. Funding for evaluation supports data collection and analysis, enabling programs to learn and improve. Funding for research expands the knowledge base, identifying what works and for whom.

Resource allocation should also address disparities in access. Communities with the highest crime rates and the greatest need for effective interventions often have the fewest resources. Policymakers should ensure that restorative justice programs are available in underserved communities and that resources are distributed equitably.

The theological significance of resource allocation lies in the biblical principle of stewardship. The resources we have are not our own but are entrusted to us by God, to be used for the common good. Allocating resources to restorative justice is a form of faithful stewardship, investing in programs that promote healing, accountability, and community well-being.

The psychological significance of adequate resources lies in research on program implementation. Programs that are under-resourced are less likely to achieve their goals, as staff are overworked, training is inadequate, and services are limited. Adequate resources increase the likelihood of successful implementation and positive outcomes.

3. Cross-Agency Collaboration

Policymakers should promote interagency collaboration between juvenile justice, education, and social services departments. Young people who offend often have needs that span multiple systems—educational challenges, mental health issues, family problems, substance abuse. Addressing these needs requires coordination across agencies.

Cross-agency collaboration can take many forms. Joint protocols can govern information sharing, referral, and case management. Cross-training can help staff in different agencies understand one another's roles and perspectives. Co-located services can make it easier for young people and families to access the support they need. Shared data systems can track outcomes and identify gaps in service.

Policymakers can incentivize collaboration through funding mechanisms that reward joint proposals, through legislation that mandates coordination, and through leadership that models collaborative behavior. They can remove barriers to collaboration, such as confidentiality restrictions that impede information sharing, and create structures that support ongoing communication and joint problem-solving.

The theological significance of cross-agency collaboration lies in the biblical vision of *shalom*, which encompasses all dimensions of life. *Shalom* is not achieved by addressing one domain in isolation but by attending to the whole person in community. Cross-agency collaboration is a way of pursuing *shalom* holistically, recognizing that the well-being of young people depends on multiple factors and that no single agency can address them alone.

The psychological significance of collaboration lies in research on coordinated care. Young people who receive coordinated services across multiple domains have better outcomes than those whose services are fragmented. Collaboration reduces duplication, fills gaps, and ensures that interventions reinforce rather than undermine one another.

4. Community Involvement

Policymakers should encourage the active involvement of community members in shaping and implementing restorative justice initiatives. Restorative justice is most effective when it is rooted in community, responsive to community needs, and supported by community members.

Community involvement can be facilitated through advisory boards that include community representatives, through public meetings that invite input and feedback, through partnerships with community-based organizations, and through funding for community-led initiatives. It requires genuine commitment to listening and responding, not merely checking a box. Community members should have real influence over program design, implementation, and evaluation.

Community involvement also means creating mechanisms for community oversight and accountability. Community members should have ways to raise concerns, to monitor program performance, and to hold programs accountable for serving the community well. This oversight builds trust and ensures that programs remain responsive to community needs.

The theological significance of community involvement lies in the biblical understanding of the people of God as a community called to participate in God's work. Israel was not a collection of individuals ruled by a distant authority but a community called to embody God's justice and mercy. The early church understood itself as a body, each member gifted for the service of the whole. Community involvement in restorative justice is an expression of this vision, recognizing that communities have gifts, wisdom, and resources for addressing their own problems.

The psychological significance of community involvement lies in research on ownership and engagement. Programs that are designed and implemented with community input are more likely to be accepted and sustained than those that are imposed from outside. Community members who are involved in restorative justice become advocates for it, spreading the word and building support.

5. Data Collection and Evaluation

Policymakers should establish data collection and evaluation processes to assess the impact of restorative justice programs on recidivism rates, victim satisfaction, and community safety. Data and evaluation are essential for accountability, learning, and improvement.

Data collection should be systematic and standardized, allowing for comparison across programs and over time. Key indicators might include recidivism rates, victim satisfaction scores, completion rates for restorative agreements, participant demographics, and costs. Data should be disaggregated by race, ethnicity, gender, and other relevant factors to identify disparities and ensure equity.

Evaluation should be rigorous and independent, using methods appropriate to the questions being asked. Randomized controlled trials are the gold standard for assessing effectiveness, but quasi-experimental designs, pre-post comparisons, and qualitative studies also have value. Evaluations should examine not only whether programs work but for whom, under what conditions, and at what cost.

Findings from data collection and evaluation should be used to guide policy and practice. They should inform decisions about funding, program design, and resource allocation. They should be shared with programs, practitioners, and the public, contributing to the collective learning of the field.

The theological significance of data and evaluation lies in the biblical call to accountability. The prophets held kings and priests accountable for their actions, calling them to account when they failed to live up to their responsibilities. Jesus taught that much is required of those to whom much is given. Data and evaluation are forms of this accountability, ensuring that programs are faithful to their mission and responsible in their use of resources.

The psychological significance of evaluation lies in research on evidence-based practice. Interventions that are supported by rigorous research are more likely to be effective than those that are not. Evaluation builds this evidence base, guiding practitioners toward approaches that work and away from those that do not.

6. Youth Diversion Programs

Policymakers should develop and support diversion programs that incorporate restorative justice practices as an alternative to traditional court processing for juvenile offenders. Diversion programs can prevent young people from becoming deeply entrenched in the justice system, reducing the negative consequences of formal processing while still holding them accountable.

Diversion programs should be available at multiple points in the justice process—pre-arrest, pre-charge, pre-adjudication—giving young people multiple opportunities to avoid formal processing. They should be grounded in restorative principles, emphasizing accountability, repair, and rehabilitation rather than punishment. They should be tailored to individual needs, addressing the underlying factors that contribute to offending.

Diversion programs should be rigorously evaluated to ensure that they are achieving their goals and not producing unintended consequences. They should be monitored for disparities in access and outcomes, ensuring that all young people have equal opportunities to benefit from diversion.

The theological significance of diversion lies in the biblical theme of second chances. Throughout scripture, God offers people opportunities to turn from their ways and start anew. Diversion programs are a way of offering second chances to young people who have made mistakes, giving them the opportunity to learn and grow without the lasting stigma of a formal record.

The psychological significance of diversion lies in research on labeling and its effects. Young people who are formally processed by the justice system are more likely to reoffend, in part because they internalize the label of "offender" and are treated differently by others. Diversion programs avoid this labeling, reducing the risk of continued offending.

7. Training and Capacity Building

Policymakers should invest in the training and capacity building of justice system personnel, including judges, prosecutors, and probation officers, to ensure they understand and support restorative justice practices. These actors make critical decisions about which cases are referred to restorative justice, and their understanding and support are essential for program success.

Training for justice system personnel should cover the principles and practices of restorative justice, the evidence for its effectiveness, the criteria for appropriate referral, and the roles that different actors can play. It should address common concerns and misconceptions, providing opportunities for dialogue and questions. It should be ongoing, not one-time, with refresher courses and updates as the field evolves.

Capacity building goes beyond training to include technical assistance, peer learning, and organizational support. Justice system personnel need ongoing support to implement restorative practices effectively, to troubleshoot challenges, and to learn from experience. Creating networks of practitioners, providing coaching and consultation, and fostering communities of practice can all support this capacity building.

The theological significance of training and capacity building lies in the biblical call to teach and equip. Jesus spent much of his ministry teaching his disciples, preparing them for the work they would do. The early church devoted itself to the apostles' teaching, learning the way of Jesus together. Training and capacity building are contemporary forms of this teaching and equipping, preparing justice system personnel to participate in restorative work.

The psychological significance of training lies in research on attitude change and behavior change. People are more likely to support new practices when they understand them, when they see them as effective, and when they have the skills to implement them. Training provides this understanding and these skills, increasing the likelihood that justice system personnel will support restorative justice.

8. Public Awareness

Policymakers should launch public awareness campaigns to educate the public, including young people, about the benefits of restorative justice and the available resources. Public awareness builds understanding and support, which are essential for program sustainability and growth.

Public awareness campaigns can use multiple channels—media, social media, community events, school programs, faith communities—to reach diverse audiences. They should provide clear, accurate information about what restorative justice is, how it works, and what evidence shows about its effectiveness. They should include stories of real people whose lives have been transformed by restorative justice, making the case in human terms. They should address common concerns and misconceptions, providing honest responses to questions and criticisms.

Public awareness campaigns should also provide information about how to access restorative justice services. Where can victims go to request restorative processes? How can young people and families find restorative programs? What resources are available for those who want to learn more or get involved? Making this information widely available ensures that those who could benefit from restorative justice know how to access it.

The theological significance of public awareness lies in the biblical call to proclaim good news. Jesus began his ministry by announcing good news to the poor, freedom for the prisoners, recovery of sight for the blind. Public awareness campaigns for restorative justice are a form of proclamation, sharing the good news that there is a different way of responding to harm, a way that heals rather than hurts.

The psychological significance of public awareness lies in research on social norms and behavior change. People's attitudes and behaviors are shaped by what they believe others think and do. Public awareness campaigns can shift social norms, making restorative justice more widely accepted and supported.

The Path Forward

The practical guidance offered in this chapter is not exhaustive, nor is it the final word. Each community, each program, each practitioner will need to adapt these principles to their own context, learning through experience what works and what does not. The key is to remain grounded in restorative values while being flexible in their application, to hold fast to the vision while being open to learning and adjustment.

The journey of implementing restorative justice is not easy. It requires patience, persistence, and hope. There will be setbacks and challenges, moments of doubt and discouragement. But there will also be moments of breakthrough and transformation, moments when you see the power of restorative justice to heal wounds, restore relationships, and change lives. These moments make the journey worthwhile.

The theological virtues of faith, hope, and love sustain us on this journey. Faith that restoration is possible, even when evidence is incomplete. Hope that our efforts will bear fruit, even when challenges seem overwhelming. Love that sustains us in the difficult work of accompanying victims and offenders through the pain of encounter and the possibility of healing. These virtues, grounded in the character of a God who is always working to restore what is broken, sustain us for the long journey ahead.

As you go forth to implement restorative justice in your community, remember that you are not alone. You are part of a global movement of people committed to a different way of responding to harm—a way that heals rather than hurts, that restores rather than destroys, that builds community rather than tearing it apart. Draw on the wisdom of those who have gone before, learn from the experiences of others, and share your own learning generously. Together, we can build a world in which restorative justice is not the exception but the rule, not a marginal alternative but the primary way we respond to young people who cause harm. Together, we can participate in God's work of restoration, bringing *shalom* to our communities and our world.

CONCLUSION

We have journeyed together through the transformative realm of restorative justice for juveniles, traversing a landscape rich with history, principle, practice, and promise. From the opening pages that introduced the concept of restorative justice to the practical guidance that equips us for implementation, we have explored the many dimensions of this approach to justice that places healing, accountability, and community at its core. As we now draw this journey to a close, it is fitting to gather the threads we have woven throughout these chapters and to reflect on the significance of what we have learned. But this conclusion is not merely a summary; it is a call to action, an invitation to each reader to become an agent of restoration in their own sphere of influence.

The journey of this book has been structured around the conviction that restorative justice for juveniles is not merely a set of techniques or programs but a comprehensive philosophy grounded in the deepest truths of theology, psychology, philosophy, and law. We have explored how the principles of accountability, empathy, and community involvement are not arbitrary inventions but reflections of the character of God and the nature of human flourishing. We have examined how practices such as victim-offender dialogues, restorative circles, and conferences embody these principles in concrete encounters between real human beings. We have documented the benefits of restorative justice—reduced recidivism, improved victim satisfaction, stronger communities—through rigorous research and compelling case studies. And we have honestly acknowledged the challenges and criticisms that restorative justice faces, recognizing that any human institution is imperfect and that ongoing learning and improvement are essential.

The theological foundations of restorative justice have been woven throughout our exploration. We have seen how the Hebrew scriptures proclaim a God of justice and mercy, who desires restoration rather than destruction, who hears the cry of the oppressed and acts on their behalf. We have witnessed how the life and teachings of Jesus embody restorative principles, calling us to love our neighbors, to forgive one another, to seek reconciliation. We have learned from the apostle Paul that we are members one of another, that when one suffers all suffer, and that the work of restoration is the work of the whole body of Christ. And we have glimpsed the vision of *shalom*—that comprehensive well-being, right relationship, and flourishing for all creation that is the goal of God's restorative work. Restorative justice, at its best, is a participation in this divine work, a sign of the kingdom breaking into the present, a foretaste of the time when all things will be made new.

The psychological foundations of restorative justice have been equally central to our exploration. We have seen how developmental psychology illuminates the unique vulnerabilities and possibilities of adolescence, calling us to respond to young offenders in ways that honor their capacity for change. We have learned from trauma research how experiences of abuse, neglect, and violence shape the developing brain and how restorative processes can create conditions for healing. We have understood the crucial distinction between shame and guilt, and how restorative practices foster the guilt that leads to accountability while avoiding the shame that leads to despair. And we have appreciated the power of empathy, perspective-taking, and social connection to transform lives and prevent future offending.

The philosophical foundations of restorative justice have provided the conceptual framework for our exploration. We have drawn on the dialogical philosophy of Martin Buber, with its insistence on I-Thou encounter as the foundation of ethical relationship. We have learned from Emmanuel Levinas about the face of the Other as the source of ethical obligation, and how restorative processes bring victims and offenders into the kind of face-to-face encounter that calls forth responsibility. We have appreciated the personalist tradition's emphasis on the inherent dignity of every human person, a dignity that is not diminished by wrongdoing and must be honored even in accountability. And we have drawn on pragmatist philosophy's commitment to learning from experience and adapting practice based on results.

The legal foundations of restorative justice have grounded our exploration in the realities of the justice system. We have traced the historical development of juvenile justice from its origins in the *parens patriae* doctrine through the due process revolution to the contemporary emphasis on evidence-based practice. We have examined the legal frameworks that authorize and regulate restorative justice, ensuring that processes are voluntary, fair, and accountable. We have explored the relationship between restorative justice and traditional legal proceedings, and how restorative agreements can be integrated into court dispositions. And we have considered the role of legislation and policy in creating the conditions for restorative justice to flourish.

As we now conclude our journey, let us reflect on the key takeaways that have emerged from each chapter, weaving them together into a comprehensive vision of restorative justice for juveniles.

1. Restorative Justice Principles

The principles of restorative justice—accountability, empathy, and community involvement—are not arbitrary inventions but reflections of fundamental truths about human nature and divine purpose. Accountability, properly understood, is not passive acceptance of punishment but active responsibility for making things right. It is the acknowledgment of harm and the commitment to repair, a process that transforms both the offender and the community. Empathy is the capacity to understand and feel the experience of another, a capacity that can be cultivated through encounter and that is essential for moral development and prosocial behavior. Community involvement recognizes that harm affects not only individuals but the entire fabric of social life, and that healing therefore requires the participation of all those affected. Together, these principles constitute a vision of justice that is more demanding and more hopeful than the punitive systems that have dominated Western legal traditions for centuries.

The theological grounding of these principles is found throughout scripture. Accountability echoes the prophetic call to "do justice, love mercy, and walk humbly with your God." Empathy reflects the divine compassion that moved God to enter human suffering in the person of Jesus. Community involvement embodies the biblical understanding that we are members one of another, that the body of Christ is made up of many parts, each essential to the whole. To practice restorative justice is to align ourselves with these divine realities, to participate in God's own work of restoration.

2. Victim-Centered Approach

The victim-centered approach of restorative justice represents a fundamental reorientation of the justice system, placing those who have been harmed at the center of the process rather than at the margins. Victims are given voice, allowed to tell their stories, to ask their questions, to express their feelings. They are given participation, involved in shaping the resolution and determining what will make things right. They are given support, accompanied by advocates and community members who care about their healing. And they are given respect, treated with dignity and consideration throughout.

The theological significance of this victim-centered approach lies in God's special concern for those who suffer. The psalmist cries out, and God hears. The prophets announce God's care for the oppressed, the vulnerable, the victimized. Jesus pronounces blessing on those who mourn and promises they will be comforted. To center victims in the justice process is to honor this divine concern, to say to those who have been harmed: you matter, your suffering matters, and we will not forget you in our pursuit of justice.

3. Offender Rehabilitation

Offender rehabilitation is not an afterthought in restorative justice but a central commitment. Restorative justice recognizes that young people who cause harm are not defined by their worst actions, that they have the capacity for change, and that the goal of justice should be to support that change. Through acknowledgment of responsibility, encounter with victims, making amends, addressing underlying factors, and community support, young offenders can be transformed—not merely deterred from future offending but genuinely changed in their understanding, values, and identity.

The theological foundations of rehabilitation are found in the biblical theme of redemption. Throughout scripture, we see God offering new beginnings to those who have failed—Adam and Eve exiled but clothed, Cain marked but protected, David confronted but restored, Peter denied but recommissioned, Paul persecuted but transformed. The message is consistent: no one is beyond the reach of God's restorative love. Rehabilitation in restorative justice participates in this redemptive work, offering young people the opportunity to become new creations.

4. Community Involvement

Community involvement is essential to restorative justice, recognizing that harm affects not only individuals but the entire fabric of social life, and that healing therefore requires the participation of all those affected. Communities provide support for victims, helping them feel less isolated and more able to heal. Communities reinforce accountability, communicating that offenses harm not only individuals but the collective. Communities offer guidance and mentorship to offenders, providing positive relationships that can support change. Communities provide resources—counseling, education, job training—that address underlying needs. And communities themselves are restored through the process, their social fabric rewoven, their capacity for collective action strengthened.

The theological vision of community is woven throughout scripture. Israel is not a collection of individuals but a people, bound together by covenant and called to embody God's justice and mercy. The church is not a gathering of isolated believers but a body, each member belonging to all the others, each gifted for the service of the whole. The kingdom of God is not a solitary experience but a great multitude from every nation, tribe, people, and language, gathered around the throne. Community involvement in restorative justice is a participation in this vision, a recognition that we are all connected and that the healing of each is bound up with the healing of all.

5. Restorative Practices

Restorative practices—victim-offender dialogues, restorative circles, restorative conferences, restitution plans, peer mediation, family group conferences—are the means by which restorative principles are embodied in concrete encounters. Each practice has its own character, its own appropriate applications, its own strengths and limitations. But all share a common core: they bring together those who have been harmed and those who have caused harm, along with their supporters and the broader community, in processes designed to address the full human reality of crime.

The theological significance of these practices lies in their embodiment of the reconciling work of Christ. Paul writes that God "reconciled us to himself through Christ and gave us the ministry of reconciliation." Restorative practices are forms of this ministry, creating spaces where those who have been estranged by harm can be brought together, where understanding can replace ignorance, where accountability can lead to repair, where relationships can be restored.

6. Benefits of Restorative Justice

The benefits of restorative justice are profound and well-documented. Reduced recidivism means fewer future offenses, fewer victims, lower costs to the justice system, and safer communities. Improved victim satisfaction means that those who have been harmed experience healing and closure rather than frustration and secondary trauma. Community building means stronger social bonds, greater trust, and increased collective efficacy—the combination of social cohesion and shared expectations for action that research has shown to be the most powerful predictor of neighborhood safety. Cost savings mean that resources can be redirected from incarceration to prevention, from punishment to healing.

These benefits are not merely practical advantages but signs of the kingdom. When recidivism is reduced, we see evidence that change is possible, that new creation can break into lives marked by failure. When victims are satisfied, we see evidence that God's comfort is real, that those who mourn can be comforted. When communities are strengthened, we see evidence that *shalom* is possible, that human beings can live together in peace and mutual care.

7. Challenges and Criticisms

Restorative justice, for all its promise, faces significant challenges and criticisms. Concerns about fairness and equity remind us that restorative processes must be designed and implemented with attention to power imbalances, selectivity, and potential disparities. Concerns about victim participation remind us that participation must be genuinely voluntary, that victims must be protected from pressure and retraumatization. Concerns about offender accountability remind us that we must distinguish genuine accountability from strategic compliance, and that rehabilitation requires addressing underlying causes. Concerns about resource limitations remind us that restorative justice requires investment—in training, in programs, in evaluation. Concerns about cultural sensitivity remind us that restorative practices must be adapted to diverse cultural contexts. Concerns about safety remind us that not all cases are appropriate for restorative processes, and that we must protect participants from harm. Concerns about limited applicability remind us that restorative justice is not a panacea and that some cases will require other approaches.

The theological response to these challenges is not denial but faithful engagement. The prophets did not ignore the failures of Israel but confronted them, calling the people to repentance and renewal. Jesus did not pretend that the world was perfect but acknowledged the reality of suffering and evil, even as he proclaimed the coming of the kingdom. The early church did not claim to have all the answers but wrestled with difficult questions, seeking the guidance of the Spirit. In the same way, we must honestly acknowledge the challenges facing restorative justice while working faithfully to address them, trusting that God is at work even in our struggles and failures.

8. Legal Framework

A sound legal framework is essential for the successful implementation of restorative justice. Legislation should authorize restorative practices, define their scope, establish standards, provide funding, create oversight mechanisms, and protect the rights of participants. Referral mechanisms should ensure that appropriate cases are identified and referred to restorative programs. Informed consent should be obtained from all participants, ensuring that participation is voluntary and informed. Rights protections should safeguard the due process rights of offenders and the participation rights of victims. Confidentiality should protect information shared during restorative processes. Documentation should create clear records of agreements and outcomes. Enforceability should ensure that agreements are honored and that there are consequences for non-compliance. Training and accreditation should ensure that facilitators are competent and ethical. Evaluation and oversight should ensure that programs are effective and accountable. Community collaboration should ensure that restorative justice is rooted in and responsive to the communities it serves.

The theological significance of legal frameworks lies in the biblical understanding of law as a gift from God for ordering community life. The law is not an end in itself but a means of shaping a people who embody God's justice and mercy. Legal frameworks for restorative justice, at their best, serve this function, providing the structure within which restorative practices can flourish while leaving room for the spirit of restoration to animate the letter of the law.

9. Case Studies

Case studies bring restorative justice to life, showing how principles become practice in real situations with real people. The story of Alex, whose participation in a school peacemaking circle transformed him from a source of conflict to an agent of peace, illustrates the power of restorative practices to address underlying causes and foster personal growth. The story of Sarah, whose victim-offender dialogue with Mr. Chen led to accountability, restitution, and mutual healing, illustrates the importance of victim participation and the transformative potential of genuine encounter. The story of the Jefferson Heights community conference, which brought together young offenders, victims, and community members to address a pattern of gang-related crime, illustrates the power of community involvement to heal not only individuals but entire neighborhoods.

These case studies are contemporary parables, stories that illuminate truth and inspire action. Like the parables of Jesus, they invite us to see the world differently, to imagine new possibilities, to recognize the presence of God's restorative work in the most unlikely places. They remind us that restorative justice is not an abstraction but a lived reality, experienced by real people in real communities, with all the complexity and messiness that entails.

10. Global Perspectives

Restorative justice is a global movement, with practices and programs in countries around the world. New Zealand's family group conferencing model, grounded in Maori traditions, has influenced restorative justice globally and demonstrated the power of culturally grounded practice. Norway's emphasis on rehabilitation and its integration of restorative principles into a strong welfare state model show how restorative justice can be embedded in broader social supports. Canada's restorative justice programs, developed in partnership with indigenous communities, show how restorative practices can address historical injustice and promote reconciliation. Australia's restorative justice initiatives, adapted from the New Zealand model, show how restorative practices can be adapted to diverse contexts.

These international perspectives remind us that restorative justice is not a Western invention to be exported to the rest of the world but a set of principles and practices that resonate with diverse cultural traditions. They remind us that we have much to learn from one another, that the exchange of ideas and practices across cultures enriches us all. And they remind us that the need for restorative justice is universal, that young people everywhere deserve responses to their offending that promote healing and accountability rather than punishment and exclusion.

11. Future Directions

The future of restorative justice holds exciting possibilities. Integration into mainstream juvenile justice systems will make restorative justice available to more young people and embed restorative principles in the fabric of the justice system. Early intervention and diversion programs will prevent young people from becoming deeply entrenched in the justice system and address problems before they escalate. Customization and tailored approaches will ensure that restorative practices are culturally appropriate and responsive to individual needs. Research and evidence-based practices will deepen our understanding of what works and guide continuous improvement. Technology and accessibility will extend the reach of restorative justice to underserved populations and make participation more convenient. Community empowerment will strengthen the role of communities in addressing their own problems and building their own capacity. Restorative education in schools will cultivate restorative values and skills in the next generation. Victim services and support will ensure that those who have been harmed receive the care they need. International collaboration and exchange will facilitate learning across cultures and accelerate the global spread of restorative justice. Restorative legislation and policy reform will create supportive legal frameworks. Cross-sector collaboration will ensure that restorative justice is part of a comprehensive response to youth offending.

The theological vision that animates these future directions is the vision of the kingdom of God—that new order of reality that Jesus announced and embodied, in which the last are first, the lost are found, the broken are healed, and all things are made new. Each of these future directions is a way of opening ourselves more fully to the kingdom, of allowing its reality to shape our practices more completely, of participating more deeply in God's work of restoration.

12. Practical Guidance

The practical guidance offered in this book provides a roadmap for individuals, professionals, and policymakers who are committed to implementing restorative justice. For individuals and community members, this means educating themselves, advocating for restorative justice, engaging with local institutions, promoting restorative values, and supporting victims and offenders. For professionals and practitioners, this means pursuing training and certification, collaborating with other professionals, developing cultural competence, assessing and evaluating programs, and conducting community outreach. For policymakers and government officials, this means developing legislation and policy, allocating resources, promoting cross-agency collaboration, encouraging community involvement, establishing data collection and evaluation processes, supporting diversion programs, investing in training and capacity building, and launching public awareness campaigns.

This practical guidance is not merely technical but moral, grounded in the conviction that how we respond to young people who cause harm matters—matters to them, matters to victims, matters to communities, matters to God. Every step we take to implement restorative justice is a step toward a more just and compassionate world, a world in which healing is prioritized over punishment, accountability over retribution, restoration over exclusion.

The Call to Action

As we close these pages, it is crucial to emphasize that restorative justice is not merely a concept to be understood but a call to be answered. It beckons us all—individuals, professionals, policymakers—to champion its cause, to become agents of restoration in our own spheres of influence. This call comes to each of us in different ways, depending on our roles, our gifts, our opportunities. But it comes to all of us, demanding a response.

To individuals and community members, the call is to become educated about restorative justice, to advocate for its implementation, to engage with local institutions, to embody restorative values in daily life, and to support those who have been harmed and those who have caused harm. You may not be able to change the entire system, but you can change your corner of it. You can be the one who speaks up for a different way, who offers a listening ear to a victim, who mentors a young person at risk, who models restorative values in your family and neighborhood.

To professionals and practitioners, the call is to pursue excellence in your practice, to collaborate with others, to develop cultural competence, to evaluate your work, and to engage with the community. You are on the front lines of restorative justice, facilitating encounters, supporting participants, managing programs. Your skill, your wisdom, your commitment make the difference between processes that heal and processes that harm. Embrace this responsibility with humility and dedication.

To policymakers and government officials, the call is to create the conditions in which restorative justice can flourish—through legislation, funding, policy, and leadership. You have the power to authorize restorative practices, to provide resources for their implementation, to ensure that they are available to all who could benefit from them. Use this power wisely, guided by evidence and by the voices of those most affected by the justice system.

The call to action is urgent. Every day, young people enter the juvenile justice system and are processed through punitive approaches that have been proven to fail. Every day, victims are marginalized and left without healing. Every day, communities are weakened by crime and by responses to crime that exacerbate rather than address underlying problems. The need for restorative justice is great, and the time for action is now.

But the call to action is also hopeful. We are not asked to solve all problems overnight or to achieve perfection in our lifetimes. We are asked to take the next step, to do what we can with what we have, to trust that our efforts, joined with those of others, will bear fruit in God's time. The work of restoration is slow and patient, like the growth of a seed, like the rising of the sun. But it is real, and it is happening, and we are invited to participate.

The Vision

The vision that sustains this work is the vision of a world transformed—a world in which restorative justice is not the exception but the rule, not a marginal alternative but the primary way we respond to young people who cause harm. In this world, young offenders are held accountable in ways that promote growth and healing, not punishment and alienation. Victims are supported and empowered, their voices central to the process of resolution. Communities are engaged and strengthened, their social fabric rewoven through collective responses to harm. The justice system is no longer a source of trauma and exclusion but a source of healing and restoration.

This vision is not naive optimism but hope grounded in evidence and faith. The evidence shows that restorative justice works—that it reduces recidivism, improves victim satisfaction, strengthens communities, and saves money. The evidence gives us confidence that our efforts are not in vain, that we are building on a foundation of proven effectiveness. But the vision also transcends evidence, reaching toward possibilities that have not yet been fully realized. It is a vision of what might be, of what could be, of what, with God's help, will be.

The faith that sustains this vision is the faith that God is at work in the world, restoring what is broken, healing what is wounded, reconciling what is divided. This faith does not blind us to the reality of suffering and evil; it enables us to face that reality with hope rather than despair. It does not guarantee success in every endeavor; it assures us that our efforts have meaning, that they are caught up in something larger than ourselves. It does not offer easy answers to difficult questions; it invites us to live the questions, trusting that the answers will emerge in God's time.

The Journey Continues

This book has been a journey through the landscape of restorative justice for juveniles. We have explored its history, its principles, its practices, its benefits, its challenges, its legal frameworks, its case studies, its global perspectives, its future directions, and its practical guidance. We have drawn on the deepest resources of theology, psychology, philosophy, and law. We have listened to the voices of victims and offenders, of practitioners and policymakers, of researchers and advocates. We have seen the power of restorative justice to transform lives and communities.

But the journey does not end here. For each reader, the journey continues in new directions, shaped by your own context, your own gifts, your own opportunities. Some of you will go on to facilitate restorative processes, sitting in circle with victims and offenders, creating space for healing and accountability. Some of you will advocate for restorative justice in your communities, speaking up for a different way and building support for change. Some of you will develop policies and legislation that create the conditions for restorative justice to flourish. Some of you will conduct research that deepens our understanding of what works and why. Some of you will educate others, teaching the next generation of restorative practitioners. Some of you will simply embody restorative values in your daily lives, modeling empathy, accountability, and respect in your relationships with others.

Whatever form your journey takes, know that you are not alone. You are part of a global movement of people committed to a different way of responding to harm—a way that heals rather than hurts, that restores rather than destroys, that builds community rather than tearing it apart. Draw on the wisdom of those who have gone before, learn from the experiences of others, and share your own learning generously. Support one another in the difficult moments, celebrate together in the moments of breakthrough, and keep faith with the vision even when the path is unclear.

A Benediction

As we conclude, let me offer a benediction for all who have journeyed through these pages and who will continue the journey beyond them:

May the God of restoration, who created all things good and who is working to make all things new, bless you and keep you. May the Spirit of wisdom and understanding guide your steps as you seek to implement restorative justice in your own context. May the love of Christ, who reconciled us to God and gave us the ministry of reconciliation, inspire your encounters with victims and offenders, with colleagues and community members, with allies and opponents. May you know that your efforts are not in vain, that every act of restoration, no matter how small, participates in God's great work of making all things new. And may you experience, in your own life and in the lives of those you serve, the healing, accountability, and community that restorative justice seeks to achieve.

Go now, and be agents of restoration. Go now, and participate in God's work of making all things new. Go now, and help build a world in which justice heals, relationships restore, and communities flourish. The journey continues. The work is before us. And the One who began a good work in us will be faithful to complete it.

Amen.

www.ingramcontent.com/pod-product-compliance
Lightning Source LLC
LaVergne TN
LVHW052243200926
848481LV00002B/257